90 0725399 2

KW-467-197

SEVEN DAY LOAN

This book is to be returned on
or before the date stamped below

15. JAN. 1996

22. JAN. 1996

CANCELLED

23. 1996

20. JAN 1997

CANCELLED

CANCELLED
-3. JUN 1997

CANCELLED
DEC 1997

- 7 DEC 1999

1 0 MAY 2000

UNIVERSITY OF PLYMOUTH

PLYMOUTH LIBRARY

Tel: (01752) 232323

This book is subject to recall if required by another reader
Books may be renewed by phone
CHARGES WILL BE MADE FOR OVERDUE BOOKS

FROM
UNIVERSITY OF PLYMOUTH
LIBRARY SERVICES

BRITAIN AND THE EEC

Recent Section F publications include

Jack Wiseman (*editor*)   BEYOND POSITIVE ECONOMICS?
Lord Roll of Ipsden (*editor*)   THE MIXED ECONOMY
M. Gaskin (*editor*)   THE POLITICAL ECONOMY OF
  TOLERABLE SURVIVAL
W. Beckerman (*editor*)   SLOW GROWTH IN BRITAIN
E. Nevin (*editor*)   THE ECONOMICS OF DEVOLUTION
W. Leontief (*editor*)   STRUCTURE, SYSTEM AND ECONOMIC
  POLICY

BRITAIN AND THE EEC

Proceedings of Section F (Economics)
of the British Association for
the Advancement of Science
Liverpool 1982

Edited by the Rt. Hon. Roy Jenkins, MP

© The British Association for the Advancement of Science 1983

All rights reserved. No part of this publication may be reproduced or transmitted, in any form or by any means, without permission

First published 1983 by
THE MACMILLAN PRESS LTD
London and Basingstoke
Companies and representatives
throughout the world

ISBN 0 333 34690 4 (hardcover)
ISBN 0 333 34691 2 (paperback)

Filmsetting by
Vantage Photosetting Co Ltd
Eastleigh and London

Printed in Great Britain at
The Camelot Press Ltd, Southampton

PLYMOUTH POLYTECHNIC
LIBRARY

04

Accn. No	151956 -1
Class. No	337. 142 BRI
Contl No	0333346904

Contents

Acknowledgements

I should like to acknowledge the assistance I received from Dr David Reisman, Recorder of Section F, in the preparation of this book. I would also like to thank the local organising committee and the University of Liverpool for their hospitality to the British Association during its 1982 conference.

R.J.

Notes on the Contributors

Francis Cripps is a Senior Research Officer at the Department of Applied Economics, Cambridge, and a leading member of the Economic Policy Group in the Department which, since 1970, has developed a distinctive critique of national and international macroeconomic policy. His main publications have been in the form of empirical analyses and policy assessments contributed to the Group's Economic Policy Review.

Geoffrey Denton is Reader in Economics and Chairman, Graduate School of Contemporary European Studies, University of Reading.

Robert Grant lectures in business economics at the City University, London. Previously he was economic adviser to the Monopolies and Mergers Commission and lecturer in economics at the University of St Andrews. His publications have been on the subjects of competitive behaviour in industry, anti-trust policy and industrial policies.

Roy Jenkins is Leader of the Social Democratic Party. He is a former Chancellor of the Exchequer and Home Secretary, and a former President of the Commission of the European Communities. He is Member of Parliament for Glasgow, Hillhead.

John Marsh is Professor of Agricultural Economics, University of Aberdeen. He is in addition Honorary Secretary of the Agricultural Economics Society, Independent Member of the Economic Development Council for the Food Manufacturing Industries, and Minister's Appointed Member of the Potato Marketing Board. His research work has been concerned with small farms, contract farming, the organisation of the market for cereals, and the problems of agricultural policy in Europe.

Roger Morgan is currently Head of the European Centre for Political Studies at the Policy Studies Institute. He is also an Associate Member of Nuffield College, Oxford, Visiting Professor at the University of Surrey, and Visiting Professorial Fellow of the University College of Wales, Aberystwyth. He has written and edited a dozen books on European and international affairs, of which the most recent is *Moderates and Conservatives in Western Europe.*

F. S. Northedge was educated at Merton College, Oxford, Nottingham University and the London School of Economics. He has been a member of the Department of International Relations at the School since 1949 and Professor of International Relations since 1968. He is the author of numerous books on twentieth-century British foreign policy and the theory and practice of international politics. He is also a frequent broadcaster on the BBC World Service.

John Pinder is the Director of the Policy Studies Institute, London. He was formerly Director of Political and Economic Planning (PEP) and head of the economics section at the College of Europe, Bruges. His main publications have concerned the European Community, industrial policy and East–West trade. He has recently been co-author of *Policies for a Constrained Economy* and *National Industrial Strategies and the World Economy.*

Christopher Tugendhat is Vice President, Commission of the European Communities. He was a leader and feature writer for the *Financial Times*, 1970–6. He is the author of *The Multinationals* and of numerous other books and articles.

David Wall is Professor of Economics at the University of Sussex. A graduate of the London School of Economics, he was a Postdoctoral Fellow at the University of Chicago. He has travelled extensively in the Third World as a consultant to various governments and international agencies. His current research interests include the determinants of international allocation of industrial activity.

Martin Wolf is Director of Studies at the Trade Policy Research Centre, London. After taking the MPhil in economics at Nuffield College, Oxford, he was a staff member of the World Bank from 1971 to 1981. During that time he was for three years Senior Economist in the India Division and was also a member of the core team for the first World Development Report. He is co-author of *Textile Quotas against Developing Countries* (1981) and author of *India's Exports* (1982).

Geoffrey E. Wood is a graduate of Aberdeen and Essex Universities. He is currently Director of the Centre for Banking and International Finance at the City University, London. His previous posts have been at Warwick University, Bank of England and the Federal Reserve Bank of St Louis. He has published articles in, among other places, the *Journal of International Economics*, the *European Economic Review*, the *Journal of Money, Credit and Banking* and the *American Economic Review*.

Introduction

ROY JENKINS

The essays in this book are about Britain and the EEC. They attempt to assess the impact of membership on our economic and political institutions and to clarify the choices open to us. Economics, after all, is about choices – and the changes which they involve. So, for that matter, is politics.

This book (which has its origins in the 1982 meeting of Section F of the British Association for the Advancement of Science) opens with the text of my own Presidential Address. I argue there that 'our future prosperity and success depend, in my view, upon building up our growing European base' and try to demonstrate how greatly we as a nation in fact benefit from our full and active membership in the Community. One important inference to be drawn from my paper – and from some of the others in this book as well – is that the Europe which we have joined is not fixed and unalterable for all time, but rather evolving and open to new initiatives. Choices involving changes are being made every day on issues which are vital for Britain and for the whole of Europe.

My Presidential Address on the present and future is followed by an historian's analysis of the past. The subject of F. S. Northedge's paper is the development of British attitudes towards the process of integration in Europe since 1945 (a process which culminated in the formation of the EEC in 1957). It examines the different reasons which made the acceptance of supranationalism difficult for Britain; suggests that British entry into the EEC in January 1973 was less the result of belief in integration than of the failure of other options in foreign policy; and concludes with a call for a firm and conclusive decision about our future relationship with the Community.

The Common Agricultural Policy has been one of the most developed – some would argue overdeveloped – topics of Community activity. This book accordingly includes two essays on that important

1

topic. The first, by John Marsh, suggests that the Common Agricultural Policy cannot survive unchanged because the momentum of its own operation will cause growing cost to the Community, increasing friction among member states and continuing frustration for farmers. The second, by Christopher Tugendhat, acknowledges the existence of costs, frictions, criticisms concerning trade distortions; but points at the same time to the fact that the Community, aware like the rest of us of its weaker as well as of its stronger points, has already begun the task of reform from within. Such reform, needless to say, will require an effective – and cost-effective – regional policy at EEC level; and the nature of such policy is considered by Geoffrey Denton in his own wide-ranging contribution to this volume.

The elimination of trade barriers has resulted in a substantial redirection of British trade towards the EEC. This development has, however, been accompanied by some deterioration in Britain's balance of manufacturing trade with the Community. Robert Grant, in his paper on industry and trade, seeks to explain that deterioration, and also the limited impact of EEC membership on the growth performance of the UK manufacturing sector. He does so in terms of people rather than things: the apparent absence of any beneficial effect of the EEC on British industrial performance, he argues, would appear to be less a consequence of entry than the result of failure on the part of British governments and politicians to exploit the opportunities presented by Community membership.

Close trading links present opportunities but they also create problems, and Francis Cripps in his contribution on macroeconomic policy draws attention to the way in which they make independent demand management difficult. He maintains, relying on a general model of the interdependence of trade and macroeconomic policies for support, that joint reflation by European countries could go further than unilateral reflation before giving rise to unsustainable trade deficits. He concludes, moving from the general to the specific, that mechanisms to shift the balance of trading advantage between individual countries are necessary if the full potential of reflationary policies is to be realised.

The potential conflict between national policies and multinational considerations has in the past been a significant obstacle to the introduction of a common Community currency. Geoffrey Wood analyses the European Monetary System, assesses its success to date, but argues that the benefits so far attained are the result of special factors unlikely to persist. He makes clear that his own preference is for a floating rate system and an announced monetary rule for each country; but also suggests that a European Money be launched, in parallel with existing currencies, so that freedom of individual choice might be the ultimate arbiter on whether (perhaps also when) Europe was sufficiently integrated economically for the use of a common currency to be beneficial.

The EEC is the world's largest trader and has, as such, an unavoidable responsibility for the health of the international trading system. It has none the less become a source of considerable international strain because of its growing interest in discriminatory protection against successful and therefore disruptive outsiders. Martin Wolf, while aware that some analysts are in favour of still greater protection, warns that their arguments are fallacious: a Community that adopted dramatically defensive policies would be ravaged by internal conflicts over assignment of the costs of protection and by external conflicts over the disruption created thereby in other countries. David Wall, while recording that Britain has become a leading voice among the countries in Europe which are seeking greater protection *vis-à-vis* the Third World, argues that the statistical data are ambiguous, and that no clear conclusion can be drawn as to whether or not British membership has improved overall trade prospects for Third World countries.

With interests in such a multiplicity of fields – agriculture, industry, the regions, macroeconomic and monetary policy, trade – it is clear that the Community will need solid but flexible political institutions. John Pinder argues that the institutions in their present form are not likely to deal effectively with new responsibilities and recommends that the European Parliament's new proposals for a system of co-decision with the Council of Ministers (a system which would give each of the two bodies similar powers) therefore be seriously considered. Another new development of a political nature is, of course, political cooperation (in the sense of an organised system of diplomatic consultation between the foreign ministries of the member states), and this is discussed by Roger Morgan in the chapter which concludes this book. Dr Morgan lists a number of shortcomings of political cooperation as currently practised – not least the fact that it is essentially a system of *diplomatic* cooperation rather than one of all-embracing political and administrative interaction – and argues that an act of political will is necessary if the member states are to fulfil their joint potential as an actor on the world political scene. So here again choices involving changes must be made.

The issues raised in this book are of great importance for Britain and, indeed, for the whole of Europe. That is why I deeply regret the extent to which public debate on the topic of Britain and the EEC is in this country all too frequently obscured by doubtfully informed and polarised comment. And that, in turn, is why I chose Britain and the EEC as the general theme for Section F's discussions in the year in which I was honoured to serve as its President. The present book is the result of those discussions. I believe that it provides a thoroughly considered, and considerable, contribution to current debate.

1 Britain and the EEC: Present and Future

ROY JENKINS

The background to our discussion is, on the one hand, one of intense international unrest and upheaval, with the towering prospect of escalating violence and global military tension in the future. The appalling events in the Lebanon in the recent past have shown us, all too clearly, the unlimited human suffering and the sickening destruction that modern urban warfare leaves in its wake, killing thousands of innocent civilians and devastating a whole civilised city. The toll of oppression and aggression throughout the world looms increasingly large – Afghanistan, Poland, Iran and Iraq, El Salvador and now the South Atlantic, stand out most prominently amongst a whole host of other current or potential trouble spots. Behind these more military concerns, there remain the equally urgent economic problems of the developed and the less developed countries alike, exacerbated since the oil crisis. The growing gap between North and South, with all its implications for the future, has been highlighted all too cogently by the Brandt Commission; yet the constructive proposals put forward, with a wholly necessary sense of urgency, in the Brandt Report, have been studiously left in limbo exactly by those very countries, including Britain, that should have taken the initiative to implement them. The World Bank and the IMF met recently in Toronto in peculiarly dangerous financial conditions but without much evidence of a mood of response to the challenge.

Whilst the international situation is fraught, closer to hand we face daunting problems of our own. There is the depressingly bleak economic outlook in general, but particularly that of ailing traditional industries, pressing for protectionist tariffs and financial aid to shore up their plummeting profits. Coupled with that there is the grim figure of 13.8 per cent of the population, 3 292 702 people – many of them young people and 40 000 of them graduates – condemned to involuntary unemployment, at the direct financial cost to our community of over £13 million a year. The very welcome, if overdue and modest, fall in American interest rates has quickly percolated through to our European economies and roused a flurry of overblown optimism from the government, which hailed the news as much needed evidence that we are finally on the right path.

Would that were so. Inflation has happily fallen from its previous heights, if at unacceptable social costs in terms of unemployment. But the most fundamental indicators of Britain's real economic state remain profoundly gloomy. National output in the second quarter of 1982 was no higher than it had been six months earlier; and a mere 0.9 per cent higher than at its low point in the spring of 1981. The output measure of gross domestic product, one of the most reliable guides to short-term changes in the economy, only rose by 0.2 per cent, and that was wholly accounted for by record North Sea oil and gas production. The output of the British economy now stands 6.5 per cent below its peak in spring 1979, with no real sign of movement out of the recession; a view underlined by the sceptical reception given to the government's rosy forecasts by the CBI and more recently by the Association of British Chambers of Commerce. I consider it to be singularly appropriate that our discussions should this year and for the sixth time in the history of the British Association, take place here in Liverpool, where the realities of urban and industrial decline, with all the consequential and concurrent social problems that that gives rise to, are starkly apparent.

Faced with such grave circumstances, it is all too easy to search for scapegoats to provide an explanation for our failings at home, and to cast around to blame others for our own predicament. Starting from this premise, some seek to persuade us to bury our heads in an isolationist sand; to try to cut ourselves off in a self-dependent economic cocoon of tariff barriers and import controls; to try to deceive ourselves into believing that, in some way, we are not inextricably bound up within the economic and political future and fortunes of those around us; that we can go it alone, ignoring our past and present reliance on trade with the rest of the world for our prosperity and survival. To my mind, it is overwhelmingly apparent that if Britain cannot succeed within the European Community, where there are no tariff barriers and where non-tariff restrictions are also mostly although not completely removed and with access to a market of 300 million people compared to our own market of only 56 million, it is difficult to see how Britain could succeed outside the Community.

In the 1980s, there is no real option of reverting to a purely national economy; and it is self-delusory to imagine that our problems would evaporate overnight if our membership of the Community were to end. In reality, the reverse is true. In my view, there are four major and overwhelming reasons for this. First, because the European Commission is able to act jointly for all the Community countries as their representative in multilateral trade negotiations, of such increasing importance in controlling and stabilising world trade. Since the Community countries jointly represent one-third of total world trade, the Commission is ensured a powerful position within international trade circles which would be denied to Britain, or to any other of the EEC member countries, were they to try to go it alone. It is no coincidence that, apart from the USA and Japan, most of the world's trading countries have formed themselves into trading blocks – COMECON, ASEAN, OPEC, the Group of 77. As the effects of recession and of increased oil and energy costs bite deeply right across the world, there are growing pressures in all the more industrially developed countries – and not just in Britain – to resort to protectionist measures to shore up their struggling industries whilst the less developed countries, so dependent on exporting to those more industrially developed countries, bitterly resent any such clamps on their precarious economies.

The continuing, lengthy negotiations that are taking place on the Multifibre Agreement, which will determine import and export quotas on textiles up to July 1986, have shown up all too clearly the strains upon maintaining an amicable balance of interests, between the essentially conflicting aspirations of the major participants. Throughout the negotiations, in which Britain has a crucial interest, our case has been put jointly with our fellow Community partners by the EEC Commission. Even within the Community there was considerable shading of opinion between those wishing for relatively liberal import quotas on a range of textile products, and those wishing for much tighter controls. Throughout these extremely complex and tense negotiations, I believe that Britain and our fellow Community partners were well served by the Commission. I am equally sure that the opportunity that we had to put our case and to reach some measure of compromise was substantially strengthened by our position within the Community.

Nor was this an isolated instance. The dangerous state of relations between the European Community and the United States, with the ailing US steel industries pressing for protectionist tariffs and reduced import quotas for steel exports from Britain and the Community to the

USA, highlighted once more the importance of concerted pressure from all the Community countries, acting jointly to protect our common interests. British attempts to negotiate bilaterally got nowhere. Furthermore, the forthcoming meeting of GATT trade ministers representing eighty-seven different countries, scheduled to take place in November of this year, will demonstrate once more that our membership of the European Community gives added weight and importance to Britain's otherwise minor status in multilateral trade negotiations. The meeting of trade ministers is intended to relaunch talks on the General Agreement on Tariffs and Trade, in an attempt to initiate new moves to stem protectionism, and to settle outstanding trade disputes between any of the eighty-seven contracting partner countries on such sensitive sectors as steel, agriculture, textiles and cars. What strength would Britain's isolated voice have on the world's trade negotiating stage, without the backing we automatically enjoy from our membership of one of the world's major trading blocks?

The second major reason that I would put forward in support of our continued Community membership is that Britain's trade has become increasingly directed towards the other member states and those surrounding countries with which the Community has special agreements. Trade with the Community now accounts for over 43 per cent of our trade with the world as a whole. This compares with the start of the 1970s, before our membership, when our trade with the Community accounted for less than 30 per cent. In 1980, West Germany replaced the United States as our main export market, although the United States has since edged ahead once more; but as the US has nearly four times the population, the striking fact is that there should be a fluctuating race between them; and with the exception of Greece, most of the other Community countries are among the top ten British export markets. Between 1972 and 1980, the value of British exports to the Community increased by 480 per cent, whilst for the USA the figure was 234 per cent, for Japan 237 per cent and for the rest of the world 295 per cent. Looking at recent trade figures, for the first five months of 1982, British exports to the EEC amounted to £9500 million compared to £2500 million of exports to the United States. After a relatively modest net surplus of £700 million on its intra-Community trade in 1980, the figures have slipped back to a relatively modest net deficit over the first five months of 1982 of £800 million. I think that it is clearly apparent from all this that British trade, and the future success of British industry, are now primarily dependent on its access to the European Community with its market of 300 million people.

Because of this, it is equally apparent that if Britain were to decide to withdraw from the EEC, withdrawal would have – at the very least – a considerable disruptive and destructive effect on British industry, and perhaps particularly on our increasingly important service industries. In turn, it would be bound to have an equally devastating effect on jobs. There has been a running and acrimonious dispute between proponents and opponents of the Community as to precisely how many thousands or even millions of jobs might be at stake if Britain were to leave the EEC. I consider this a somewhat unquantifiable dispute and I equally consider it fairly grotesque, given the current appalling levels of unemployment, seriously to consider a policy that would in any way, and to any extent, exacerbate employment prospects further. When the full extent of our energies should be concentrated on creating new jobs, and bringing stability to those employees whose future employment is clouded with uncertainty, it seems folly in the extreme to embark on a policy so deliberately disruptive and counter to the settled direction of Britain's major trading thrust.

It is not only British industry which considers our continued Community membership to be vital for our future. It is quite apparent that a significant percentage of inward investment in Britain by non-EEC countries is due, in considerable part, to the fact of our EEC membership. Overseas investors looking for European sites consider potential sites right across the EEC, and Britain faces severe competition in attracting investment. To most overseas investors, a major factor must be the size of the EEC market, and the importance of establishing a base within the EEC to compete successfully within the tariff-free market. In general, production costs in Britain are higher than elsewhere: to take one well-publicised current example, new car prices in West Germany and across Europe are approximately 20 per cent lower than in Britain, thanks principally to lower production costs. It is claimed that for certain products it would actually be cheaper to export direct from the United States or from Japan to the EEC rather than to continue exports from the UK to the EEC were Britain to withdraw and be obliged to pay EEC tariffs.

The significance of this becomes more striking if one considers in more detail the extent and importance of inward investment in Britain by non-EEC countries. In 1978, the last year for which figures are available, £1152 million was invested in Britain by other countries. Of this, 77.6% came from countries outside the EEC, and in particular from the United States and from Japan. At the end of 1978, US assets in British industry (excluding oil, banking and insurance) amounted to 59.5 per cent of all foreign investment. Since Britain joined the EEC, the American share of overseas investment in Britain has risen, although it was declining prior to our membership. Indeed, 50% of all American non-oil direct investment now comes to the European Community countries, compared to less than 33 per cent in the 1960s; and of half of the total US non-oil direct investment, 39 per cent was invested in the United Kingdom in 1977/78, rising to 44 per cent in 1979. Significantly, US investment both in Britain and in the rest of the EEC is heavily concentrated in manufacturing: in Britain this accounts for 84 per cent of total investment, excluding again oil, banking and insurance. Clearly the fact that Britain has tariff-free access to the whole EEC market must be a vital factor in any US decision to invest in UK manufacturing. This is borne out if one then considers the export figures to other EEC countries of overseas companies based in the United Kingdom. It is clear that the UK market alone would not provide sufficient incentive for many companies to base themselves in Britain: Britain is clearly chosen as an European company base, supplying the entire European market. If Britain left the EEC, equally clearly such companies would reconsider investment prospects in Britain with a new, more jaundiced eye.

A recent study on inward investment in the United Kingdom, commissioned by the European League for Economic Cooperation, gives an interesting insight into the thinking of the British management of several of the largest American and Japanese subsidiaries with manufacturing bases in Britain. Questioned about the effect they thought that withdrawal from the EEC would have on their parent companies' future investment policy towards their British subsidiaries, the message was unequivocally gloomy. The more optimistic felt that their company would freeze further growth: others feared that their company would pull out of Britain altogether, and move to another country within the EEC. The study also quotes figures from the 1977 Census of Production, the most recent available, showing that whilst foreign-controlled manufacturing in Britain constituted only 2.5 per cent of the whole, it accounted for nearly 14 per cent of jobs, 15.8 per cent of pay, 19 per cent of total manufacturing output and 18.7 per cent of net capital spending. When the Census for 1979 becomes available, it is likely to show even higher percentages, as part of a growing long-term upward trend.

Our future prosperity and success depend, in my view, upon building up our growing European base, and not suddenly and wilfully casting aside all that has been accomplished in this respect over the past decade. In the coming years, Britain and the other EEC countries will jointly be faced with the traumatic upheaval and challenge that the new technologies pose, both to our industries and our societies. We can perhaps draw grim comfort from the fact that, to a greater or lesser degree, many of the problems that we face also confront our Community partners. Urban deprivation and inner-city decline; unemployment amongst the skilled and unskilled, both young and old; the decline of traditional industries. They are also the side-products of the overall dilemma facing the entire Community: how best to avoid being squeezed between, on the one side, the most technologically advanced countries, the United States and Japan; and, on the other side, by the newly industrialised countries, which can now produce more competitively than we can those very goods on which our industrial success has traditionally been based.

The third major reason that I would give for our continued Community membership is that I believe that we stand a greater chance of success if we grapple for new initiatives jointly, rather than struggle on in our own separate ways.

I mean this in no negative sense. Indeed, if we are to respond to the challenge, it will require renewed determination to work together, both on political and technical or industrial fronts. Previous efforts at industrial cooperation have tended, all too frequently, to be concentrated on defending our declining Community industries – I have already mentioned the important role played by the Commission in negotiations to protect the interests of the Community's steel and textile industries. Although these are, of course, important and necessary Community activities, they must be regarded as short-term, stop-gap measures, designed to get those industries back to being competitive and essentially somewhat negative in purpose. If we are to compete successfully on the world market, we should also be seeking new opportunities to work together on positive initiatives, making use of the wider Community market to develop in ways denied by the more limited scope and resources of our individual national markets. The scope for a Community-wide venture in the field of technological innovation, for example, is clearly apparent. It is estimated that Britain, or any other of the Community countries taken as an individual national market, would only provide 5–10 per cent of the market required to justify the investment necessary for any new major technological project. Any new technological development therefore needs to have a European-wide market as its base; and we should surely grasp the opportunity to develop that market for ourselves, rather than watch our competitors rush in to fill the gap.

Quite evidently, we have a lot of ground to catch up. In 1965, the Community exported 40 per cent more electronic-based products than it imported; in 1976, the Community only broke even. Meanwhile, the Japanese, in 1976, exported nine times as many such products as they imported. The situation today is worse still, as the balance of trade in computers alone shows. That is of growing concern in the long term is the relative drop in the number of patents taken out by Community nationals: this dropped by 20 per cent between 1965 and 1977, whilst the Japanese took out 400 per cent more patents in the same period. I very much hope that the proposals on technological innovation and the Commission put forward to the Council in June 1982, as part of the Mandate exercise, will be seized upon with due sense of urgency. For the proposals are a constructive series of measures, designed to encourage Community cooperation in a variety of ways. In particular, I believe that there is particular scope for greater pooling of the resources available for research and development work – relatively limited resources by American or Japanese standards – to avoid wasted duplication of effort. This is true as much in the field of technological innovation as in energy research – and doubtless in many other areas too; and the Commission's efforts to promote joint ventures in these areas, and to encourage the mutual exchange of research and technical information, should be warmly supported. Only by acting jointly in this manner will we be able, in my view, to carve out a viable economic future – and thus avoid being squeezed into an increasingly precarious and unsatisfactory position between the innovative leaders – the United States and Japan on the one hand – and the increasingly competitive industries of the developing countries on the other.

I turn now to the fourth aspect of the Community which I regard to be of major importance to Britain and that is the growing significance attached to political cooperation. In recent years this is the area in which there has been perhaps most success in developing and expanding a common Community interest and a public voice. In a sense this is ironic, since foreign affairs are one area for which the Community has no theoretic or defined responsibilities. In another sense it was perhaps inevitable – and I certainly regard it as a most important and desirable development – since many policies for which the Community does have responsibility have inevitable foreign policy implications. For example, agricultural exports to non-EEC countries, and in particular to the USSR; food and development aid to sensitive areas in the Third World, such as Cambodia; trade sanctions against Iran and more recently, Argentina. In these instances and others, the importance of a consensus on foreign policies is clearly apparent; and this has inevitably led to the necessity for a more clearly defined structure within which to develop systematic discussion and coordination of policies.

Political cooperation is one aspect of the Community's activities for which Britain has generally shown enthusiastic interest. Hedged in between the superpowers, faced with escalating global tension and the stockpiling of increasingly effective and deadly armaments, the importance of political cooperation for Europe is increasingly apparent. I consider it to be of immense importance to Britain that, through the Community, and as part of the Community, we have a more authoritative and respected voice in world affairs than could today be secured by Britain alone. Of equal importance is the fact that the Community's voice has an independence, separate from if friendly towards the United States; and recognised as such by the rest of the world.

In view of this, I very much hope that Britain will not lag behind and delay the serious discussion of the important and far-reaching proposals put forward under the so-called Genscher/Colombo Plan, proposed jointly by the Foreign Ministers of Germany and Italy. Whatever the reservations, which I do not myself share, but which I must recognise as considerable, I believe that the proposals for greater coordination of security policies, which carry important economic as well as political implications, should be closely and sympathetically considered. Such an initiative would be separate from, but complementary to, our existing commitments within NATO; and would be intended to strengthen our position both as a Community and as individual members of NATO. Such an initiative would have considerable implications for our respective defence industries and national defence procurement programmes, which would need to be considered carefully; but a move in this direction, with all the repercussive effects it would have, not least in stimulating technological cooperation, would to my mind be a welcome development. In an expanding Community, with Greece now a member and Spain and Portugal close to joining, the relevance of expanding the Community's role in this respect is obviously great. I greatly hope that Britain and other member states will respond with due vigour.

Indeed, I personally believe that the wide political implications raised by the Genscher/Colombo Plan, taken in conjunction with the entirely separate proposals put forward by the French government, the latter concentrated mainly on economic matters and employment, clearly show that the Community is not a static and stagnant entity, incapable of change and reform. It is significant that it is the German, Italian and French governments which are seeking to expand the Community's role and to shift its concentration away from an unbalanced preoccupation with agriculture and the Common Agricultural Policy and towards wider concerns. No comparable initiatives come from Britain, the fourth major power of the Community. Britain should seize this opportunity to steer the Community towards policies more relevant to her interests, and work with our partners to launch a revamped and revitalised Community, starting from the constructive basis provided by these various proposals. For we cannot have our cake and eat it. We cannot seek a minimalist Community, in which we take a minimalist interest, and then turn round and accuse our Community partners of playing the game at our expense. It is in Britain's interests and I believe in the Community's too, to develop the Community's activities on regional and social policies, industrial innovation, energy conservation and the development of renewable resources of energy. But to do this, we cannot always take a minimalist line. I do not believe that it is in Britain's interests to say rigidly that we will never consider raising the current 1 per cent VAT ceiling; that we want the right of the individual country to be as absolute and extensive as possible. That is no way to get the Community to change. We cannot criticise the Community incessantly for failing to recognise our own special interests and yet fail ourselves to put forward positive and constructive measures for the Community's development that would shape it more along the lines on which we in Britain want it to go and from which we would benefit.

After the rancour surrounding the budget discussions in May 1982 and the consequential sense of mutual exasperation and incomprehension clouding our relations with the rest of the Community, the summer holidays provided a welcome breathing space. I greatly hope that the British government will seize the opportunity to come forward with a set of positive proposals to prove our commitment to the Community and to its future development. Such an initiative is long overdue. But the timing is now ripe and should not be missed, if the Community is to develop in the shape of which it is capable, with Britain a committed and active Community member.

2 Britain and the EEC: Past and Present

F. S. NORTHEDGE

Britain has been a member of the European Economic Community (EEC), or, to give it its current name, the European Community or EC, since January 1973, but has derived little satisfaction from the experience. Opinion polls conducted by the EEC Commission have shown that opponents of British membership of the Community in Britain have for several years outnumbered supporters two to one, the same proportion as that by which supporters outnumbered opponents in the referendum on the issue conducted in this country in June 1975. One of the two traditional British political parties, the Labour Party, was committed by a vote of 6 213 000 to 782 000 at its last Annual Conference to taking Britain out of the Community.[1] The recent Falkland Islands crisis served as a temptation to many British people, including leader writers of *The Times*, to entertain ideas that the country might serve its interests better by relaxing continental commitments and turning once more to the 'silver sea'.[2]

Traditionally, of course, the British have never had much love for Europe, which is a place for holidaying, not for politics. The House of Commons select committee on foreign affairs found that only half of the diplomatic staff in the British embassy in Paris were proficient in French, and only a third in the embassy in Bonn could speak German with any fluency. The unfamiliarity of British politicians with continental politics, indeed their distaste for them, is a theme of British history, symbolised by Lord Derby's admission, when Prime Minister in the 1850s, that 'we can trust none of these European governments', by Churchill's description of Stanley Baldwin in the 1930s as 'knowing little of Europe and disliking what he knew', and by Enoch Powell's dismissal of Europe as a 'seething cauldron of resentments, ambitions and hostilities' and of the EEC currency plan as an 'elephant pit' prepared by France and West Germany for Britain to fall into.[3] Perhaps, too, the association in British minds of Europe with the dead of the two world wars has not made its image any more congenial.

One refers to British mental detachment in regard to Europe as 'traditional', but it is in fact relatively recent, being a consequence of Britain having acquired an empire covering a quarter of the land surface of the globe and embracing a quarter of its people. In the last decades of the nineteenth century the empire became bigger than the government in London could supervise, and connections with Europe dropped in importance accordingly. But for centuries after the Norman Conquest in 1066 England and the continent formed an undivided political community. As late as the eighteenth century a British commander, Marlborough, led European armies to victory in the heart of Europe. Wellington did the same somewhat nearer home at the beginning of the nineteenth century. It was George Canning, the British Foreign Secretary, who recognised the former Portuguese and Spanish colonies in Latin America as independent states in the 1820s and so 'called the new world into existence to redress the balance of the old', as he somewhat strangely put it, and who led Britain away from Europe; and the expansion of empire, the industrialisation of Britain and the growth of overseas trade made it possible for him to do so. With the decolonisation of the British empire after 1945, it would be natural to expect a reversion to the ancient position of involvement in European politics. But old habits die hard, especially in a conservative country like Britain.

Coupled with the British sense of awkwardness in dealing with things European has gone a distinct indifference, and in many people a positive hostility, towards the idea of political, or any sort of, union among the European states, especially if it is supposed to involve this country. Ernest Bevin's famous phrase about the Council of Europe in the late 1940s sums up the feeling: 'once you open that Pandora's box you'll find it full of Trojan horses'. True, from the end of the Second World War British governments were in the forefront of efforts for West European economic recovery and collective defence. No one worked harder than Bevin as Foreign Secretary in the first Labour government after the war to build West European international institutions for economic recovery on the basis of Marshall Aid from the United States in the years 1948 to 1951. The Organisation for European Economic Cooperation (OEEC), of which Britain was the foremost architect, is now the Organisation for Economic Cooperation and Development (OECD) with headquarters in Paris; it includes the

United States and Japan among its members, and is the most important body for economic cooperation among the industrialised non-communist nations. Again, it was more due to British initiatives than to those of any other state that the Brussels treaty for economic, social and cultural collaboration and for collective self-defence in Western Europe was signed in March 1948, and this provided the embryo of the North Atlantic treaty signed by 12 Western nations in Washington on 4 April 1949.

All this British-sponsored international cooperation was on traditional lines. National sovereignty was firmly safeguarded and no concession was made to the growing number of people in Western Europe at the end of the war who wanted a step forward towards pooling sovereignty, so that decisions in international bodies could be taken on the basis of majority voting, a sort of limited federation. British politicians had always been nervous about this: they strongly opposed the French Prime Minister Aristide Briand's plan for European union in 1930 and worked energetically in the different European capitals to get it rejected.[4] Ten years later, when France was on the brink of capitulation in the Second World War, Prime Minister Churchill agreed to the offer of union with France, when it was put to him, only with the greatest reluctance and as a 'dramatic announcement to keep the French going'.[5] It came too late to be put to the test.

After 1945, Britain, with a supporting ring of Scandinavian states, was the chief opponent of schemes of European cooperation which involved any handover of sovereignty. The Council of Europe, eventually consisting of 18 West European member states and based on a statute signed on 5 May 1949, was scaled down from a quasi-federal body with 'limited but real powers', as they were called, in the hands of its two principal organs, the Committee of Ministers and the Consultative Assembly, to the talking shop which it largely is today, through British influence for the most part. The Schuman Plan for the pooling of coal and steel industries in Western Europe, which the French proposed in May 1950, was rejected by Britain because it assigned supranational powers to its High Authority. Britain sympathised with, but refused to join, the European Defence Community (EDC), a treaty for which was signed in 1952 by the six states which accepted the Schuman Plan for the coal and steel community (Belgium, France, the Federal German Republic, Holland, Italy and Luxemburg), British objections being, again, to its supranational features. In the end, the French National Assembly refused to ratify the EDC treaty when it was put to the vote in August 1954 and the Community failed to come into existence. Socialist members of the Foreign Affairs Committee of the National Assembly said afterwards that they would have voted for the EDC treaty, thus ensuring its success, if Britain had shown any enthusiasm for it.[6] Finally, when the Rome treaty was signed in March 1957 for the creation of an economic community among the Six, Britain again took no part: instead, she formed the European Free Trade Association (EFTA) in 1959 with Austria, Denmark, Portugal, Norway, Sweden and Switzerland – afterwards called the Seven – a body framed on traditional international lines, unlike the supranationalist EEC, and intended to bring pressure to bear on the Six for the abandonment of supranationalism and a reversion to traditional practice.

This opposition to supranationalism was not a party issue; it is hard to see how it could have been, considering the long-standing British lack of enthusiasm for schemes of European federation. It is true that, to some extent, the familiar right-to-left political spectrum in Britain corresponds with the spectrum of pro-European to anti-European leanings, a situation at first sight puzzling in view of the time-honoured association of socialists with internationalism. The interests of the business world, with its habitual support for the Conservative Party, in a wider market for exports, however, may be presumed to have given British right-wing politicians their sympathy for the EEC, while Labour politicians can be presumed to recoil against the relatively high food prices in the Community, and to argue that the working-class family would be better served by more distant food supplies, as for instance from within the Commonwealth. But it should be emphasised that the right–left pattern of sympathy for and coldness towards the EC respectively represents gradations within a general climate of indifference. If the middle-of-the-road British Conservative MP is warmer towards the Community than the middle-of-the-road Labour MP, he is at most only marginally so. A classic illustration of this was furnished during the debates in Britain over the Schuman Plan. Mr Churchill (as he was then) chided Attlee for lukewarmness on the European issue, being especially critical of the Labour leader's refusal to send representatives to the conference proposed by the French for setting up the coal and steel community. But in the House of Commons exchanges on the Schuman Plan on 27 June Mr Churchill made it clear that he objected to the supranational elements in the Schuman Plan quite as much as Attlee.[7] In August 1950 Harold Macmillan unfolded the Conservative Party's plan for a European coal and steel organisation at the Consultative Assembly of the Council of Europe: it was based on the traditional international model. British Conservatives,

Macmillan stressed, 'agreed in principle' with the aims of the Six for coal and steel, to which the author of the French plan, Robert Schuman, retorted that 'he who agrees with me in principle disagrees with me in fact'.[8]

The exception to the rule of British party politics that supranationalism in Western Europe has been more opposed than welcomed is, of course, the Liberal Party and, after its formation in March 1980, the Social Democratic Party, the present allies of the Liberals. It is doubtful whether Liberal support for British membership of the Community (which is in any case not entirely uniform within the party) has played any measurable role in keeping the party small as a parliamentary force, considering that pro-Europeanism is not an asset for any British political group. It is the vagaries of the electoral system, together with the predominance of the two major parties over so many years, which have probably been the main factors in Liberal weakness, and it is ironically owing to this very fact that British Liberals have been able to indulge the luxury of a pro-European policy. If the party had had larger parliamentary support (we are referring to the period before the emergence of the SDP and the formation of the Liberal–SDP alliance) it would almost certainly have had to consider more carefully the effect on its standing of its backing for a European Community policy. The popularity of the SDP from the moment of its birth, despite its pro-European policy, is harder to explain. One must assume that exasperation with the two traditional parties was running so deep in Britain (though the Falklands crisis has served to reduce it for the ruling Conservatives) that any group which aimed at 'breaking the mould' of British politics would be taken to the voter's heart, almost whatever it stood for, including support for the Common Market. Later, when the Liberal–SDP alliance has established itself more soundly and passed through the fires of a general election, its leaders may feel compelled to pause and count the price they pay for being saddled with a pro-European policy. In the meantime, there is no clear evidence of the Alliance actually being weakened by that policy.

Strong dislike

THE ROOTS OF BRITISH AVERSION FOR EUROPEAN INTEGRATION

mixed feelings.

British ambivalence towards, or half-heartedness about, the European Community is bedrock and basic, underlying all the bickering about budgetary questions, fishing and so on. It is rooted in history, in the way in which the British political system grew up, in British interests and sources of national strength and prosperity, and in all the mental habits which have developed along with such things. At the risk of oversimplifying, British attitudes to European integration may be said to have originated in four or five national experiences which, taken together, have made the process of British association with the movement towards unity in Western Europe more painful than it has been for any other country.

Firstly, for two centuries at least Britain has been the thalassic, maritime, sea-going power *par excellence*, protecting its scattered empire and worldwide trade by a navy equal (until 1921) to the two next biggest navies in the world combined. The British had interests as a premier naval power and trader too extensive for them to be cabined and confined in Europe. If they had a choice, as Churchill often used to say, between the European continent and the open sea, they must always come down on the side of the latter: that was where their empire and trade lay, and that was the highway to allies, especially the United States, without the help of which survival, after the First World War at least, would have been problematical. This notion of Britain as a worldwide oceanic power was intensified, if anything, by the experience of the Second World War. Britain, after all, survived that conflict, whereas continental Europe, and in the end Germany, too, went down in defeat and disaster. It was hard for British politicians who had seen their country at the very pinnacle of world power at the Yalta and Potsdam conferences in 1945 to accept the idea that the West European countries then in such sore straits had it in them to launch any great innovation like European unity, or that Britain, in all its wartime glory, should stoop to join forces with such down-and-outs. Later, when the down-and-outs were recovering and making a greater success of their economies than Britain, it was deeply humiliating to have to admit that perhaps, after all, European integration had played some part in their success. For Britain in the late 1940s and early 1950s, the rejection of Europe was the prerogative of one of the world's greatest powers, and was doubly gratifying for being so: seeking membership of the EEC in the 1960s was the symbol of decline, and that was one of the things which made it displeasing.

Secondly, for as long as the British folk-memory went back, governments at Westminster had worked for *disunity* in Europe, not unity. The traditional British policy towards Europe, natural to a small island anchored off a politically turbulent continent, was the balance of power, or the organisation of international coalitions against the most threatening state of the day, the France of Louis XIV and Napoleon, the Germany of the Kaiser and Hitler. The unification of Europe could never be a project dear to British hearts because a united Europe would be able to disarm on land and invest the resulting savings in sea power, which would bring the independence of Britain into question. So ingrained was the habit of the balance of power in the British mind that in 1962, when Harold Macmillan, the then Prime Minister, was applying for British membership of the EEC and was warned that President de Gaulle of France might veto the application (as he did in January 1963), Macmillan retorted that in that case Britain would have no alternative but to organise a 'peripheral coalition' against France, just as it had done in Napoleon's time.

The fact that since 1918 so many schemes of European unification had their origins in France (just as they had for centuries before) is a third reason for British lack of enthusiasm about them. French support for European integration since 1945 has been at once highly imaginative, as the contribution of the French master-builder in this field, Jean Monnet, shows, and acutely self-centred. The French took the initiative in the 1950s with the Schuman Plan, the Pleven Plan for a European army, the drive to relaunch the process after the failure of EDC in 1954. At the same time, integration has had to serve French national purposes, especially French determination to control Germany, or rather its rump, the Federal Republic, and prevent it again becoming a threat to peace, and to control the pace of integration so as to accord with French wishes concerning the abandonment of sovereignty. This policy was often pursued with a brutal realism and disregard for others. In May 1950, for instance, when the French launched the Schuman Plan, they did their utmost to ensure that Britain did not join it, giving her little time in which to make up her mind and demanding that the principle of supranationalism be accepted in advance of the conference to agree on the coal and steel community. It is true that Attlee's Cabinet had no wish to accept the principle of supranationalism, but the French made it easy for them to reject it with a good conscience by the tactics they adopted. Later, the French twice turned down British applications to join the EEC without consulting their partners in the Community. Between de Gaulle's two vetoes came his boycott of the Community, bringing its work virtually to a standstill until he had his way in the form of the Luxemburg compromise in January 1966, which allowed a state to nullify Community proposals which it regarded as inconsistent with its own national interests. In May 1982, as a result of French pressure, the

EEC refused to allow Britain to avail itself of the Luxemburg procedures in the matter of the adoption of the Community's farm prices.

The fact that the French have taken the lead in European integration
since 1945, and have been the country with which Britain has had most
to do in seeking admission to the EEC, has not made the problem of
Britain's Community membership easier. The history of Anglo-
French relations from as far back as 1066 has been studded with
hostilities and disagreements. There are infinite sources of friction in
the partnership, arising from psychological and cultural differences,
clashes of hard national interest and ingrained habits of thinking and
feeling. It is not an exaggeration to say that, over the years, only one
thing has enabled British and French politicians to overcome their
dislike for one another, and that is their common fear of Germany.
Once Germany (or rather the Federal Germany of Adenauer) and
France made their partnership the foundation of their efforts to
construct the EEC, the *raison d'être* of Anglo-French friendship
disappeared. So long as President de Gaulle had a friend in Adenauer,
he did not need Britain, and the British, if truth be told, received that
news almost with a sigh of relief. When de Gaulle fell from power in
1969 and was succeeded by Georges Pompidou, Franco-German
relations moved back, though not fully, to their former state of mutual
suspicion. Britain was then welcomed into the EEC by the French
authorities and accordingly entered that body in January 1973. The
British and French, in short, are not the world's most natural collaborators, and Britain's difficulties in learning to see the Community
as a means of solving its problems have been aggravated by the fact
that it is the French that the British have always found on the doorstep
of Community Europe, deciding whether Britain should be admitted.

Fourthly, Britain embarked at the end of the Second World War on
a programme of social and economic reconstruction for which the
Labour government under Clement Attlee considered that they had
received a mandate in the general election in July 1945. To achieve this
programme the Labour Party had waited thirteen years in the wilder-
ness since its dramatic defeat in the 1931 election and the formation of
a predominantly Conservative government, tranformed into the wartime coalition government under Churchill in May 1940. Reconstruction involved the creation of a new social service system to shield the
unemployed, the sick and other victims of social misfortune, the
maintenance of full employment and the taking into public ownership
of key sectors of the economy as a means of fulfilling these objectives.
The state was to be the agency for the transformation of Britain into a

more equal and compassionate society. It was therefore ironical that, after dreaming for years of such an opportunity, Labour leaders should be confronted by the suggestion from Western Europe, where moderately right-wing regimes now predominated, that the national control of basic resources should be relinquished, and that these resources should be handed over to bureaucracies which hardly seemed answerable to anybody. Hugh Dalton, the Attlee government's first Chancellor of the Exchequer (he was succeeded by Sir Stafford Cripps in November 1947) expostulated that 'we are determined not to put these gains' – that is, the social progress achieved under the government – 'in peril through allowing vital decisions on great issues of national economic policy to be transferred from the British Parliament in Westminster to some supra-national European assembly ... We intend to hold what we have gained here in this island.'[9] Such protests nevertheless raised awkward questions for socialists, even of the more moderate British variety: a Labour Cabinet might redistribute national income more fairly, but when that income began to seem meagre compared with that of countries joining the European integration movement, would Labour face a choice between social services increasingly difficult to finance and the economic success which seemed to be the reward for Community membership?

Finally, there was the question of sovereignty. The British have found it harder than most people to accept the idea of the divisibility of sovereignty, parts of it remaining at home, parts being signed away to other authorities in Brussels or elsewhere. In British constitutional practice, power to make law lies with the monarch advised by ministers responsible to Parliament, and that is about all there is to be said on the subject. The British constitution, in so far as one can be said to exist, is one of the most centralised in the world: but for the fact that the government of the day is supposed to seek the electorate's approval for another term of office every few years, it can virtually do what it likes, with no Supreme Court and hardly any constitutional restraints to stand in its way. The government's power over legislation was inherited from the absolute monarchs of the past and is comparable only with theirs. The British, unlike the Americans, the French, the Germans and other people, have never deliberately drawn up a constitution for themselves, allocating powers to the centre and the periphery. Power has remained always with the centre, and the centre gave away as much of it to other authorities as it liked, it being understood that it could be taken back again if the centre felt like it. Moreover, sovereignty in Britain has been a continuous tradition from times too distant for people now to recall. It has never been appropriated by any foreign state, as the sovereignty of all the European states, except for the Soviet Union, was at one time or another sequestrated in the course of the Second World War. Once sovereignty has been lost, it is not too hard to get accustomed to the idea of losing it again. Britain, on the other hand, remained a *virgo intacta* throughout the Second World War, as it had been from time immemorial. As Hugh Gaitskell once said, for Britain to abandon her sovereignty, or any part of it, meant 'the end of Britain as an independent European state ... the end of a thousand years of history'.[10]

HOW BRITAIN CAME TO TERMS WITH EUROPE

Considering the strength of forces in British history and institutions which argued against entry into supranational bodies such as the EEC (however much supranationalism in that organisation may have been diluted with the passage of time), the remarkable thing is how Britain succeeded in effecting an entry at all. Many British people still wonder how and why it was done. And about the manner of Britain's entry into the Community two things may be said which have affected the British experience of the Community ever since. In the first place, the process of entry was a painfully protracted one, with starts and stops, goings forward, comings back and general bewilderment as to where we were going, if anywhere at all. Other countries, such as the original Six, or Denmark and Ireland, who joined with Britain in January 1973, or Greece, who entered eight years later, simply decided to join and were admitted. Norway, urged by its government to join, decided by referendum to stay out, and that was that. The process of entry in Britain's case was vastly more complicated.

The British attended as observers the Messina conference to frame the EEC which met in 1955, then decided not to sign the Rome treaty which created it in March 1957. Another year was spent in attempting to persuade the Six to convert the new body into a traditional free-trade area for industrial goods only, or to accept Britain and the other West European countries which objected to supranationalism in a kind of free-trade annexe to the EEC. When France refused to carry on these so-called Maudling negotiations, Britain and the other objectors to supranationalism formed EFTA as a way of strengthening their bargaining position *vis-à-vis* the Six Rome-treaty states. But it soon became evident that, with her extensive trading interests, Britain could not feel at home in a Europe divided into the Six and the Seven, and in 1961 Prime Minister Macmillan decided to take the plunge and to apply for EEC membership. Negotiations began with the Six with a view to full membership but with safeguards for British agriculture, the financing of which was quite different from that of the EEC system, for Britain's partners in EFTA, who must not be left in the lurch, and for the Commonwealth countries, which had enjoyed a preferential position within the British home market since 1932. The talks were ended with a resounding 'no' from President de Gaulle in January 1963 and an almost audible sigh of relief went up in Britain. Almost two years later, in October 1964, Harold Wilson formed the first Labour government for thirteen years, after a general election which gave him a six-seat majority in the Commons. Wilson and his colleagues had no strong admiration for European integration, but a severe economic crisis in 1966, which was to culminate in the devaluation of the pound by 14.3 per cent in November 1967, brought about a change of tune and in May 1967 the second British application to join the EEC was made. This time de Gaulle was able to use Britain's painfully obvious economic troubles as a reason for rejecting the application, and this was done at the general's press conference in November.

De Gaulle himself, however, was unseated as a result of student and trade union unrest in France in 1969 and an opportunity was thus created for Britain to try again. By this time, Harold Wilson, very much a sceptical convert to European integration, had lost an election in Britain on 18 June 1970 (symbolically, the date of the battle of Waterloo) and a Conservative government under Edward Heath, the strongest supporter of the European case in either of the two traditional British parties, made a third, and this time successful, bid to join the EEC. The fact that the Heath government's term of office was marked by intense industrial strife in Britain, which at one time put the country on the basis of a three-day working week and ultimately led to the government's fall in 1974, distracted attention from Britain's momentous move into the EEC in January 1973. Wilson's return to office, however, had the effect of bringing the Labour Party face to face with the inevitability of a British entry into Europe about which most of its senior members had serious doubts, and which caused feelings little short of consternation among its rank-and-file. The party found in fact that it could stomach the EEC only on two conditions, the first being that the terms of entry agreed to by the Heath government must be renegotiated, and the second that public opinion must be canvassed in the form of a referendum, the first in British history.

The renegotiation was conducted on the British side by Foreign Secretary James Callaghan and proved to be a perfunctory affair: the original terms of entry were modified in no substantial respect. As for the business of making entry into the EEC acceptable to British public opinion, this was achieved by a two-to-one majority in a nationwide poll held on 25 June 1975. There prevailed over the country on that occasion almost a festive atmosphere, the day being exceptionally fine, and voters perhaps gratified by a sense of relief that Britain was at last in the Community and the acrimony and disappointments of the past were over. People seemed to enjoy going to the polling booths to vote in unusual circumstances on an unusual issue, though it was significant that their opinions were being asked after the event rather than before. At any rate, a process of entry which had extended over fourteen stop–go years now seemed to be completed, though no one could foresee that before long many people who had voted 'yes' to entry would want to get out again.

The other important thing about Britain's entry into the EEC was that it had every appearance of being a policy of last resort, adopted, one might almost say, when all other expedients had failed. There was no suggestion of it being hailed as a brilliant success, or a success at all; the impression remained that it was brought about in humiliating circumstances and when other options in foreign policy had lost their convincingness. For continental Europeans who had looked forward to the opportunity to build a united Europe during long years of Nazi occupation, bodies like the Council of Europe, the Coal and Steel Community, the Economic Community, were the fulfilment of a dream. For Britain, joining organisations such as these represented the disappointment of expectations, of hopes of better things. In their inmost thoughts the British were never really convinced about the merits of European unity: unity was all right as a slogan, Attlee might talk about the need to 'federate or perish', but it was not a programme for practical action. It was 'sublime mysticism and nonsense', to use Castlereagh's phrase about the Holy Alliance. But, astonishingly, the EEC succeeded, especially in the early 1960s, taking Federal Germany and France to levels of affluence unheard of in Britain: even in Italy economic recovery was something to wonder at. Britain, on the other hand, plunged in 1966 and 1967 deeper into the economic mire.

That Britain visualised Europe as a 'home of last resort' was true in certain senses even more important than the economic. After 1945 there was a strong tendency in political quarters to visualise British foreign policy as proceeding within the three circles of Europe, the

Commonwealth and the Atlantic Community, the latter being understood mainly as the Anglo-American 'special relationship'. The 'three-
circle' concept is mainly thought of as one of Churchill's
brainchildren.[11] But the basis of it was obvious enough. So long as
Britain was able to maintain an influential position within these three
international associations, her say in world affairs was likely to remain
important, and, considering the country's still considerable position in
international trade and politics, British governments were bound to
work hard to preserve it. But in time two of the circles, the Commonwealth and the Anglo-American connection, weakened and did so,
significantly, at about the same time, that is, the early 1960s, as a
British Prime Minister first began to think it necessary to apply to the
EEC for membership.

The weakening of the Commonwealth became evident with its
growth in size as decolonisation proceeded. The cohesion of that
institution was bound to be affected, but this was much more so as the
economic interests of the new Commonwealth countries diverged
from Britain's, and so did their political interests. The new Afro-Asian
countries aimed at development, with which Britain, with her endemic
economic problems, was not well placed to help; they had no desire to
see their economic future sacrificed to British interests and wanted to
move ahead under their own steam. Their political outlook, too, could
hardly be more different from Britain's. She was involved in the Cold
War, in building up collective defence systems against the perceived
danger of Soviet aggression, in rearmament. African and Asian ex-
colonies regarded such concerns as irrelevant to their interests and
derived no satisfaction from the prospect of serving as mercenaries in
wars waged by one group of white nations against another. Moreover,
in South Africa the black Commonwealth countries had an enemy far
more real to them than the USSR, and one with whom, as it happened,
Britain saw no overwhelming grounds to quarrel. British governments
and people, Conservative and Labour alike, had no liking for the
apartheid system, but the British economic stake in South Africa was
too great for them to join Afro-Asian countries in drumming that
country out of the international community.

A significant development occurred in March 1961, when the South
African government decided to leave the Commonwealth in the face of
opposition by black African Commonwealth states to a South African
request to be allowed to remain a Commonwealth member despite
having become a republic. The black states, and indeed a great part of
the world, had been deeply shocked by the casualties suffered by black

South Africans when police opened fire on demonstrators at Sharpeville in March 1960. Macmillan, the British Prime Minister, had already advised South African whites to come to terms with the 'growth of national consciousness' in Africa in his 'winds of change' speech before the two Houses of the South African Parliament on 3 February 1960.[12] But it is doubtful whether, on balance, most British people approved of internal affairs being made a test of fitness for Commonwealth membership: it had never been the custom in the past. To that extent, South Africa's enforced departure from the Commonwealth in 1961 was a turning-point in British attitudes. Much as the British continued to regard the Commonwealth with pride and affection, warmth of feeling towards it declined, and that decline has not been seriously interrupted since. Macmillan must have given wide-ranging thought to the case for and against a British application to join the EEC before making that application in June 1961. But the change in British sentiment towards the Commonwealth engendered by the debate about South Africa cannot but have fortified his thinking.

British relations with the United States, the second of Britain's partners in the 'three-circle' concept, also began to undergo important changes in the early 1960s. Britain's alliance with America has been the sheet-anchor of her foreign policy since the Second World War: it is more important to her than it is to the United States, and the British have made more sacrifices to preserve it than have the Americans. But the early 1960s saw far-reaching changes. The Federal German Republic outstripped Britain economically, and American politicians, while retaining their old affection for Britain, began to look to Bonn as their strongest ally in Europe. It was essential, too, for the United States to cultivate West Germany after the shock it suffered when the Berlin Wall was built in August 1961 and the Americans offered no resistance to it. De Gaulle, on his side, showed the strongest interest in supplanting the United States in the affections of the German people if their interests did not receive a higher place in American thoughts.

Moreover, Britain's role in American decision-making, and not merely the perception of her strength as an ally, began to change. Ever since the United States joined the Grand Alliance in December 1941, British leaders tended to see themselves as standing at the ear of American government, advising it on the great issues with which America must now grapple as a world power, albeit without the experience to do so, warning it against recklessness in the use of the awesome destructive power of which it now disposed. Clement Attlee's famous flight to talk with President Truman in December 1950, when rumours were rife of American intentions to use atomic bombs against the Chinese, was a classic example. President Kennedy, however, who entered the White House in January 1961, was not a man who looked as if he needed a British tutor to guide him through the labyrinths of world politics. As his conduct during the Cuban missile crisis in October 1962 showed, he seemed wholly capable of conducting a dialogue with the other superpower, the Soviet Union, without external advice, though it must be added that his relations with Harold Macmillan were closer than those with any other foreign statesman.[13] With J. F. Kennedy in the White House, the United States seemed to 'come of age' in foreign policy. His successor, L. B. Johnson, was too deeply involved in the Vietnam War to be much influenced by British views on the conflict, while Johnson's successor, Richard Nixon, had a foreign affairs adviser and subsequently Secretary of State in the person of Henry Kissinger who seemed to have little regard for European ideas on foreign policy, British or non-British.

None of this meant that the Atlantic partnership, represented by NATO, with its Council, Military Committee and joint commands, counted for less in British policy: but Britain's special place in Washington as the confidant and mentor of its policy-makers began to undergo a change and, as a result, Britain's connections with her European neighbours came up for reconsideration. It is significant that Kennedy's accession to office, like South Africa's departure from the Commonwealth, occurred in the same year, 1961, as Britain's first application to join the EEC. The first two of these events were too close in time to the third for them to have determined it. But, with the weakening of those two other circles of British policy, the third was bound to take on greater importance. At the same time, the existence of the other two circles became less of an obstacle to Britain's developing her base in the third.

Britain's entry into the EEC being in some measure the result of the waning of alternatives, it is easy to see how disadvantageous her position was in the negotiations about the terms of entry. It is not merely that Britain was admitted into the EEC late – fifteen years after the Community came into existence – and therefore had to make herself at home in arrangements devised to suit the interests of others. But the fact that Britain's options in external policy had been reduced as a result of the waning of the circles of the Commonwealth and the Anglo-American special relationship gave to her entry into the EEC the appearance of being an unwelcome, though unavoidable, alternative when more attractive ones were failing. It might almost be said that Britain entered Europe (or, more correctly, joined the EEC) in 1973 because she had nowhere else to go, rather as the unicellular animalcule, the amoeba, is said to find its food, not by seeking it directly, but by being repelled by environments which do not contain food. It is true, of course, that no one in Europe in the early 1970s talked about Britain having no convincing options in foreign policy outside Europe, and therefore settling for the European option which she had disdained for so long. But it was plain to all that that was the situation. And it was this which seriously weakened Britain's bargaining strength. Of all the negotiating postures in international affairs, the best is one in which other states are asking you to do something and you are in a position, if need be, to say 'no' to all of them. The worst case is one in which you are asking other states for something and they know you can hardly take 'no' for an answer. Such was Britain's position during negotiations for entry into the EEC. It was similar to that of a person who asks for another's hand in marriage, and the courted person knows that the suitor has already been rejected by other eligible mates. The courted knows that he (or, more likely, she) can afford to lay down almost any terms for the match.

BRITAIN IN THE COMMUNITY

One might have supposed that the British, after such contorted efforts to join the EEC, would have settled down to make a success of their membership once the process of joining was complete. True to the whole record of British experience of the Community, this has not happened. The European Community is wildly popular in none of its member states (soon to include Spain), but in Britain its standing is perhaps lowest of all. Like Denmark but more so, Britain remains the odd man out in the Community and in the rest of the Community a sense of unease about Britain has been rising year by year.

One reason for this is that EEC membership seems to have brought Britain neither the expected losses nor the expected gains, and hence it has been difficult to form any positive judgement about it on which future policy could rest. In the years before entry, Conservative and Labour governments brought out White Papers on the implications of membership which concentrated on the costs in terms of higher food prices, and the effects of these on the price, and hence the prospects, of British exports to the rest of the world.[14] When entry came, however, the British, like many other people, found themselves caught up in a rising spiral of inflation which swept away the carefully compiled forecasts of price rises likely to result from EEC membership. To all outward appearance, the British people are on about the same living standards as when they joined the EEC, plus the effects of the sort of growth rates one would expect of any developed industrial country. It might be argued that they would have been worse off had they not joined, but the difficulties of proving that are practically insurmountable. As for the effects of the European Common Market on British exports, the available facts are equally inconclusive. It seems unlikely that British export prospects have not in some way drawn benefit from access to a market of some 300 million people, all of relatively high purchasing power, but the statistics of Britain's balance of payments with the Community do not provide much evidence of this, nor do the reports of individual British business men on their experience of the Common Market.

However, it is rarely the carefully compiled tables of statistics which determine the way in which people at large think about the international bodies they agree to belong to. It is often the more colourful, easily visualised pinpricks and irritants which engender resentments, especially where there is an ingrained bias against such organisations to begin with. And of these there was an abundance in Britain's contact with the EEC. One of the most highly publicised was the announcement in 1975 that a Danish film producer intended to come to Britain, as he was entitled to under the terms of the Rome treaty, to which Britain had acceded two years before, to make a film about the sex life of Jesus Christ. A wave of horror swept the country, the Queen describing the film as 'odious' (and that was before it was made), all the more so since many people realised, for the first time, that Britain was now in the Community and hence that this sort of thing could lawfully happen. The film itself was never made.

A somewhat similar rumpus, equally trivial and equally significant, was the EEC Commission's decision to make the tachograph (or 'spy-in-the-cab') compulsory for all trucks in the Common Market, thus hoping to reduce road accidents by limiting the time a truck driver could be at the wheel of his vehicle to forty-eight hours in any period of seven days. Truck-owners objected to the Commission's directive because the tachograph cost £100 or more to install and about half that sum every year to service. Truck-drivers resented a device which had the effect of limiting their earnings. Other examples of EEC interference in economic life in Britain included the standardisation of the size of eggs by rules different from those formerly in operation in this country, the regulation of the constituents of ice cream and of the ingredients in beer exports. A more serious bureaucratic intervention was the vetoing of a British nuclear materials agreement with Australia worth £1000 million. No wonder there has been a decline in the popularity of the EEC in Britain; no wonder, too, that the 'faceless bureaucrats' in Brussels are held to be chiefly responsible.

These are relatively minor irritations. Looming at the intergovernmental level are bigger questions in which Britain has faced her EEC partners in angry confrontation. Foremost among them is the Common Agricultural Policy (CAP) with all its iniquities. The CAP is regarded in Britain, though British farmers do well out of it, as a device by which the Community as a whole handsomely subsidises inefficient French farmers, on whose behalf, it might almost be said, the EEC was originally brought into existence. High farm prices mean high subsidies from the Community budget, to which the British complain that they make excessive contributions: even so, highly priced food produced in the Community remains unsold, hence has to be stored and refrigerated in the form of butter 'mountains' and wine 'lakes', all at Community expense, and then, the supreme absurdity, is unloaded at knock-down prices on communist-block countries against which Western states are organised in hostile array. Of the Common Market budget, 80 per cent is spent on the CAP, and because Britain has a big import trade with non-EEC countries, and by the Community's rules pays a proportion of the import duties of such trade into the Community budget, is in the position of being the largest contributor to the budget while having the lowest (with Italy) GNP per head of all member states. The maximum amount Britain has ever contributed to the EEC budget (£1200 million) is infinitesimal in comparison with Britain's own annual budget (£121 000 million); it has moreover been scaled down this year to just over £500 million, thanks to Prime Minister Margaret Thatcher's shrill appeals for financial justice. But the budget issue, besides giving anti-Common Market forces in Britain another stick with which to beat pro-Common Market groups, tends to give the EEC the appearance of being a clique of mutually jealous, not to say greedy, states quarrelling about financial dues rather than collaborators in a common endeavour.

Britain's disputes with the other EEC states have extended to fishery and fish conservation matters, the British complaint being that, in acquiescing in the throwing open of waters round Community territory to the general fishing interests of member states, the British fishing industry is deprived of exclusive access to waters from which its previous income was derived. Milk marketing arrangements have been another subject of lively debate between Britain and her Common Market partners, and Britain has also taken a detached position in declining to participate in such schemes of monetary stability in Western Europe as the European Monetary System (EMS) which the major EEC states have formed. Almost the only area of EEC cooperation in which Britain has proved herself to be in favour of going forward rather than standing still has been that of the enlargement of the Community: British ministers, generally speaking, have supported a larger rather than smaller Community. But this, it is suspected, is not so much because they believe the Community to be such a good thing that they want its benefits to be more widely shared, but because they prefer a loosely-knit, less well-integrated system, and think that a larger Community is a way of achieving this.

It is a curious fact, however, that the British authorities have recognised possibilities of development of the Community system in another area, which, as it happens, hardly appeared in the structure created by the Rome treaty in 1957, namely political cooperation, sometimes known as the coordination of foreign policy. Of course, external relations, or dealings with non-EEC states, have always been an integral part of the business of the EEC; no one has suggested that the Community can be isolated from the rest of Europe or the world. Moreover, it is not always easy to draw a line between such relations and foreign policy properly so-called, that is, the traditional domain of foreign offices and ministries of external affairs. Perhaps we would be right in speaking of foreign policy (and the coordination of the foreign policies of different states) as having to do with such matters as sovereignty and title to territory, the recognition of states and governments, war and peace, the settlement of international disputes, the regulation of armaments, alliances, alignments and such matters, whereas 'external relations' have to do with every kind of relations between states, but especially with trade, finance, the safeguarding of business interests, or what are sometimes referred to as 'low politics'. In areas of foreign policy such as the Middle East and its many problems, East–West relations in the context of the Helsinki agreements signed in 1975 and subsequent conferences to review the working of those agreements, and the application of economic measures against trouble-making states, such as the Soviet Union in the matter of Afghanistan and Poland, and Argentina in the matter of the Falkland Islands, the EEC countries have achieved a considerable degree of likemindedness. This has been more the case the more divergences on a wide range of foreign and defence questions have become evident between the West European countries and the United States under the Reagan Administration.

British ministers since 1945 have generally considered it their responsibility to try to hold together the Western alliance by acting in an intermediary role between the Common Market countries and the United States: they did so in 1954, even before the Common Market existed, when the French rejected the EDC and Britain stepped into the breach by using West European Union (WEU) as the instrument for bringing West Germany into the NATO structure, acquiring in the process the heavy commitment to keep forces in Germany on a more or less permanent basis. Before his resignation during the Falkland Islands crisis in April 1982, Lord Carrington had been making special efforts to place Britain in the forefront of the movement for political cooperation among the EEC countries.[15]

THE FALKLANDS AND THE REVIVAL OF OLD QUESTIONS

Although Britain's partners in the EEC agreed to support her in the Falkland Islands crisis in the early summer of 1982 by voting in favour of economic measures in restraint of trade with Argentina, they did so in a limited and restricted way: two of them, Ireland and Italy, dissociated themselves from those measures. When Britain objected to the raising of Community farm prices during her conflict with Argentina, there was some suspicion in Britain that the prices were being raised as the *quid pro quo* exacted by the EEC for the support afforded to Britain against Argentina. Britain insisted that there was no connection between the Falklands crisis and farm prices. When, however, the other EEC states went to the point of raising farm prices despite British objections, thus, in the British view, violating the rule embodied in the Luxemburg compromise of 1966, which stated that France considered that, 'where very important issues are at stake, discussion must continue until unanimous agreement is reached', they argued that the Luxemburg rule was not applicable. Britain, on the other hand, contended that there was a link between the rule established in 1966 and the farm price issue. Thus, though the Falklands crisis seemed at first to strengthen Britain's ties with the EEC by creating a consensus on economic measures against Argentina, in the end the effect was probably to revive the strains surrounding her general position in the Community.

But the Falklands crisis also seemed to affect Britain's position in the EEC by leading many British people to believe that, in working for better relations with the EEC, especially in the field of political cooperation, the Thatcher government had subordinated more geographically distant concerns to those which happened to be closer at hand. The resignation of Lord Carrington as Foreign Secretary shortly after the crisis broke at the beginning of April was significant. Lord Carrington felt he had to resign primarily because of allegations that he had misread clear indications in March of the impending Argentinian invasion of the islands. But he had been closely associated with the movement in the Foreign and Commonwealth Office to give priority to Europe.[16] When the Argentinian invasion took place, he was in the Middle East, pressing forward EEC ideas on a settlement of the Palestinian problem. He used the phrase that 'you cannot be thinking about the Falklands twenty-four hours a day', and it would not be rash to assume that he, like other Foreign and Commonwealth Office officials, regarded the Falklands as an irritant in Anglo-Argentinian, and also perhaps Anglo-American, relations, which should be eased or removed by negotiations on the status and future of the islands. The mission by Mr Richard Luce, a junior FCO Minister, to New York in February 1982 to discuss with an Argentinian team the future of the islands seemed to be in line with such considerations. The fact that Lord Carrington was not a member of the House of Commons, and was therefore less aware than others of the strength of feeling in the House about the Falklands, may have led him to think such relics of empire were negotiable in the press of his work for a more active role for Britain in Europe.

The Falklands war, if it was a war, came and went. For Britain, it was an astonishing success, contrasting strongly with the record of British reverses in one field after another after the Second World War. The medicine of showing the flag which had worked so well in the South Atlantic might work as well elsewhere. The Falkland Islands were bound to become a heavier commitment for Britain than ever before: more money would have to be spent developing the islands if the British argument for retaining them was to sound plausible; they would have to be better defended in future, with substantial forces stationed in and around them. Other outlying fragments of empire, such as Gibraltar, Hong Kong and Diego Garcia, would need to be looked at again and their defences against another General Galtieri overhauled. Almost inevitably, all the old distaste for Europe might surface again, all those people in Britain waiting for an excuse to dodge under the European barriers and make a getaway to 'fresh fields and pastures new' would take heart and see in the revival of an oceanic role for Britain an escape from the ungracious problems of the Common Market.

Perhaps this vein of reverie in the editorial chair or Commons bar or tearoom is a mere *jeu d'esprit* without long-term implications. But the fact that the British are so inclined to teeter on the brink of Europe without the resolution either to jump in or jump out suggests that it needs but the slightest temptation for them to retrace their steps to the beginning of the European road, on which most of them seem to wish they had never set foot. If the Falklands crisis brings to the fore the dangers of Britain drifting back into an oceanic role, from which she painfully extracted herself ten or so years ago, it will have served a useful purpose. But the crisis is equally likely to saddle Britain with dreams of lost grandeur which have little relation with present-day problems.

The besetting disability in Britain's relations with the EEC has been, and still is, schizophrenia, an inability to decide, once and for all, what the country's proper place in the world is. Britain, having entered the Community, not so much through conviction of its merits but from a sense of despair about alternatives, found much to object to in the Community system, especially the CAP and budgetary arrangements. These she tried to alter so that they would suit her purposes better. And all the time the impression was given that, after changes in such institutions and practices had been made to suit Britain's interests, and no doubt at some cost to other EEC states, she was just as likely to leave the Community as to stay in it. The effect on our continental neighbours must have been the same as that of the obscure and tergiversatory Woodrow Wilson on French Prime Minister Clemenceau at the Paris peace conference in 1919, when the latter at length burst out: 'M. le President, êtes vous pour ou contre?'

Perhaps it would be true to say that, in their inmost thoughts, most British politicians and civil servants know they cannot leave the Community, though it could leave them by ceasing to exist. An increasing amount of British trade is done with the EEC, 45 per cent, as compared with the 30 per cent when the Community was formed, 60 per cent if trade with states associated with the Community is included. Some of Britain's closest diplomatic partners are situated in Western Europe; the idea that Britain should be shut out of talks on world issues with such countries as France and Federal Germany is unthinkable. The pretence that this is possible goes on, though nobody believes it. It does not necessarily follow, however, that Britain's partners in the

EEC understand this point. Their call to Britain must be that she has to make up her mind once and for all: either to leave the Community and make the best terms she can with other states outside it (running the risk that the Common Market could become a trade bloc shut against Britain), or to stay in, but to do so determined to make a success of the enterprise, if that is humanly possible. This means that Britain must devote herself to participating in the search for means to make the EEC succeed, not be for ever looking for ways of making membership more financially lucrative to herself and muttering threats to leave if it is not. Analogies between the affairs of states and the affairs of individuals are notoriously misleading, but no marriage can be sound if husband or wife spend most of their lives instructing their lawyers to prepare a divorce.

NOTES

1. *The Times*, 2 October 1982.
2. Leading article, 'Strategy in a Silver Sea', *The Times*, 21 June 1982.
3. *The Times*, 4 October 1978.
4. *Documents on British Foreign Policy, 1919–1939*, ed. E. L. Woodward and Rohan Butler, Second Series, vol. I (London: HMSO, 1946) chapt. IV.
5. W. S. L. Churchill, *The Second World War*, vol II (London: 1949) p. 183.
6. Anthony Nutting, *Europe Will Not Wait* (London: Hollis and Carter, 1960) p. 65.
7. 476 H. C. Deb. 5s. Col 2159.
8. Council of Europe, Consultative Assembly, Second Session, Seventh Sitting, 14 August 1950.
9. Report of the 49th Annual Conference of the Labour Party, Margate, 1950, p. 166.
10. *Britain and the Common Market*, text of speeches made at the 1962 Labour Party Conference (London: The Labour Party).
11. W. S. L. Churchill, *Europe Unite. Speeches, 1947–1948*, ed. by Randolph S. Churchill (London: 1950) pp. 409–24.
12. Harold Macmillan, *Pointing the Way, 1959–1961* (London: Macmillan, 1972) p. 156.
13. See David Nunnerley, *President Kennedy and Britain* (London: Bodley Head, 1972).
14. For example, *Britain and the European Communities. An Economic Assessment*, Cmnd 4289 (London: HMSO, February 1970).
15. See his article, 'European Political Co-operation: America Should Welcome It', *International Affairs*, The Royal Institute of International Affairs, vol. 58, no. 1 (Winter 1981–2).
16. See article by David Spanier, 'Foreign Policy: the Change of Emphasis that is Putting Europe First', *The Times*, 26 November 1980.

3 The Common Agricultural Policy

JOHN MARSH

For some people in Europe the Common Agricultural Policy is seen as one of the principal achievements of the Community. Linking together through formal policy the activities of all member countries in one particular sector it is regarded as a pattern for the closer union foreseen in the preamble to the Rome treaty. This view would be greeted with astonishment by most who live in the United Kingdom and with growing scepticism amongst adherents of the Community elsewhere. The Common Agricultural Policy seems to have become a symbol of the divisiveness, inefficiency and collective stupidity of the Community. Far from being an integrating device, it promises to prove the explosive which finally wrecks all hope of European unity. This chapter tries to explain why, despite the good intentions of those who created the Common Agricultural Policy, it has not led to heaven. It will also suggest that there are other policies which could achieve more nearly what the authors of the treaty and the CAP intended.

THE DEVELOPMENT OF AGRICULTURE IN EUROPE

Three factors are central to any understanding of the dilemma facing agricultural policy-makers in Europe. They are the implications of growth in the EC economy as a whole, the application of new technology within the agricultural sector and the static nature of demand for agricultural goods.

Low income elasticities of demand for agricultural products at a time of rising per capita incomes inevitably mean that the autonomous rate of growth of farm revenues as a whole lags behind the rate of growth in the revenues of other sectors. Further, since the rest of the economy's expansion may require some of the resources currently engaged in agriculture, the costs which agriculture has to pay for its purchases from other sectors, or to retain labour or capital in competition with other sectors, will tend to rise at a rate broadly proportional to the growth in incomes in the economy as a whole. The consequence, in the absence of any positive policy, would be a tendency for farm incomes to lag behind those of other sectors. They might even fall in absolute terms. This, of course, does not mean that individual farmers may not achieve higher incomes or that in some years the income of farms as a whole may not rise, whilst other incomes fall. Such are the vagaries of weather and the inequalities of performance amongst farmers that both developments are possible within an overall trend towards lower relative farm incomes. Isolation makes it more difficult for people engaged in agriculture to move into new occupations than for most people in other declining sectors. Thus agricultural decline tends to lead to regional decay. Against this background the social and political pressures for intervention in agriculture may be more important than considerations of economic efficiency.

At high levels of income, extra spending on food tends to emphasise convenience, variety and meals eaten out. Such changes in demand do not lead to marked increases in demand for goods at the farm gate. However, given higher incomes, consumers may be even less ready to adjust to changes in price by reducing or raising the quantity they purchase of particular foods. Such price inelasticity remains one important cause of widely fluctuating prices to producers. Wide price fluctuations matter to governments; when food prices rise greatly, hardship results for the poorest members of society. Sharp price increases in products, which weigh heavily in the retail price index, may, at least according to some theories, help to stimulate higher rates of inflation.

In recent years relatively rapid improvements in agricultural technology have been a major source of disequilibrium. Output has increased most dramatically in dairy farming, cereal production and intensive livestock. The result is that the same agricultural area can now produce much more food. Recent technical improvement has not been neutral so far as the types of resource required are concerned. It has tended to substitute capital for labour and to a lesser extent for land. Much of the new technology requires relatively large units if it is to achieve potential economies of scale. In Europe the structure of farming is often small and fragmented. Many of the improved methods are most readily applicable in lowland farming, thus farmers in hilly or mountainous areas may become increasingly disadvantaged and whole areas be threatened with depopulation. For some onlookers modern farming methods are made even less attractive because of the sheer power of technology to change not only output but the established appearance of the countryside itself. Part of the concern stems from objective factors such as alterations in the water table resulting from land drainage, increased calls on water resources for irrigation and the possible pollution of streams by agricultural chemicals. Equally articulate but less easy to evaluate are subjective anxieties about changes in the countryside. These include its appearance, the existence of a varied wild animal and plant life and the accessibility of country areas for urban recreation. Increasingly governments are drawn into these issues and find conflicts between the pressures to create an efficient pattern of farming, to sustain farm incomes and the social and aesthetic priorities of the non-farming public.

To summarise, the development of agriculture in Europe faces a policy-maker with problems of a social and political nature in relation to farm incomes and the impact of technology on the structure of farming and the environment. It has not removed anxiety about price instability but it has provided an opportunity to remove the fear of scarcity and to release resources to be used elsewhere in the economy.

THE WAY IN WHICH THE COMMON AGRICULTURAL POLICY WORKS

The designers of the Common Agricultural Policy sought to implement goals specified in the Treaty of Rome. These goals embodied the perception of agricultural policy needs of the 1950s. They emphasised the need for greater productivity, the wish to raise the incomes of those who worked in agriculture, concern about price stability and the security of supplies and a wish to ensure that prices to consumers were 'reasonable'. Later more emphasis has been given to regional aspects of agricultural problems and most recently and unofficially there is a questioning of the goals of greater efficiency and a wish to bring environmental concerns to the fore.

Initially the policy-makers relied almost wholly on the manipulation of the prices of important agricultural commodities to achieve these goals. In essence they tried to establish a common internal price level more stable and higher than that which prevailed in the world market. To do so they deployed, for major commodities, an all-embracing system of protection. For some, tariffs were imposed. More important, however, were the variable import levies inserted between the lowest world offer price and a price thought to be appropriate for the Community. In so far as these variable levies are effective, goods from abroad cannot compete on price with those produced within the Community.

For such important commodities as cereals, milk and beef, the Community reinforced this protection by agreeing to intervene in the domestic market if farmers' products did not find a market at an acceptable price. Such intervention puts a floor in the internal market. It is financed by the European Agricultural Guidance and Guarantee Fund from the common budget of the Community. To enable EC produced goods to be exported, restitutions, subsidies which bridge the gap between high Community and low world prices, may be made available to traders.

Any restraint on output, provided it can be produced at costs up to EC administered prices, is removed by intervention and export restitutions. Thus this system enabled the level of production to grow as technology improved regardless of the much slower growth of demand within the Community itself. Initially the effect was simply to displace imports. Ultimately, however, when the domestic market could no longer absorb all that was produced, goods had to be sold abroad or taken off the home market by intervention. Once self-sufficiency is reached, the full cost of the difference between the world and EC values on extra output falls on the budget. The consequences can be readily seen in the development of expenditure on Community price policy during the past twenty years (Table 3.1).

Following the creation of its price policy the Community has introduced a variety of structural policies. These policies embody rather than resolve a contradiction. Towards the end of the 1960s under the influence of the so-called 'Mansholt Plan', the Community began to evolve a series of structural directives which were intended to facilitate the mobility of manpower within and out of agriculture and the modernisation of agricultural structures. It was hoped that this strategy would eventually remove the need for continued income and price support by enabling those remaining in the industry to derive satisfactory incomes from the market itself.

In the course of the 1970s, however, the emphasis of structural policy shifted. In part this was a recognition of the need to discriminate between regions well placed to produce at low cost and those where natural conditions were especially difficult. A number of directives

TABLE 3.1   *Total guarantee expenditure*

1967/8	1968/8	July/ Dec '69	1970	1971	1972	1973	1974
1 313.0	1 995.9	1 554.4	2 363.0	2 346.5	2 737.2	3 657.5	3 097.9

1975	1976	1977	1978	1979	1980	1981	1982 (provisional)
4 727.4	5 570.0	6 662.4	8 672.4	10 440.7	11 314.9	11 610.5	13 217.3

NOTES   1967/8–1977 million ua
1978–9 million EUA
1979–82 million ECU

SOURCE   1967/8–1977 EEC Food and Agricultural Statistics, MAFF, various edns.
1978–80 SOEC Agricultural Situation in the EC (1981).

gave additional assistance to the so-called 'less favoured areas'. These included parts of all Community countries and their implementation depended on the initiative and energy of the governments and farmers in the country concerned. More recently, as growing problems of unemployment have made the prospects of mobility out of agriculture less attractive, attention has been focused on the possibility of integrated development programmes. These seek to revitalise and sustain the economy of hard-pressed areas by comprehensive interventions in agriculture and related activities. Both approaches represent, in contrast to the 'Mansholt' concept, an attempt to resist autonomous economic forces rather than to work with them.

Expenditure on structural policy has remained a relatively minor part of total Community agricultural expenditure (Table 3.2). Unlike the open-ended commitment to price policy, structural policy is strictly constrained within the funds made available by the Council of Ministers. Although its effect may be enhanced by expenditure from national budgets, it displays a much more cautious attitude towards agricultural policy than that applied to commodity prices.

TABLE 3.2 *FEOGA guidance expenditure*

1967/8	1968/9	July/Dec '69	1970	1971	1972	1973	1974
285.0	285.0	142.5	285.0	285.0	285.0	325.0	128.4

1975	1976	1977	1978	1979	1980
185.3	209.0	292.1	161.4	224.0	275.0

NOTES and SOURCE as Table 3.1.

It would be misleading to leave this brief sketch of the character of the Common Agricultural Policy without noticing some of its important achievements. These include:

1. Much greater freedom of movement of agricultural goods between Community countries. Intercommunity trade in agricultural goods has grown substantially (Table 3.3).
2. An effective means of insulating Community prices from fluctuations in world market prices.
3. A substantial transfer of resources towards the agricultural sector from the rest of the Community.
4. The establishment of the Community itself. Whilst it is certainly possible that a different agricultural policy might have allowed the

TABLE 3.3   *The development of trade in agricultural products*

A.   *EC6 – Trade in agricultural products*

	1958 million EUR	1972 million EUR	1972 as % 1958
Total imports	9 683	23 425	242
Imports from EC6	1 243	9 425	758
Imports from non-EC	7 440	14 000	188
Total exports	3 139	14 116	450
Exports to EC6	1 213	9 434	777
Exports to non-EC	1 926	4 682	243

SOURCE *Yearbook of Agricultural Statistics 1974* (Luxemburg: Eurostat, 1974).

B.   *EC9 – Trade in agricultural and food products*

	1973 million EUA	1980 million EUA	1980 as % 1973
Total imports	39 857	78 552	197
Imports from EC9	15 486	36 342	235
Imports from non-EC	24 371	42 210	173
Total exports	22 620	55 792	247
Exports to EC9	15 242	36 271	238
Exports to non-EC	7 378	19 521	265

SOURCE *The Agricultural Situation in The Community* (Brussels–Luxemburg: European Commission, 1976 and 1981).

original members to form the Community, this particular one enabled them to do so. If no policy had been evolved for agriculture the Community itself would have failed.

Additional achievements are sometimes claimed. More realistically it seems that, in these cases, the CAP allowed such developments to occur, rather than caused them to happen.

1. Production and productivity within the Community's agriculture has increased. Increases in output are mainly the consequence of improvements in technology. Improvements in productivity stem both from extra output and because people left the sector. The effect of the CAP is ambivalent. By creating expectations that

incomes would be higher the CAP may have tended to slow down the rate of departure from agriculture. Higher prices may have encouraged investment in improved methods but an artificial hierarchy of prices has tended to distort the pattern of production. In particular, cereals have been more favoured than livestock.

2. It is claimed that by increasing EC self-sufficiency the CAP has ensured security of food supplies. Such a claim implies hypothetical judgements about world food production and supplies and the level of EC production had prices been lower. It would be necessary to show that since 1958 insecurity was a substantial possibility. This seems doubtful. As one of the richest areas in the world the Community can afford to buy food even if prices are high. The technology which has raised its output is also applicable in other countries. Only in 1974–6 was there a serious threat of worldwide shortage and for a time high prices for several commodities. For some products for a short time import prices actually exceeded the internal price level of the Community. Subsequently world prices have fallen well below EC levels. It seems at least possible that the Community could have ensured satisfactory food security at lower cost to itself by a combination of lower internal prices, an approach to international trade which maintained Community preference at levels similar to that enjoyed by industrial products, and by trade and investment policies which encouraged more production in lower-cost regions of the world. It is not even certain that had internal prices been nearer world levels the level of output within the Community would have been reduced. Within such an environment the share of agricultural resources controlled by the most efficient producers would have increased.

3. A third achievement claimed for the CAP is an increase in the EC's agricultural exports. Part of this is 'food aid'. Part is the result of subsidised price-cutting in competition with lower-cost agricultural exporters. It is hard to believe that this is an intended achievement. So far as food aid is concerned, an equivalent investment located in the recipient countries themselves or in lower-cost exporters would have produced more food of a type more suited to the needs of the poorer countries. Provision of food in poor countries as a policy may be a well-intentioned if somewhat inefficient form of aid; the disposal of unplanned surpluses in order to protect internal markets is less clearly acceptable. At its worst it could amount to exporting instability rather than providing help.

THE CONTRADICTIONS OF PRICE POLICY

The principal justification for paying higher than market equilibrium prices for food is the need to maintain the incomes of agricultural producers. Central to Community price determinations have been arguments about the incomes of farmers. However, an analysis of the way in which prices work within the agricultural sector suggests that such an approach is likely to be self-defeating. Although simple economic models cannot hope to explain the complexity of actual experience, the model of perfect competition provides a good starting-point for the analysis of the behaviour of farms. It requires that there should be so many producers that each has to accept the prices at which transactions occur rather than being in a position to influence them by varying the quantity put on the market. It requires, too, that there are no artificial barriers to entry or exit from the sector. Perfect competition also assumes perfect knowledge, clearly a major oversimplification of any reality. However, in the case of European agriculture, given the degree to which some prices are maintained at known levels by administrative processes and the impressive improvement in communication systems available to farmers, this simplification does not destroy the cogency of some arguments based on the model.

Within a framework of perfect competition, an increase in price will add to farm incomes only in 'the short run'. In the long term, since the return on inputs is now greater than in other uses, more resources will remain in or be drawn into agriculture. In a free market this would depress prices, since aggregate demand cannot absorb additional output at current levels. In an administered market it will lead to increased support costs, although who bears the cost, taxpayer, consumer or foreign competitor, will depend on the system of support. At the same time the process of attracting resources into the industry will tend to raise the cost. This is more than a question of higher input prices; it includes, too, the introduction or retention of resources which have lower marginal physical products. This effect is likely to be of especial significance for agriculture since one of its main inputs, land, cannot readily be increased in supply. This argument implies that over a period of time higher prices will be translated into higher costs, some of which may be payments to landowners but others will go beyond the agricultural sector as payments to the suppliers of, for example, chemicals, machinery, buildings and credit. If incomes are to be restored by price manipulation, a further increase will be needed.

However, as expansion occurs, the price of inputs is likely to rise and less efficient inputs to be drawn into production, so the margin between total revenue and total cost per unit of output tends to narrow as expansion occurs. If this occurs, a given addition to short-run income will imply that the amount by which prices have to rise will need to increase at a growing rate. However, if incomes do increase, the cycle of further cost increases will recur. Thus price manipulation is a self-defeating instrument to raise incomes in the long term in an industry as competitive as farming.

Empirical analysis of the relationship between the prices of farm products and input costs is fraught with problems. Apart from product price movements, costs are affected by events elsewhere in the economy, by the general level of inflation, by progress in farm technology and by seasonal factors unrelated to selling prices. The result is that information about actual cost movements gives no unequivocal indication of the time lag involved between raising prices and the erosion of any benefit to farm prices. Table 3.4 indicates that the trend in land prices from 1973 to 1976 rose more rapidly than either agricultural prices or consumer prices. This real increase in the price of land is not inconsistent with the view that competition for its use was intensifying in this period, although agricultural price policy could only provide one element in a total appreciation of factors influencing land prices. Table 3.5 similarly suggests that as output grew, farmers were making use of a higher proportion of purchased inputs; an observation consistent with the cost-raising tendency of high product prices but affected too by the effects of changes in the relative prices of labour and by developments in technology.

The argument developed here implies that, following attempts to raise farm incomes by putting up the prices, the initial gains to farmers will be transferred to the providers of inputs until profit levels return to normality. The critical element in determining what level of income results is what farmers and potential farmers regard as a 'normal' level of profit. This is a highly complex concept. It includes not only the money return on current business activities but perceived returns in the form of the value of appreciating capital assets, satisfaction derived from controlling one's own working day, the enhanced status which many farmers feel they enjoy because they are farmers and the sense of reward some feel in a craft which involves looking after animals and cultivating crops. Such non-material values may rank very highly in the eyes of at least some people, even in an urban community. If this is so,

TABLE 3.4   *Trends in agricultural land prices as a percent of the implicit price of agricultural production (1973 = 100)*

A.   *Trend in land prices × 100*
     Implicit price of final production

| | France | | Netherlands | | Belgium | | UK | DK |
	Arable	Grass	Arable	Grass	Arable	Grass		
1974	107	115	132	134	125	127	103	119
1975	110	118	148	153	101	123	99	124
1976	109	117	166	174	101	122	91	129
1977	112	122	207	220	120	146	104	149
1978	121	131	269	291	136	166	120	161
1979	127	138	336	370	151	184	127	187

B.   *Trend in land prices × 100*
     Consumer price index

| | France | | Netherlands | | Belgium | | UK | DK |
	Arable	Grass	Arable	Grass	Arable	Grass	Ag. land	Ag. land
1974	99.9	107.1	113.6	115.4	108.0	109.7	94.8	102.6
1975	97.8	105.0	130.2	134.4	90.4	109.6	97.3	110.5
1976	98.7	106.0	149.3	156.3	93.4	113.4	97.1	118.9
1977	100.5	108.5	174.3	185.7	97.7	118.9	98.9	126.0
1978	103.8	112.2	208.9	226.2	121.0	128.4	108.4	136.1
1979	105.4	114.7	250.6	275.9	112.3	137.2	112.6	145.9

SOURCE   A. Based on data for annual percentage charge in land prices and the implicit price of final production from *Agricultural Situation in the Community* (1981); B. index of retail prices from *Basic Statistics of the Community*.

the consequence will be that market forces will ensure the monetary return to farming, what we conventionally regard as 'income', will tend to be depressed.

The lessons of this analysis for the policy-maker are twofold. First, that by putting up prices one can only raise money incomes in the short term. In the long term, prices will have to be raised yet again if incomes are to be sustained let alone improved. Indeed, the rate at which prices are increased will have to increase itself if the right level of income is to be maintained. A long-run improvement will occur when the level of incomes farmers regard as 'normal' increases. This is likely to depend

TABLE 3.5 *Rates of increase in final production and intermediate consumption, 1973–80*

	Final production	Intermediate consumption
Germany	3.8	6.7
France	9.0	13.7
Italy	18.6	21.5
Netherlands	6.2	8.6
Belgium	3.1	5.2
Luxemburg	3.0	4.8
United Kingdom	14.0	15.2
Ireland	17.9	24.4
Denmark	9.1	11.8

NOTE Intermediate consumption includes, seeds, seedlings, animal feed, fertilisers and soil improvement, products for crop protection, pharmaceuticals, energy, cattle, farm implements upkeep, repairs, services and 'other'. Annual rate of increase in current prices.

SOURCE *The Agricultural Situation in the Community* (Brussels/Luxemburg: European Commission, 1981) p. 178, Table 05.

more upon alternatives open to them and upon changing values in society than upon any events within agriculture itself. Second, because higher prices will attract extra resources into farming (or prevent some leaving) output will be increased. Given the mechanism of the CAP, once self-sufficiency is reached for a specific commodity, this effect can have costly consequences for the budget.

It is worth noting that even the short-run benefits to income are distributed in a way highly inappropriate to the social concerns of the Community. The greatest increase in revenues accrues to those who produce most. However, large-scale farmers, provided they run their businesses efficiently, are usually relatively wealthy by the standards of most Europeans. Rural poverty affects the small farmer and the farmer in the remote, difficult, less-favoured area. Such farmers, because they have little to sell, derive relatively little benefit from increased prices, even in the short run.

These arguments, simple almost to the point of naïvety, demonstrate that price policy is not simply an inequitable device for those seeking a durable increase in farm incomes: it is also an ineffective one. To rely upon it to provide acceptable incomes is to commit the Community to an open-ended, continuously growing increase in prices of a type which is unjustified by the requirements of output and ultimately dependent upon infinitely increasing budgetary resources.

A second difficulty with the Community's price policy is its approach to a single market. The idea that there should be one price within the Community for all producers is generally accepted without question. It reflects the priority the Community gives to creating fair conditions of competition. However, the way in which the single price is applied does nothing of the sort. Those who insist on the importance of 'a single price' note that, within a competitive market, only one underlying price level could exist. Prices may vary between locations by the costs of transport but not by anything more. Thus a single price within the Community undistorted by frontiers appears to be the symbol of a competitive market. Reality is more complicated. An administered price, fixed on social grounds, and supported when supplies exceed demand, frustrates competition. It unfairly shields the high cost and allows the low-cost producer to expand at expense to the budget and consumer.

Such an administered price is precisely what the Community seeks to achieve on social and political grounds. It is equally contrary to the logic which makes a single price attractive as an indicator of competition. Competition is neither wanted nor, in the product market, is it achieved. Instead the competitive position of farmers depends upon a complex of 'member country' economic conditions and political decisions. Setting a single, common money price for commodities produced and sold in different economies does not prevent the real price received by farmers, 'what other goods a quantity of the product will buy', from varying. Part of this variation can be attributed to different relative rates of inflation, not compensated by exchange-rate changes. Part occurs because the single price operates within the context of different taxation regimes. Different systems of taxation, both direct and indirect, mean that what is retained by the farmer from a single price for a product he sells varies according to the country in which he is situated. Clearly this determines the conditions of competition just as much as the 'single' price fixed by the Council of Ministers.

Further inequity occurs because, within member countries, national governments operate, sometimes in defiance of the Community, national agricultural support systems. This is overtly the case in France. Not only has the government tolerated gross interference with the flow of trade from Italy and the UK into France, it has also supported, by domestic financial measures, the incomes of some agricultural producers. Cynically it might be worth noticing that a major part of the costs of any resulting additional output in France is borne by other members of the Community!

This analysis of some of the conceptual and practical problems associated with the 'single price' implies that the Community is wasting its efforts in seeking this goal through administered agricultural product prices. If it wishes to attain the substance which justifies its efforts to attain a single price, it must direct its energies towards economic convergence and common economic policies, not simply towards the alignment of some prices in one sector.

WHO PAYS FOR THE COMMON AGRICULTURAL POLICY

A great deal of elegant and important work has been done to analyse the costs of the Common Agricultural Policy. This chapter makes no attempt to add to this but only to indicate the nature of these costs and their significance for European agricultural policy-makers. The CAP transfers income to the agricultural sector principally by raising the prices paid by consumers and by expenditure on export restitutions and intervention purchases. The budgetary element attracts most attention because of its visibility. This emphasis is dangerously misleading. A much more important element is borne by consumers. Table 3.6 shows in schematic form the significance of notional increases in food prices. For the purposes of illustration, private, final consumption expenditure on food has been taken from OECD national accounts statistics for 1979. This has been converted into ECUs using average annual market rates of exchange. The table then shows the implications for EC consumers as a whole and in each member country of different assumptions about the extent to which food prices might be raised by the CAP. Two important messages emerge. First, given even the most modest assumptions about the price increasing impact of the CAP, the effect on consumers far outweighs the budget costs. In 1979 these were 10 670.4 million ECU – equivalent to only 5 per cent of expenditure on food. Second, the distribution of this burden is proportional to expenditure on food,. Interestingly the UK comes behind Italy, France and Germany on this score.

This illustration alerts the onlooker to examine the price-raising impact of the CAP with great care. Attempts to measure this leave considerable grounds for debate. Among the elements disputed are: (i) what would be the level of world prices in the absence of the Common Agricultural Policy; (ii) what would be the response of EC supply to lower price levels; (iii) what would be the response of EC demand to lower price levels? There is room for argument about each

TABLE 3.6   Illustration of the significance for consumers of notional increases in price associated with the CAP

	WG million DM	Fr million Fr	It billion Lira	NL million Guilder	Belg/Lux million B/Fr	UK million £	Irl million £	Dk million Kr	EC9 million EUA
1. Private final consumption expenditure on food National currencies	181 900	252 762	47 778	29 150	394 787	19 755	982	35 755	—
2. Equivalent in EUA	72 441	43 363	41 969	10 603	9 830	30 562	1 467	4 961	215 396
3. % share	34	20	20	5	5	14	—	2	100
4. Cost to consumers (EUA) assuming CAP raises food prices									
by 10%	7 244	4 336	4 197	1 080	983	3 156	98	496	21 539
15%	10 866	6 504	6 295	1 620	1 475	4 734	147	744	31 209
20%	14 488	8 677	8 394	2 161	1 966	6 312	196	992	43 079

NOTE   The data in row 1 relate to recorded consumer expenditure in 1979 and are only used as an illustrative base. The actual expenditure on CAP price support in 1979 was 10 440 million ECU.

SOURCES   Private final consumption expenditure on food: *National Accounts of OECD Countries 1962–1979*, vol II: Detailed Tables (Paris, 1981); exchange rates: *Agricultural Situation in the Community* (1980) p. 143.

of these issues. Table 3.7 shows the results of recent work done in the University of Gottingen under Professor Tangermann which examines the implications of the most recent price settlement for members of the Community. Broadly, for the Community as a whole it appears from his calculation that in the short term consumers must find an additional 10 000 million ECU, while the extra costs to the budget will be of the order of 2600 million ECU. Thus the share of the burden shown by the budget is only about a quarter of the total costs of the settlement. In the long term, as supply increases, this proportion rises to nearer 30 per cent, but it is still the consumer who bears the heaviest burden.

It is a central defect of most discussion of the Common Agricultural Policy that this balance between financial, budget consequences and the full cost borne by consumers is not commonly understood. Its implications are far-reaching. Poorer families spend a higher proportion of their income on food than do richer families.[1] Equally it is clear that expenditure on food per head varies within Europe (Table 3.8) so that the distribution of this burden will be uneven amongst European member countries and amongst European citizens in a way that is not related to their country shares in budget costs nor to the level of real income per head. Paradoxically the price-raising aspects of the CAP tax poor consumers proportionately more heavily than those who are rich. At the same time the benefits in the short term accrue to rich rather than poor farmers. This reinforces the view that the social impact of the CAP is unacceptable. If the true costs to consumers were more widely understood, it would no longer be only the British who want to change the policy.

THE NATURE OF THE THREAT TO EUROPEAN UNITY

It is ironic in view of the previous paragraphs that the main threat to European unity emerges not because of the largest and least appropriate element in the costs of the Common Agricultural Policy but because of the relatively less substantial distributional effects which occur through the budget. However, it would be misguided to underestimate the importance of the budgetary consequences of the CAP. Two features of the policy make this critical. First, the budgetary transfer is much more visible than the tax on consumers. Second, once a product reaches the point of self-sufficiency, incremental output results in extra cost to the budget, broadly equivalent to the difference between world prices and EC support prices. Given a price environ-

TABLE 3.7 Effects of Provisional Council decision to raise prices by an average of 10.6 per cent (1982)

	WG	Fr	It	NL	Belg/Lux	UK	Irl	Dk	EC
A. Short-run effects									
Consumer burden	1465	2804	2735	352	547	1626	122	237	9890
Taxpayer burden	815	639	328	135	115	481	20	56	2589
Total	2280	3443	3063	487	663	2107	142	294	12479
B. Long-run effects									
Consumer burden	1465	2804	2735	351	547	1626	122	127	9890
Taxpayer burden	1301	1020	524	216	184	768	31	90	4133
Total	2766	3824	3259	568	731	2394	154	327	14012

SOURCE S. Tangermann, Institute of Agricultural Economics, University of Gottingen (1982) private communication.

TABLE 3.8 Per capita expenditure on food among EC member countries (1979)

	WG	Fr	It	NL	Belg/Lux	UK	Irl	Dk
Total expenditure in EUA million	72441	43363	41969	10802	9830	30562	1467	4961
Population, 000	61315	53499	56888	13986	10199	55883	3365	5118
Per capita EUA	1181	810	737	772	964	546	435	969

SOURCES Food expenditure as Table 3.6; population data from Milk Marketing Board, Dairy Facts & Figures (Thames Ditton: MMB, 1980) p. 28, Table 9.

ment justified on 'income' grounds and technical progress, this means that the EC must either be prepared to find continuingly increased budget resources or else the policy will collapse. Collapse could mean either that the EC ceased to maintain some prices, without making any alternative arrangements or, more probably, that national governments intervened to support their farmers in ways incompatible with a common policy.

Until 1982 the option of substantially increasing budgetary commitments to finance the CAP was thought to be implausible. It was accepted that the United Kingdom certainly, and Germany possibly, would veto such a development. However, in the light of the 1982 price-fixing it seems possible that the Community might attempt to force through higher budget contributions on the basis of majority voting. If it did so to sustain the CAP prices, it would transfer real income from some member countries (the agricultural importers) with no basis of social justification or economic need simply because majority voting power enabled other member countries, the agricultural exporters, to extract payment. This amounts to the exaction of a tax without regard to notions of acceptability or responsibility for the welfare of those taxed. It is virtually identical with the type of colonialism which led to the war of independence and the separation of the USA from the UK. It seems highly improbable that the Community could survive should this occur. Continued British membership must already be in doubt. However, even without the United Kingdom the costs of an unchanged Common Agricultural Policy would continue to grow until eventually they became intolerable for remaining member countries, including those now seeking to join. In the longer term, either the policy would have to change or the Community would cease to function. In this case the fault is not with the British but with the policy.

The seven members of the Community who embarked upon a process of majority voting have thus accepted the onerous responsibility for the survival of the Community, not simply for UK membership. Either they must adapt the CAP or the budgetary mechanism in a way which makes it financially tolerable or alternatively they will destroy the CAP and with it threaten the continued existence of the Community. The abuse of power to defend a sectional interest and a moribund policy is not simply an affront to the UK, it is an attack on the Community itself.

Adaptation of the CAP is by no means impossible. Reform would represent not simply more concessions to particular national interests but a policy better for Europe's agriculture, for those in farming and elsewhere who are Europe's poor, and for the Community as a whole. Reform does not imply an abandonment of those principles for the CAP set out in the Rome treaty, rather an evolution of policies to give them substance in the context of the 1980s. Treated in this way, majority voting could permit the Common Agricultural Policy to escape the absurdities of the past and contribute, as intended, to the integration of the Community as a whole.

THE OPPORTUNITIES FOR CHANGE

Many of the difficulties within the Common Agricultural Policy stem from an attempt to use one type of instrument, price policy, for a diversity of purposes. The instrument itself is valuable. The purposes remain valid. What is not feasible is the exclusive use of price manipulation to meet all the diverse demands on agricultural policy.

Price policy is needed to ensure a degree of internal stability against disruption originating in world markets. It can also be used to influence the level of internal output. The devices of the variable import levy, intervention purchase and export restitution provide an administratively tidy and reasonably effective way to do this. However, if prices are manipulated in a way which provides only the degree of stability and the level of output needed by the Community as a whole, they cannot at the same time match the aspirations of farmers. As we have seen, to do so demands continually increasing prices regardless of the level of output. Prudent prices are unlikely to meet the demands of those countries which are net agricultural exporters. Many dimensions enter into any consideration of what might be an appropriate level of output for European agriculture. The concept of comparative advantage is clearly relevant. If in Europe the development of technology in agriculture raises productivity more rapidly than in other sectors, compared with its impact on relative productivity in other economies, the share of domestic EC resources which should remain in agriculture will be increased. Security of supply is critical. If Europe believes that it cannot rely for any part of its food upon imports, and cannot tolerate any shortfall in any food item, then self-sufficiency might seem a sensible target. So inflexible an approach imposes very high costs on any economic system. It is reminiscent of some of the theories which explain the abrupt disappearance of the dinosaurs. Self-sufficiency in food on this basis may hinge upon greater imports of non-food, notably fuel. It is not obviously the case that these supplies are more secure than food itself. Some argue that Europe should produce beyond its own needs in order to give food aid to other countries. The merits of this argument have already been questioned (see p. 45). However this chapter makes no attempt to come to specific conclusions on this or other issues which affect the level of output. What is relevant is that, once such decisions have been made, there is a finite quantity of farm output which can be said to be in the Community's interest. Once that is achieved no further incentives should be given to expansion, even though incomes in agriculture are too low or the distribution of agricultural activity inappropriate.

A second characteristic of an intelligent use of price policy stems from the fact that agriculture is in a period of technical change. Since markets do not exist to absorb output at current prices the industry must encounter the need for adjustment which will include a mixture of producing at lower prices and reducing the resources engaged in agriculture. The policy-maker must therefore explore potential movements of resources between uses in agriculture and elsewhere. This must relate to the levels of employment in other sectors. Even when opportunities for new jobs are not good, this does not justify a price policy which expands agricultural output beyond what the Community decides it needs. To do so is to consign other scarce resources, capital in particular, to uses of lower value than in other sectors. The result is a deterioration of the overall competitiveness of the EC economy and thus a reduced ability to sustain the aggregate level of employment. Employment problems cannot be solved by the protection of individual sectors, but transitional aids to people, who, at price levels which lead to a satisfactory level of output, cannot earn a satisfactory total income, may play a role.

Given the dynamics of supply and demand in the agricultural sector, a price level which generates the level of output needed will almost certainly eventually leave some individuals with incomes which are inadequate but with no immediate alternative employment opportunities. To cope effectively with this reality some form of direct income payment is likely to be the best solution. Payments to people need not imply that the recipients should cease to farm. Indeed provided the prices they receive are compatible with producing a volume of output which is appropriate for the Community: if they can produce part of this profitably, even though this does not itself provide a satisfactory income, the Community will gain. Direct payments which supplement personal incomes would have lower costs than policies which attempted to remove such farmers from agriculture and made the whole of their income dependent upon public funds or which attempted to solve the problem by higher prices. At the same time, so long as the payment was made to the person, and in no way conditional upon his remaining in farming or producing farm goods, there would be minimal distortion of the conditions of competition.

A third requirement is that agricultural policy should take note of growing concern about the environmental and animal welfare implications of some modern agricultural technology. Europeans may choose to make agriculture and food more costly in order to preserve some traditional features of the environment or to restrain some types of technological development. Should this be the case, it is important that those who benefit should be those who pay. There is a danger that those who press these issues most strongly represent only a small fraction of the Community's population although the measures they suggest would affect all. Higher costs will either mean higher food prices or the substitution of EC output by imports from countries with less restrictive legislation. Political debate is essential to determine what, if any, restraints are needed. Such arguments cannot be separated from social questions concerning the cost of food, the welfare of farmers or the viability of rural communities. If it is decided to preserve a particular type of agriculture in some areas of the Community or to retain some decaying technology, policy instruments to give effect to this should not simply raise the market price of food to consumers. Possible ways of doing this could include specific payments to producers in particular locations or producers who used particular techniques. Such devices would make visible the costs of such environmental or welfare priorities and so contribute to an informed political debate.

Finally, if it is to survive, the Common Agricultural Policy has to operate within the realities of an 'uncommon' Community. So far as incomes, environmental, animal welfare and population considerations are concerned the problems, needs and aspirations of the various member countries differ. The imposition of any single solution financed at a Community level brings about unjustified income transfers between member countries. This threat is particularly severe given a system in which the Council of Ministers reaches decisions by majority voting. There is a need therefore to distinguish what is best done wholly at a Community level from what is best done at a national level and integrated within a framework of Community policy. The orchestration of national aids rather than their prohibition seems more likely to meet both the Community and the national needs than attempts to eliminate national support. Inevitably there are dangers. A country which pursued, on grounds of animal welfare, a policy of banning all battery birds would either have to accept that its eggs were to be purchased from other member countries or would have to pay substantial subsidies to its own producers to enable them to compete with eggs produced by more efficient methods. This might well bring home to the governments concerned the costs of the policies they advocate. It would not impose them on the whole EC.

A major difficulty about orchestration is enforcement. Even if it could be demonstrated that taxation, national assistance on social grounds, national environmental or regional policy etc., was unfair as between producers in different member countries, this might not prevent abuse. Recourse to existing legal process is slow and costly.

One approach to this problem would be for the Community to agree a code of practice for national agricultural aids. Such a code would be administered by the Commission. In the event of a national practice being regarded as causing unfair competition, the Commission, or any individual within the Community who felt that he suffered, could take the country concerned to a specialist division of the European Court. For this purpose the Court might establish a subsection exclusively concerned with cases of 'unfair agricultural aids'. Such a body would be something along the lines of the UK Restrictive Practices Court. Should a practice be proved to be unfair, the country concerned would then have the option either of abandoning it or of paying compensation to the damaged member country or individual on a scale proportionate to the damage which was done and determined by the Court. This would certainly give rise to some interesting legal cases but it would create a basis against which a more pragmatic and practical approach to the orchestration of national aids in agriculture was realised within Europe. Should it do so, the benefits to European unity could be considerable. The costs of deviation would be visible and borne by those who wanted to be different. It would be up to each government to decide whether at these costs the offending aids were worthwhile in the national interest. Such considerations seem more likely to promote convergence among member countries than ineffective attempts to ban national aids which represent a political response to the differing national adjustment problems of agriculture but which impose costs on other members of the Community.

CONCLUSIONS

This brief review of the Common Agricultural Policy has argued that its problems are the result of fatal flaws in the implicit assumptions it makes about how the world works. The relationship of price to income and the significance of a single price for the maintenance of conditions of competition in the EC are not as the policy-makers appear to think. As a result, decisions on price policy do not produce the desired results. The consequences of failure are serious. Consumers bear a much heavier burden than is evident from the transactions of FEOGA and the budgetary inequities which result threaten the survival of the Community. The resource cost to the EC's economy tends to grow. Divisions among member states are accentuated. The risks of financial collapse are ever present.

This chapter has argued that reform is needed not to dismember past policies but to achieve through improved working of these and additional policies what the founders of the Community intended. Some specific notions are discussed. First, price determination must be related to a volume of output the Community decides it wants. This can take account of the need for secure supplies and for stable internal markets. Second, other desired goals, which affect the method and location of production, e.g. environment, animal welfare and regional economies, should be financed by specific payments from EC and national budgets. These would demonstrate who benefited and who paid, thus assisting rational political debate. Third, the level of output and payments for specific purposes are not likely to leave all farmers with socially or politically acceptable incomes. As a result, direct income aids will be needed. These should be administered and financed by national budgets but the schemes must be subject to EC control and some EC finance might be used to assist the poorer countries to implement effective policies. Such aids to poorer countries would themselves help to achieve a better balance of resource flows among member countries. Finally, it is clear that national aids are inevitable given the uncommon nature of the EC's economies. Rather than forbid them it seems better to seek to orchestrate them along agreed lines and establish procedures whereby they would be made expensive to member countries if found inconsistent with an EC code of practice.

None of these suggestions represent a rejection of the basic goals of the CAP. They do attempt to develop its policies in the light of political and economic realities. Other solutions could be found. A failure to acknowledge the need for change, an insistence that the use of a policy instrument in a particular way is an unchallengeable 'principle' of the CAP, in the end, would lead to its total destruction. Those who survive have to adapt to the world. Those who maintain that the world must adapt to them are likely to have a rude awakening.

NOTE

1. See, for example, T. E. Josing and Donna Hamway, 'Income Transfer Effects of the Common Agricultural Policy', in B. Davey, T. E. Josling and A. McFarguhar (eds), *Agriculture and the State* (London: Macmillan, 1976) pp. 180–205.

4 European Agriculture: the Way Forward

CHRISTOPHER TUGENDHAT

It is in my view an important national interest that everyone concerned directly and indirectly with public affairs should have the opportunity to broaden their knowledge and understanding of the opportunities and problems involved in British membership of the European Community. Britain's political and economic future lies in Europe. It is therefore essential that there should be the widest possible understanding of how the Community might be changed and developed and of the issues at stake.

My task in this chapter is to focus upon the Common Agricultural Policy, to analyse and comment on certain of its characteristics and to indicate ways in which it might be improved.

Before getting immersed in this subject, however, I should like to start by tackling the question of why the Community applies an agricultural policy, common to all member states. I will deal with two basic points: first, the need for agriculture to be subject to specific policy measures; and secondly, why they have to be common throughout the Community.

Before the Common Agricultural Policy was introduced, all European countries took specific measures with respect to their own agriculture. The policies applied differed, sometimes markedly, from one country to another. But in all of them, including Britain, regulation of one sort or another was considered necessary in order to strike balances between economic, social and political pressures and objectives. Nor should it be thought that the regulation of agriculture is a phenomenon unique to the countries of the Common Market. The industry is regulated in all countries where it is of any importance at all, regardless of political and economic creed – the United States, Switzerland and Japan provide three diverse examples to prove my point.

I would only add that in the West, the combined effect of agricultural policy and the efforts of the farming community invariably seem to produce surpluses, whereas in Russia and Eastern Europe, they equally invariably seem to produce shortages. Both give rise to difficulties, but as anyone who remembers the rationing and austerity of the war and post-war years will attest, the problems of plenty, however intractable, are greatly to be preferred to the problems of penury.

When the EEC was formed, it was understood from the outset that free trade in agricultural produce could not take place in an harmonious manner if each member state retained responsibility for its own independent agricultural policy. Free trade and divergent national regulatory systems are simply incompatible. Were national policies to be applied, each country would feel obliged to prevent its own system from being undermined by the effects of policies carried out by its partners.

Again, this is not a problem peculiar to the Community. For example, the member countries of the European Free Trade Association also recognise that trade between them in agricultural produce cannot be free in the absence of a uniform agricultural policy. They decided not to apply such a policy and agricultural trade is excluded from the provisions of EFTA. Furthermore, the General Agreement on Tariffs and Trade recognises that the objectives of liberalising trade have to take special account of differences in agricultural support mechanisms. This is shown by the fact that the GATT incorporates specific derogations and waivers for agriculture from what are otherwise general rules.

Theoretically, the Community, like EFTA, could have developed a common market in industrial goods without a Common Agricultural Policy. Politically, however, that was impossible. Because of the balance of interests between the original member states, the two were regarded as two sides of the same coin and they remain so still. There are other practical reasons why a common market in agricultural goods is in the general interest. Although agriculture contributes less now to gross domestic product than it did when the Community was set up, it is still important. Taking the Community as a whole, the figure is just under 4 per cent of the combined GDP. In France it is 4.2 per cent, in Germany 2.0 per cent, in Denmark 4.4 per cent, and in Britain 2.1 per cent. Over eight million Community citizens, or around 7 per cent of the working population, are involved directly in agriculture, or around 20 per cent of the total employed in manufacturing industry. There are also many others who supply goods and services to agriculture who depend on the industry for their livelihoods. In Britain, the figure for those directly engaged in agriculture is 2.8 per cent with, of course, many more working in related activities.

In recent years, intra-Community trade in agricultural and food produce has grown rapidly – the annual rate of increase was about 14 per cent during the 1970s and the total is now valued at about £20 billion or about £80 for each Community citizen per annum. The performance of British exporters is one of the unsung success stories of our economy.

The need for a common policy for agriculture cannot of course be invoked to justify any given common policy measure. It is important to draw the distinction between the need for, and the nature of, the common policy. Debate at all levels is often made unnecessarily difficult when suggestions for changes in the nature of the policy are misrepresented as an attack on the need for a common policy. Conversely, there is nothing inconsistent in supporting the view that a common policy is needed but simultaneously to advocate that changes should be made in the operation of the policy.

In order to put into context the changes that I consider should be made, I would like to say a few words about the manner in which support may be provided. Basically, the choice is between the extent to which the burden of support falls on taxpayers or on consumers. The debate then fans out to cover such matters as the relative merits of selective forms of income support, the reasonableness of prices paid by consumers, and the burden of the policy on the Community budget.

Debates over who should pay – taxpayers or consumers – for agricultural support in the Community, especially in the United Kingdom context, are not infrequently put in terms of extremes. The CAP is sometimes misleadingly depicted as putting the entire burden on consumers. Although it is quite true that for certain products the burden of support falls essentially on consumers, this is not true in all cases. Indeed for an increasing number of sectors, the Community system places little or no burden on consumers. For those products such as cereals, milk, beef and sugar, where there is a consumer burden reflected in the application of import levies, this burden must be put into perspective. For example, the consumer price of bread in the United Kingdom increased by 17.9 per cent per annum from 1973 to 1980 but during this period the annual increase in wheat prices fixed under the Common Agricultural Policy in the United Kingdom was far lower at only 5.3 per cent. A similar result is found with other important products such as milk, where the corresponding figures are 18.8 per cent and 5.8 per cent, for beef 14.6 per cent and 7.6 per cent and for sugar 19.5 per cent and 5.8 per cent. In other words, by far the largest part of the increase in consumer prices is due to factors such as distribution charges which have nothing to do with the Common Agricultural Policy. Consequently, great care should be taken when assessing the impact on consumers of the CAP to attribute to the policy only that for which it is responsible. Unfortunately, the public has often been led to believe that the CAP is the culprit and consequently unjustly labelled as such.

In this connection it is salutary to note that in the period 1973 to 1980 the annual rate of increase in consumer prices of potatoes in the United Kingdom was more rapid than for beef. Why do I choose these products as examples? There are two reasons: the first is because the increase in the price of beef is often cited as some form of proof of the burden of the CAP on consumers; the second because potatoes are the one main agricultural product where national, rather than Community, measures apply. In other words, for potatoes, where policy is in British hands, the increase in consumer prices, and incidentally in producer prices, has been higher than for a product the price of which is often criticised and for which the Community is responsible.

Whilst on the point of consumer prices, I would just like to say a word about the price of butter, which is also often used, or rather misused, as an indicator of what is wrong with the Common Agricultural Policy. It is claimed that butter is far too expensive. It is implied that were it not for the Community we could return to pre-1973 prices. I do not think a return to pre-1973 prices for butter under any form of agricultural policy is any more likely than, for example, the price of a British Leyland Mini, which incidentally has increased far more rapidly than butter, also returning to pre-1973 levels. To those who are not persuaded that a return to pre-1973 prices is possible, but who none the less feel that the price of butter is too high, I offer the following figures: they were collected in November 1981 by the United States Department of Agriculture. They show the price of butter in ten capital cities in various industrial countries including the United States, Australia, Canada, Japan, Switzerland and Spain. The highest price was over eight dollars per kilogramme and the average of the remainder well over five dollars. I wonder if anyone would care to guess where on this scale the London price came? I will tell you: it was second lowest, with only Australia recording a cheaper price. This is a very satisfactory rating, particularly as prices far higher than in the United Kingdom were recorded in countries noted for their criticism of the Common Agricultural Policy.

There is of course a world of difference between the relevance of the various mechanisms employed in the Common Agricultural Policy and the precise ways in which these measures are applied. Agreeing to support markets by, for example, intervention, does not mean either that the price at which intervention takes place, or that the level of protection against third countries is appropriate. Several indicators cast doubt on the correctness of the way in which some of the instruments of the Common Agricultural Policy have been applied. For example, the degree of self-sufficiency – in other words, the proportion of what we consume which is produced in the Community – has for a range of products increased significantly over the past decade.

The increase in self-sufficiency reflects two phenomena. First, there is the dynamism of agricultural output. Scientific advances in animal and plant breeding, in disease and pest control and in husbandry have often been output-increasing and so production has risen significantly year by year. Farmers have proved far more adept and rapid at applying new technology than most manufacturing industries.

In many cases, increases in output are far more rapid than consumption increases. Thus, milk production in the United Kingdom has increased since 1973 by getting on for 2 per cent a year despite an annual reduction in cow numbers of nearly 1 per cent. These figures may sound small. Perhaps they are, but their consequences are not. Dairy output throughout the Community is increasing at about the same rate as in the United Kingdom, equivalent to over two million tonnes of milk a year, whereas consumption is virtually static.

It is in a way fortunate for the Community that productivity in some member countries lags well behind the average. Again taking the dairy sector, output per cow is in some countries only about 75 per cent of the Community average. If those below average achieved the current average performance, something they are quite capable of doing, the Community milk surplus would shoot up by some eight million tonnes per year – or by nearly 50 per cent. The dairy sector is not alone in recording massive increases in output. Yields of wheat, for example, have shot up by about 30 per cent over the past decade.

A significant consequence of these production increases has been some extraordinary changes in the Community's place and influence upon world markets. Our exports of agricultural products have grown far faster than total world agricultural trade – in other words, our market share has increased significantly. For example, for beef in 1977 Australia exported about seven times as much as the Community, but now we export three-quarters as much as they do and we have overtaken Argentina and New Zealand, which traditionally exported much more than the Community. The Community is now the world's third largest exporter of wheat. For skimmed milk powder, our share of exports to the world market has increased from about one-fifth in the mid-1970s to approximately one-half now. For butter-fat the development is even more spectacular: increasing from less than one-tenth to getting on for two-thirds over the same period.

In a world where acute hunger is a continuing problem for millions, such developments might be judged as entirely desirable. But it is hypocritical to pretend that Europe is helping the Third World by offloading on to it cut-price surpluses produced at high cost as a result of political and social pressures. What the developing countries require is help to enable them to grow the particular types of food their people need and that their land is best adapted to produce. Europe's role should be confined to providing what they cannot produce for themselves, to giving help until their output is increased and, of course, to assisting in emergencies.

The increase in Community agricultural output has led to a spectacular growth in Community expenditure on agriculture guarantee, or to give it its French acronym, FEOGA guarantee expenditure. In the mid-1970s, FEOGA guarantee expenditure was equivalent to about 5 per cent of the value of final agricultural production in the Community. By 1977 it was over 7 per cent and in 1980 about 10 per cent. In other words, real costs per unit of output have doubled in half a decade. In addition, the burden of FEOGA guarantee expenditure in relation to Community gross domestic product, although of course still very small, increased by nearly 50 per cent during the second half of the 1970s. During this period the proportion of total expenditure accounted for by exports increased from a low of under 20 per cent in 1974 to a peak of over 50 per cent in 1980. Last year it was just below 50 per cent.

In absolute terms, expenditure on FEOGA guarantee increased in the second half of the 1970s at an annual rate of well over 20 per cent. This rate of increase ran the real risk of bursting the budget because the rate of increase in resources potentially available to finance the budget – in other words, import duties and levies and an amount equivalent of up to 1 per cent VAT applied on a uniform basis – developed far less rapidly.

Fortunately, in recent years there has been a considerable reduction in the rate of increase of FEOGA guarantee expenditure. This is due in part to policy decisions and better management, but to a large extent to a firming up of world markets, notably for dairy products. To achieve this price change, a careful coordination of dairy export policy involving the Community and New Zealand, the two main exporting countries, has operated to the benefit of both. This coordination can, I think, be introduced for some other products, notably beef, in a manner that would not only reduce budget costs but bring a desirable increase and stability in world prices.

None the less, the vagaries and volatility of world markets are well known and as a greater proportion of Community agricultural production now goes on world markets, changes in world conditions have a more marked impact on the Community budget than was the case in the past. With 60 per cent or so of the budget taken up by FEOGA guarantee expenditure, of which about half is now spent on export refunds and thus determined by world prices, the impact on the entire Community of a possible slide in international market conditions is obviously significant. The risk of a slide is, I fear, taken more seriously by finance than by agricultural ministers. Finance ministers, aware of the risks, are now reluctant to allow what the Commission considers to be a reasonable development of Community expenditure policies in areas other than agriculture. Consequently, the current modest development in agricultural expenditure is not facilitating as much as one would expect a broadening of the Community's financial responsibilities.

The development of Community output has not only given rise to budget problems, it has also led to serious friction with our trading partners. Above, I gave figures for the changed position for the Community for certain exports to world markets. For many products our share has increased rapidly. Where this increase has been due to a genuine competitive advantage of our producers over others, no criticism is called for. Praise, in fact, is due. But where improved performance is attributable not to an inherent competitive advantage but to the benefits exports derive from export refunds, our trading partners have cause for complaint, provided of course their hands are clean – which is not always the case.

The increasingly venomous nature of trade disputes is worrying. It worries me as Budget Commissioner when the Community budget is called upon to pay subsidies equivalent to a significant part of the market price for products in order to market otherwise unsaleable produce.

In the case of, for example, skimmed milk powder, these subsidies now cost up to two-thirds of the market price. It also worries leaders in all countries involved, either as importers or exporters of agricultural products. For example the United States considers that their exports to third countries are being undercut by unfair and aggressive trade practices carried out by the Community. They also consider that access for their exports to the Community is being made more difficult. I agree with the sentiment often voiced in the United States that nations should solve their agricultural difficulties internally and not shift the burden of domestic measures and problems on to third countries. We need to take very seriously the criticisms made concerning distortions of international trade and be aware that what may seem reasonable to us may not be so judged by others.

But the various accusations and counterclaims must be kept in perspective. No country, not even the United States, has an agricultural production and trade policy as neutral and as open as those it would like other countries to apply. Australia also vigorously criticises the Community for what it considers to be excessive import restrictions. I wonder, though, whether Australia genuinely advocates trade freedom because, when I take the important example of motor cars, I see that the Community applies a 11 per cent duty without quotas, whereas Australia has a tariff barrier over five times this level at 57.5 per cent and operates a quota system. This no doubt reflects the particular characteristics of the Australian motor industry. Criticism must therefore also take account of the economic and political circumstances facing the agricultural sector in different parts of the world. There are real differences in circumstances that justify differences in policy. For example, the policy applied in parts of the world with intense population pressures and where agriculture has been practised for centuries, is likely to need different measures to those justified where land is relatively abundant and the agriculture 'new'.

For budgetary, trade, as well as other reasons, the Commission has advocated policies involving a narrowing of the gap between Community prices and those applied by its main competitors, coupled with modifications of the price hierarchy and a limit on the open-ended nature of agricultural support measures whereby guarantees would be diluted in the event of production exceeding set thresholds. These objectives appear to have the support of heads of state and governments and I hope will be applied by ministers of agriculture in the Community in the decisions they take in the coming years.

In 1982's prices' decision we saw what may well turn out to be the first real progress towards cutting off the open-ended nature of agricultural support whereby Community guarantees will no longer be totally independent of the level of production. A second innovation was to introduce direct income support measures for certain producers so that their revenues could be protected without the need for a further increase in price. This is a very positive step towards supporting conflicting demands of, on the one hand, market balance and on the other, income support. These demands clearly cannot be accommodated in price policy alone.

I should, however, point out that the income support measures that have been decided are more costly, in budget terms, than operating a similar degree of support through the price mechanism. In this respect, the policy has been made somewhat more expensive in budget terms. None the less there is widespread agreement that this type of measure is preferable to a further price increase.

It is thus important to bear in mind that a cheaper CAP in budget terms would not necessarily be a better one. A cheaper one could be achieved by transferring a larger part of the burden of support on to consumers by reducing production and consumption aids. Measures could also be taken to limit imports and promote exports. Both these approaches would have the effect of forcing up internal market prices. Any such development would in my view be regrettable and I am sure that few would disagree. Of course the total budget cost of agricultural support is of undoubted importance, but within this constraint what matters is not just how much is spent but how it is spent. This does not, however, mean that the way the CAP is financed could not be improved so as to make it fairer as between the member states. Indeed, I believe it should be. A renationalisation of agricultural policy would not however necessarily reduce the cost, a point I would like those who advocate a renationalisation of agricultural policy to bear in mind. Apart from spelling the probable end of the free market in industrial goods, it would also be extremely costly, as I will seek to show in a moment.

Having outlined the possible direction in which agricultural policy in the Community may move, I would like in conclusion to comment on some of the possible consequences for the United Kingdom of returning to a national agricultural policy. Those who favour British withdrawal from the Community generally talk in terms of an alternative system of agricultural support that would closely resemble the one we had before joining the Community and this is therefore the one on which I intend to concentrate.

A policy based essentially on deficiency payments would undoubtedly be extremely expensive. The actual cost would of course depend on the measures applied and on world market conditions. But in my view, the figure would be about £2 billion a year. I first mentioned this figure at the Oxford Farming Conference in January 1982 and it has since been widely commented upon.

The Opposition Spokesman on Agriculture, Mr Norman Buchan MP, has come forward with a lower figure: £1 billion. The reason for the difference appears to be entirely due to different but very important assumptions about world prices. I have assumed that they do not rise because I do not believe it would be in the national interest for Britain's agriculture to contract. Thus, as total world food supplies would be unaffected by the withdrawal, world prices should remain virtually unchanged. Mr Buchan has estimated that were the United Kingdom to withdraw, world prices would move up and close about half the gap between world and British prices. For prices to move so significantly, either supply or demand would need to change markedly. I cannot imagine that the British people would wish to eat much more simply because they had left the Common Market and I can therefore only assume that the cause of this increase in world prices would be a marked contraction in British agricultural output.

Obviously, such an increase in world prices would also make it virtually impossible to achieve the significantly lower food prices which we are so often told would result from British withdrawal, especially when it is remembered that the cost of the basic raw material represents a steadily diminishing percentage of the final price to the consumer.

I make these points not in any spirit of acrimony but because I wish to bring home the fact that in this branch of economic policy as in so many others, there are no easy options. The Common Agricultural Policy does not provide the only means by which British agriculture can be organised. As I have explained, it can and should in any case be improved and modernised in several respects. But it should also be remembered that the most likely alternative is also expensive and fraught with difficulty. Just as the Communist countries never seem able to solve their perennial problem of increasing production to the point where it can satisfy demand, so the Western countries – the Community, the United States, Japan, Switzerland and others – are still searching for a way to bring surpluses and costs under control. I believe that if the governments of the member states would only follow the Commission's ideas and build upon them, the Community would be well on the way to achieving that elusive goal.

5 Regional Problems and Policy in the EEC

GEOFFREY DENTON

INTRODUCTION

There has been a phenomenal increase of interest in regional problems, science, measurement and policy in Western Europe over the past forty years. The shaded areas showing problem regions have spread from small beginnings until they threaten to cover the whole map; regional organisations have made more than their fair contribution to initialitis; swarms of regional geographers and economists have been bred; regional policies have proliferated, and expenditure on programmes of regional aid has soared. What is the definition of a 'region'? What is the origin of regional problems? Are regional problems and policies really permanent, or are they merely temporary phenomena related to a particular phase of social and economic life in European countries? What are the objectives of regional policy? What are its true costs? How does one measure its success? What is the correct balance between subsidising regions to solve their problems, and controlling such subsidies in order to preserve free and fair competition?

While most of the burgeoning industry of regional affairs has remained within the separate jurisdictions of the national governments, the European Community of the Six became involved after 1958, and its involvement has grown with the successive enlargements of the EEC. How does integration affect the fortunes of particular regions? What contribution can the Community itself make to solving regional problems? Should a proportion of Community GNP be redistributed from richer to poorer regions, and on what principles should such generosity be organised?

The questions are innumerable, and the available answers, despite much research and discussion, too few and too vague. In the hope of contributing to a reassessment of the situation, this chapter briefly reviews the present state of knowledge about regions and regional problems, the effect of integration on them; the assessment of regional policy, its costs and effectiveness, and its relationship with competition and trade policy.

THE DEFINITION OF REGIONS AND OF REGIONAL PROBLEMS

The first difficulty in even starting to discuss these issues is that no one has yet been able to find a satisfactory definition of a region. Geographical and historical features have created separate political structures and have helped to create regional consciousness, and it is sometimes suggested that a region can best be defined as an area whose population thinks it is a region. But a region based on such a narcissistic definition will not be assisted financially by outsiders unless it can produce some objective evidence of special problems arising out of its separateness. Such problems usually prove to be, in the broadest sense, economic, and an economic definition of a region is therefore essential.

Putting it very crudely, economists have usually defined a region as an area within which capital and labour are quite mobile and across whose boundaries they are less so. Economic differences arising between the region and surrounding areas are said to persist because the lack of external mobility prevents the automatic adjustments that would otherwise correct them. There are many problems with this approach. What happens if one factor is mobile, but the other not? What difference is made if mobility is only in one direction? Mobility may also vary as between one sector and another. Since mobility is clearly relative rather than absolute (there is always *some* movement), one is involved in examining not only the types but also the degrees of mobility. The definition in terms of factor immobility also results in a confusing hierarchy of 'regions'. There are local regions defined by the absence of short-term and short-distance mobility across their boundaries, larger regions defined by the absence of longer-term and longer-distance mobility, and even vast continental regions distinguished, as for example in the literature on optimum currency areas, by the ability to adjust an imbalance in foreign payments by altering the exchange rate. Thus, a region may mean anything from a local employment area, to a subregion (such as East Berkshire) to a region (such as the Northwest) to the whole United Kingdom (possessing its own flexible currency), or even the whole of the EEC (if this is judged to be an optimum currency area).

And the problem regions defined by governments in determining policy interventions apart even from euphemistic changes, such as from 'depressed' to 'special' to 'development' areas, have enjoyed a bewildering variety of nomenclature with the mostly simultaneous existence of development, special development, DATAC and intermediate or 'grey' areas, development districts and enterprise zones, not to mention the requirements of Industrial Development Certificates (IDCs), and areas where they might or might not be granted. One reason for this bewildering variety of regions is that regions have an unfortunate habit of changing their status over time. Thus the major problem regions of the UK since the 1930s were the boom areas of the Victorian era; while from 1945 to about 1975, Belgium has experienced an even more rapid and remarkable switch, in which the Walloon and Flemish regions changed places in the economic league table between the 1950s and the 1970s.

The indicators or criteria for recognising the existence of a regional problem are numerous and often contraindicative. Some of the most frequently cited are: unemployment rates, activity rates (the percentage of the population actively seeking work), income per head, rates of emigration, rates of growth, age and class structures, industrial structures, congestion and environmental conditions. Each of these criteria raises complex issues of comparability. For example, the statistical computation of unemployment is notoriously variable between one country and another and even within one country over time. Even if comparable statistics could be obtained, the relative incidence of regional problems would still be difficult to measure since social preference patterns vary from one country to another and what is perceived as a problem in one country or region may not be so regarded in another. Even indicators as similar as unemployment and activity rates can give contrary indications: a region may have high unemployment but low activity rates, or vice versa. Incomes per head are not well correlated with unemployment rates. Outward migration of labour raises difficulties because it tends to reduce the level of other indicators such as unemployment. It is therefore debatable whether outward migration is a symptom or a cure of the regional illness. What is certain is that there is no single regional problem to be defined by a certain concatenation of these indicators; rather, there are a number of different regional problems which can each be defined by a selection from the list. It follows that different problem regions may have little in common and that solutions may have to differ widely.

While these problems are sufficiently keenly felt at national level (for example, the very different nature of the regional problem as between the industrial Northeast of England and the agricultural Scottish Highlands), they are magnified at the level of the European Community. It is difficult to find a common basis for discussion as between the United Kingdom, where regional disparities have been high in unemployment but small in incomes per head, and the Italian Mezzogiorno, where not only is unemployment much higher than in the North, but incomes are relatively extremely low.

The problem of definition is exacerbated when one considers the EEC as a whole, in that regional statistics are collected according to regional boundaries that are defined by essentially administrative rather than economic criteria. Thus, in the German Federal Republic, Hamburg and Bremen are treated as separate regions only because they have the constitutional status, based on their historical role as city-states, of *Länder* within the federation; in the UK there are only eleven regions, the economic planning regions, including the Southeast, which, including as it does London, has a population of about nineteen millions. In France there are twenty-one, in Italy twenty, while in Spain, which may be a member of the EEC in a few years, the statistics distinguish each of fifty separate and administrative provinces in a separate region. Thus, in the comparisons of income per capita throughout the EEC published by the EEC Commission from time to time, Hamburg is usually at or near the top of the league, only because it is administratively separate from its poorer hinterland, and the rankings of many other regions similarly are questionable given the irrelevant criteria on which the statistics are collected on a more useful basis.

THE ORIGINS OF REGIONAL PROBLEMS

Since in the past populations have tended to grow in areas where industry or agriculture were successful, regional problems frequently originate in the decline of an industrial sector which previously provided employment to an existing population, or even attracted immigrants from outside the area. Therefore, many regional problems develop in areas where important industries are in decline. The decline may be due to natural causes, such as the exhaustion of a raw material (for example, coal), or from economic causes, such as the international competition of textiles and shipbuilding, which has created serious difficulties over many years for regions in Western Europe which rely on these industries. Loss of competitiveness of regional industries may be caused by low growth of productivity relative to other regions, or by rigidities in the labour markets causing the maintenance of too high wages. The regional economy may also be undermined by an appreciation of the national exchange rate, based on the higher productivity of other regions within the national economy. However, regional problems are by no means caused solely by too low productivity. If productivity grows faster than demand for the product, then regional unemployment may result, as in the case of West European agriculture, where a combination of rapid technological progress with a low income elasticity of demand have created a much reduced demand for labour.

Whatever the origin of a regional problem, its persistence can only be explained by analysing the reasons why the industrial structure of a region is not adapted by new industry replacing the declining sectors. Some regions have come through periods of stagnation to a new prosperity based on new industries. The case for regional policy is largely that it can assist and speed such transformations. Other regions, however, may have little chance of viability in changed technological or market conditions (for example, the areas of worked-out coalmining in West Durham), and an important task for regional analysis is to distinguish the regions that can be nursed back to prosperity from those that can only be assisted to wind down. In view of the problems of defining a region in the first place, and of specifying the problems that justify intervention, it is not surprising that there is much confusion on this matter. The failure to attract new industry can be explained in general terms as a failure to offer low enough costs of production to business. Costs are relative to other conditions in the regions, such as a peripheral location remote from materials or markets, unattractive environment, poor industrial relations, etc. However, since in principle all such disadvantages of the location may be offset if actual production costs can be kept low enough, the fundamental cause of continued difficulty may be ascribed to excessive wage levels relative to these other conditions.

The pattern of regional problems found in the EEC has changed with the two major enlargements of the Community. In the original EEC, the Six, there were only two major problem regions, the Mezzogiorno (the South of Italy) and Southwest France. Both were geographically peripheral regions of declining agricultural employment, which had failed to attract industry. They suffered, therefore, from high unemployment, low incomes per head of the population and high rates of emigration.

The entry of Denmark, Ireland and the UK into the EEC in 1973 added a further peripheral poor agricultural region, Ireland, to the two already mentioned. More significantly, it brought into the EEC major declining industrial areas in the North and West of England, Scotland, Wales and Northern Ireland.

The accession of Greece, and the prospective accession of Portugal and Spain, is tilting the balance of the EEC's regional problems back towards the rural problems of the original Six. Greece and Portugal both have one major industrial region centred on the capital, and an outflow of labour from the agricultural, unindustrialised regions that constitute most of the remainder of the national territory. In Spain, though there is greater spread of industrial development over three to four industrial areas, similar problems of rural decline and indeed 'desertification' affect much of the interior of the country.

However, by 1982 the general economic situation of the EEC had changed so dramatically that the pattern of regional problems had evolved rapidly independently of the changes brought about by the successive extensions of the membership of the Community. General economic recession affected not just the 'declining' industries of coal, textiles and shipbuilding, which had largely accounted for the UK's regional problem; it also affected previously prosperous industries, such as steel, motors and many parts of the engineering sector, and therefore created high rates of unemployment in many regions that had been prosperous at least until the mid-1970s.

THE EFFECTS OF INTEGRATION ON REGIONAL PROBLEMS

There are two reasons why the European Community as such may be held to have a responsibility towards problem regions. First, the integration of the national economies and harmonisation of policies may be shown to create or to exacerbate regional problems. Secondly, the Community spirit may become sufficiently developed eventually as to create acceptance of a common responsibility towards poorer regions. This second reason is probably more relevant to a possible future economic union, and for the present it is more realistic to concentrate on the effect of the Community itself on regional problems.

In the original customs union of the Six three reasons were adduced why the Community might worsen regional problems of its members. First, it was held that increased *competition* caused by the removal of tariffs and other barriers to trade would drive out of business inefficient and high-cost firms, many of which would be located in problem regions. The poor locations that had already made them uncompetitive within their national economies would make them even less able to compete in the wider market. A second suggested reason was that as a consequence of increased trade deriving fom the customs union there would be a tendency towards an eventual equalisation of factor earnings throughout the Community. Although this might improve the income per head of those in employment in problem regions, it would increase unemployment by reducing still further the competitive strength of the region, and might reduce the overall regional average income per head. Thirdly, it was claimed that the main determinant of the competitive position of any region was its distance from the market centre. The enlargement of the market by the removal of tariff and other barriers at the national level, while it would make some problem regions, such as the Saar and Lorraine, more central than in the previous separate markets, would make others, such as the Mezzogiorno and Southwest France, more peripheral and therefore even less able to compete.

To these overlapping arguments was added Myrdal's concept of cumulative causation, whereby loss of competitive strength would create a 'vicious circle', leading to a progressive decline in the regional economy, with an accelerating outflow of capital and labour.

Although these arguments for the effects of integration on some regions are plausible, they are based on theories that are not easily tested and made operational. To all the conceptual problems of defining regions and regional problems are added the difficulties of estimating the effects of tariff removal and policy harmonisation. As has been found in the debates about British membership of the EEC, it is not easy to calculate the effect of integration on each industry, let alone to work through the regional industrial structure to assess its regional effects.

THE OBJECTIVES OF REGIONAL POLICY

The objectives of regional policy at the national level may be simply stated as being to reduce regional disparities. However, given the difficulties of defining regions and regional problems, it is not easy to proceed beyond such a meaningless generalisation. At EEC level there are two possibilities. Policy may at the minimum be limited to undoing any effects the Community itself may be thought to have in widening the disparities. Or, if a more forward policy is proposed, based presumably on a more optimistic view of the possible development of Community spirit, the objective may be held to be synonymous with that at the national level.

There are in fact immense differences in attitudes towards regional policy in each country. At one extreme, the keenest protagonists of regional policy appear almost to be proposing, though without always realising it, that the objective of policy must be the complete elimination of each and every disparity between one region and another. Such an objective would be impossible of attainment, given the continual emergence of new regional problems, and the lags in identifying them and devising and implementing appropriate policies. The attempt to achieve such an ambitious objective would in any case be likely to incur high costs in economic efficiency. At the other extreme, the advocates of 'workers-to-the-work' insist on leaving matters to the free play of market forces, often ignoring that we are nowadays usually in the economists' second-best situation, in which the market is already distorted in many ways, and that leaving regional problems to solve themselves is not socially and politically acceptable. The right solution must lie somewhere between these two extremes.

In the UK the overriding objective since the 1930s has been the elimination of all but minor disparities in unemployment. Though more sophisticated long-term objectives, such as creating an industrial structure less vulnerable to import competition or to cyclical fluctuations, have influenced policy, the real impetus to regional policy has come in periods of recession when a rapid increase in unemployment, with specially heavy incidence in the problem regions, impelled governments of all complexions to immediate 'fire-brigade' action. Perceptions of the regional problem appear very impervious to success in reducing it, and as one objective is attained, a more difficult one is added. Outside the UK, the major objective of regional policy has been the prevention of high rates of outward migration from agricultural regions by inducing the location of new industries in such regions. But in view of the importance of internal migration in the industrial development and economic growth of France and Italy, the objective could not be defined in terms of preventing any net emigration from the regions. And if it is not so defined, one is left with a vague target to reduce emigration by some unspecified amount, as with the general unemployment objective in Britain.

Attention to the costs of too much concentration of economic

growth in the prosperous regions, especially in the Southeast of
England and in the Paris region, led to the elaboration of hypotheses
suggesting that regional policy is not only good for the problem
regions, but also for the 'congested' prosperous areas, and indeed that
it is in the interests of the economy as a whole since it increases the
available labour supply and assists in controlling inflation. While
considerable evidence has been adduced in support of these proposi-
tions, they remain controversial. It is not entirely clear that congestion,
on which the argument hinges, really is worse in the Southeast of
England than it is in the Northwest, or in central Scotland. And if this is
doubtful, there remains a suspicion that policy to overcome impediments to the mobility of labour, such as the housing situation, would do
even more for the national GNP than providing jobs for the unemployed in locations that firms do not choose voluntarily.

Considering the argument about mobility at the EEC level can only
increase the uncertainty about this kind of issue. When movement
across national frontiers is in question, the stakes are raised both ways;
the social costs, and benefits, to workers who move are greater, but so
are the costs of failure to achieve the most efficient locations within the
larger market. On which side the costs are raised more is impossible to
answer. At the professional and executive level there are many signs of
willingness and even a positive desire to move. But the major problems
about mobility of labour have always been at the shopfloor level,
where the costs of movement appear much greater in comparison with
the improvement in remuneration that can be obtained.

TYPES OF REGIONAL POLICY

Regional policy takes many different forms in different member states
of the EEC, and changes frequently even within one country. A full
account of this diversity is beyond the scope of this chapter, but a brief
summary may be helpful. Four main types of regional aid may be
distinguished. The greatest concentration of government action, especially in the UK, has been on the subsidisation of investment projects.
Subsidies have taken many different forms: outright grants, special
depreciation provisions providing additional relief from taxation,
cheap loans to reduce the cost of borrowing to finance investment.
These and other incentives to investment have been based on the
assumption that the introduction of new industry was the best way to
improve employment opportunities, increase real incomes per capita
and reduce emigration.

A second main strand of policy has consisted in giving priority in problem regions to the provision of public infrastructure, roads, ports, colleges, (advance) factories, even the building of new towns. Thirdly, general incentives or subsidies have been provided to bring about a general reduction of costs in the assisted regions. General subsidies to the use of labour, such as the UK's regional employment premium, have been justified on the ground that it was better directly to encourage the use of labour in areas of high unemployment than to subsidise the use of capital through subsidies to capital investment.

Finally, regional policy has employed negative as well as positive inducements. Especially in the UK, but also in France and elsewhere in the EEC, controls over industrial location have been used to deter industry from building new factories or offices in the prosperous areas, in the hope that this would induce firms to expand instead in the problem regions.

EEC REGIONAL POLICY

EEC regional policy during the first fifteen years of the existence of the Community consisted only of the allocation of a high proportion of loans from the European Investment Bank (EIB) to the Italian Mezzogiorno, and a similar concentration of Social Fund spending on retraining and mobility of workers. Grants in aid of regional industrial development did not become available until after the UK joined the EEC in 1973. The European Regional Development Fund (ERDF) was established for three years in 1975, and was renewed in 1978 and 1981 for further three-year periods. It is funded by the general budget of the EEC but at a very low level, taking less than 10 per cent of a budget that totals only about £12 000 million (1983 draft budget), or less than 1 per cent of the GDP of all the Community members together. The ERDF is allocated, as to 95 per cent, through predetermined national quotas. The UK quota was 28 per cent in 1975–7, 27 per cent in 1978–80, and 23.8 per cent for 1981–3 (following the accession of Greece with a quota of 13 per cent). Other relatively poor member states (Italy with 40 per cent in 1975, now 35.5 per cent, and Ireland originally 6 per cent, now 5.9 per cent) also have quotas well in excess of their share in financing the Community budget. However, the Commission have argued that too much of the ERDF expenditure goes to countries with GDPs per capita above the EEC average, who also face less serious regional problems, and have therefore proposed that from 1983 quotas should be removed from Germany, France,

Denmark, Netherlands and Belgium, and spending concentrated on the more needy states. ERDF grants are administered through national administrations, and in further support of projects already included in national programmes for regional aids, approved by the EEC Commission. Given that there is little independent role for the EEC as such, it is highly questionable whether the existence of a Community regional fund provides any net addition to the level of assistance that would in any case be provided through regional policies financed at national level. Since 1978 a small proportion of the ERDF, 5 per cent, has been non-quota, that is, available to the Commission to use in accordance with Community-wide criteria. But this provides a quite insignificant sum for EEC policy to deploy, and the Commission have proposed that this non-quota section should be increased to 20 per cent of the total fund.

In addition to this 'positive' policy at EEC level, the Community also operates an important 'negative' policy, to police national regional aid programmes in order to ensure that they do not conflict with the objective of free and undistorted competition throughout the Common Market. Under Articles ninety-two to ninety-four of the Treaty of Rome, the Commission must be notified of all national programmes, and it controls both any distortions to trade and the problem of 'competition' or 'overbidding' between regional aids in different member states, by controlling the levels of subsidy that may be given in different types of region. Higher levels of subsidy, expressed as the total subsidy as a percentage of total costs of a project, are permitted in more peripheral regions than in the more central regions of the Community.

THE COST AND EFFECTIVENESS OF REGIONAL POLICY

At the simplest level, the costs of regional policy are the sums spent by governments on the various forms of subsidy used to induce industry to stay in, to relocate in, or to expand in, a region. Tax allowances, concessions or interest rates, and other forms of indirect aid can be calculated in terms of a 'subsidy-equivalent' and added to direct operating subsidies. The total of all forms of subsidy can be divided by the total number of jobs created to arrive at a 'cost-per-job' measure, and they can be expressed as a percentage of total turnover to indicate the effect on the cost prices of firms in the regions. But such measures are highly suspect. Many indirect subsidies, such as giving preferences to the regions in public infrastructure programmes, are virtually impossible to measure. The estimation of the number of jobs created is beset with difficulties, such as that of knowing whether or not a job might have been created even without a subsidy, how permanent the job is going to be, and how many jobs might be created by multiplier effects from the increased activity brought about by the initial job creation. While these measures may be useful for choosing between different forms of subsidy, they are of little value in deciding whether to subsidise or not.

Savings of expenditure under other heads, such as social security (especially unemployment) benefits, should be offset against the cost of regional subsidies to arrive at a net budgetary cost. This kind of calculation has sometimes led to the conclusion that the budgetary cost of regional subsidies is close to zero, or even that it is negative. But this is still by no means the whole story. Budgetary costs of regional aid programmes are only a part of the overall economic cost of regional policy. Costs to firms and to any workers transferred into the regions must be added. If productivity is, and remains, lower in the region than in the economy as a whole, if higher transport costs for components and finished products are incurred by operating branches in different parts of the country, or by location entirely in a remote region, these costs must be added. And if locational or other disadvantages of the region persist, the costs of firms may be loaded far into the future. Whether or not subsidies to induce a move to a region are justified must therefore depend on the results of cost-benefit studies of a magnitude so vast and a time horizon so distant that any regional problem would have evolved out of all recognition by the time they had been completed.

Measuring the effectiveness of regional policy must depend on the definition of the objective. Even counting the number of jobs provided runs into the familiar problem of defining the situation that would have come about if there had been no regional policy. A difference between the total unemployed ten years ago and the total unemployed today is the consequence of many causes, and the isolation of the effect of one cause, regional policy, is difficult. Since relatively high unemployment in the British regions has appeared in most cases to persist, the conclusion is suggested that we have been 'running very fast to stay on the same spot', implying that regional policy has succeeded in preventing the situation from worsening. Assuming such a modest objective, it may be possible to 'prove' effectiveness in this way, though many doubts remain. It is not certain that the situation would have got worse without any regional policy; or alternatively, it may be possible to claim great success for a regional policy if it can be argued convincingly that it prevented a complete disaster even though it could not prevent an increase in unemployment. The effectiveness or success of policy to prevent or slow down outward migration is just as hard to measure. As already mentioned, in the economic conditions of French or Italian agriculture, and industry, over the past twenty-five years a massive net emigration from agricultural regions was probably inevitable and even desirable. To say by how much regional policy ought to have slowed it down must be impossible.

The methods used for measuring the employment effects of regional policy are similar to those used in studies of the trade effects of tariff removal, and are indeed basic to all studies of employment effects. The micro method is to question all firms about how their behaviour has been affected by policy. This method raises many uncertainties, including the cost of comprehensive surveys, the problem that firms may not know too well how their decisions have been reached, the possibility of 'strategic response' – that is, that firms may give the response they consider will best alter future policy to their advantage. The macro method, statistical analysis of aggregative data, is more satisfactory, but faces the problem of separating and identifying the effects of one policy from the effects of other policy and economic variables affecting unemployment. This kind of analysis centres on the definition of a 'reference situation' with which the actual outcome may be compared in order to derive, as a residual, a measure of the effect of policy. The standard methods are assessment of trends, shift-share standardisation, and regression models. The trend method has the virtue of simplicity, but not much more to recommend it. Definition of a date at which a change of trend may be identified, and ignorance of variables such as differences in the industrial structures of different regions, create many difficulties in assessing a change of trend and attributing it to the effects of policy. Standardisation techniques take account of regional variations in industrial structure. Expected employment is estimated for each region on the assumption that it grew at the same rate as for that sector at the national level. The difference between this estimate and the observed growth in regional employment in that sector is assumed to be the regional policy effect. (This method can be tested by comparing the actual and the estimated values in a previous period, before the policy was introduced.) Regression analysis requires the specification of a complete model of the determinants of employment, and the availability of adequate data for each of the variables. If these requirements can be met, then this technique can provide more accurate estimates of the effects of policy. It can also be combined with two methods, by putting a trend, or shift-share, variable into the model. All these methods have problems, and none can be categorically regarded as superior, though the potential for the econometric model is greatest.

Studies carried out in the UK suggest that regional policy may have created some 25 000 to 35 000 jobs per annum in problem regions in the 1960s and early 1970s. However, there is also evidence that the effectiveness of policy may have declined in the 1970s, possibly to a level of only 10 000 or so jobs per annum. These job creation effects are gross effects, not net effects for the whole economy. That is, they measure only the addition to jobs in the assisted regions, and make no allowance for any effects of regional policy in reducing employment in other parts of the national or the wider EEC economy. Especially in periods when aggregate demand is tightly constrained, jobs created in assisted regions may be at the expense of loss of jobs in other regions, which will face subsidised competition with their own costs burdened by taxes which have to be levied to finance regional subsidies.

The effects of the EEC's Regional Development Fund (ERDF) on employment in the member states must have been very slight. First, although the expenditures from the Fund are in principle additional to the regional policy spending of the national governments, in practice there is no way of ensuring that they are. Given the fact that the Fund is distributed mainly in the form of national quotas and to the national governments, there is every reason to believe that much of the expenditure is used to replace national expenditure that would otherwise have been allocated to regional policy. Only in the case of the 5 per cent of the Fund which is distributed by the Commission outside the national quotas is it likely that most of the spending is truly additional. Secondly, the Regional Fund is very small in relation to national government spending on regional assistance. In the case of the UK, which had in 1978–80 a national quota of 27 per cent of the Fund, the gross receipts were only about £50 million p.a. compared with national spending on regional aids of about £500 million. Given the estimate that UK regional policy in the 1970s created 10 000 jobs per annum, EEC spending in the UK, even if all of it had been additional, would have created only about 1000 jobs per annum. More relevant than the operations of the Regional Fund are likely to have been the overall effects of the financing of the EEC Budget, which makes net transfers among the member states considerably greater than those of the regional fund, and therefore affects the ability of the member states to finance their own regional policies. (However, the effects in Ireland, a much smaller EEC member state with a large proportional share in the ERDF, have been much more significant.)

6 The Impact of EEC Membership upon UK Industrial Performance

ROBERT GRANT

INTRODUCTION: EXPECTATIONS AT THE TIME OF ENTRY

During the years immediately prior to Britain's accession to the European Community, considerable attention was devoted to the likely effects of membership upon the British economy. Despite the controversy generated in the debate over membership, a substantial degree of consensus emerged as to the probable economic impact. It was clear, for example, that budgetary contributions and higher food prices would involve a substantial outflow on the balance of payments and would boost the rate of inflation during the transition period. The impact on the industrial sector was less clear-cut. It was generally considered that the effect of the elimination of tariffs between Britain and the EEC combined with a loss of Commonwealth, EFTA and Irish preferences would result initially in an adverse movement in the balance of trade in manufactures. The 1970 White Paper, *Britain and the European Communities, An Economic Assessment*, estimated an adverse movement in the non-food trade balance of between £125 million and £275 million. With higher import prices for food and the large net budget contributions, an adverse movement in the balance of payments of up to £1000 million was foreseen.

However, these impact effects of entry were generally regarded as being of less significance than the longer-term consequences for the rate of growth of the British economy. The nature and sources of the dynamic effects of entry were seldom made explicit. The most prevalent argument of the pro-marketeers was that Britain's incorporation into the Community would cause her rate of economic growth to converge towards the higher rates experienced by the EEC(6).[1] The mechanism envisaged by the advocates of entry was that EEC membership would increase the potential for export sales, enabling the country to embark upon the desired strategy of 'export-led growth'. Not only did the EEC provide a large and affluent market on Britain's doorstep, whose growth of income per head exceeded that of Britain's traditional export markets, but Britain's prospects among her established customers were becoming increasingly gloomy due to erosion of Commonwealth preferences and the imposition of trade barriers by industrialising Third World countries.

A more detailed consideration of the dynamic effects of membership was provided in the 1970 White Paper. The potential for increased economic growth was seen as arising not only from the ability of British industry to expand exports of manufactured goods but also from (i) the stimulatory effects of increased competition; (ii) the increased investment which would arise from increased competition and export expansion; (iii) the exploitation of scale economies, in particular, the benefits to technologically-based industries from the ability of British companies to grow to the size required for adequate R & D.[2]

Belief in the beneficial character of the dynamic effects of EEC entry was far from unanimous. For example, Professor Kaldor, while endorsing the nature and the importance of the dynamic effects of entry, considered that the adverse static effects of entry in terms of an increasing trade deficit, a rise in domestic prices and costs, large net budget contributions, and loss of real income would be so severe as to result in dynamic effects of entry which would depress rather than stimulate economic growth (Kaldor, 1971).

Despite these differences of opinion as to the quantitative impact of the different effects, it is apparent that at the time of Britain's entry to the EEC there were some clearly formulated notions as to the nature of the impact of membership on British industry which were based upon the forecast of changes in UK trade and a diagnosis of the sources of Britain's low rate of economic growth. In this chapter I shall reexamine the arguments concerning the impact of the EEC upon British industry in the light of almost a decade of membership, drawing upon recent research into British trade performance and the deficiencies of growth and productivity in British industry. The main body of the chapter is in two sections: first, a summary of the principal changes in UK trade associated with Community membership; second, an examination of the principal ways in which the EEC has influenced the growth of the UK industrial sector.

THE TRADE EFFECTS OF EEC MEMBERSHIP

The influence of EEC membership on British industry has occurred principally through the changes in UK overseas trade which have resulted from incorporation within the Community. Despite considerable research into this topic, definite conclusions about the impact of the EEC on UK trade cannot easily be drawn. All that can be observed are the changes in the volume and pattern of trade since entry. Not only are the separate 'trade-creating' and 'trade-diverting' effects predicted by the theory of custom unions empirically inseparable, but it is impossible to distinguish the effects of EEC membership from the effects of the oil price shocks, recession, North Sea oil, and the various other factors which have since 1973 so radically altered the international economic climate and the trading position of the UK.

The principal effects on UK trade have arisen from the changes in UK tariff rates consequent upon EEC entry. But even here it is difficult clearly to identify those changes which have directly resulted from Community membership. At the time of entry, Community membership promised a substantial fall in protection for British industry – not only were tariffs between the UK and EEC to be eliminated, but the Common External Tariff of the EEC was on average below the average UK tariff on manufactures. However, the historical fall in UK average tariffs since 1973 overstates the impact of the EEC since tariff rates were declining worldwide during the 1970s as a result of the multilateral tariff negotiations. Of the reduction in UK average tariff rates between 1959 and 1977 only between one quarter and one third were the result of EEC membership (Morgan, 1980). Since the late 1960s the average tariffs of the OECD countries on industrial products were reduced by 36 per cent in the Kennedy Round and by 34 per cent in the Tokyo Round, reducing rates of tariffs on most manufactures to very low levels (as shown in Table 6.1).

Thus UK entry into the EEC did not involve quite so drastic a change in Britain's commercial relations with the rest of the world as appeared in 1973. Certainly the notion of the EEC providing an 'expanded home market' for British manufacturers and a secure springboard for export sales to non-EEC markets fails to take account of the low tariff rates on manufactured goods throughout the indus-

TABLE 6.1 *Post-Tokyo Round average tariffs on all industrial products (excluding petroleum)*

	per cent
US	4.3
Japan	2.7
EEC	4.6
Austria	7.7
Finland	5.5
Norway	3.1
Sweden	4.0
Switzerland	2.2

SOURCE OECD

trialised world and of the non-tariff barriers and characteristic differences between national markets within the EEC.[3]

Despite these various factors which might be expected to limit and obscure the impact of the EEC on UK trade, the evidence on the changing pattern of UK trade after 1973 shows a remarkable shift in both imports and exports towards the EEC (9) (Table 6.2).

TABLE 6.2 *UK visible trade with the EEC as a proportion of total UK visible trade*

	Exports to EEC as % of total UK exports	Imports from EEC as % total UK imports
1970	29.7	28.4
1971	28.1	30.7
1972	30.2	33.8
1973	32.3	35.7
1974	33.8	35.3
1975	32.2	38.5
1976	35.5	38.4
1977	36.8	40.0
1978	38.1	43.3
1979	42.6	45.2
1980	43.1	42.7
1981(Q4)–82(Q1)	42.1	43.2

SOURCE The United Kingdom balance of payments, 1981, OECD internal paper (1982) based upon GATT data.

How far was this shift in British trade towards the countries of the EEC the result of Community membership? David Mayes has measured the EEC effect by comparing the actual EEC shares of UK trade in individual product groups with the shares which would have occurred if the trends of 1962–72 had continued. Figure 6.1 gives the results for just three product categories.

For almost all categories, the share of EEC (6) both in UK imports and the UK exports rose substantially above the extrapolated trends. Exceptions were imports and exports of raw materials which were not subject to any significant tariff changes and broadly followed the trend lines, exports of machinery and transport equipment whose increases were broadly in line with pre-1973 trends, and UK imports of transport equipment, the EEC share of which had fallen, largely due to UK imports of Japanese cars.

In addition to a diversion of trade towards the EEC, Community membership has resulted in a substantial growth in the volume of UK trade. Between 1972 and 1978 the ratio of total trade to GNP of the UK rose from 33.5 to 48.5 per cent, compared with a rise for the EEC (6) from 36.6 to 45.3 per cent.

The effect of these trade changes upon the total output of UK industry depends most directly upon whether EEC membership has increased exports by more than imports. Table 6.3 shows that EEC membership coincided with a substantial worsening of the balance of trade both with the EEC and the world as a whole. For manufactured goods there is a similar worsening of the trade balance with the EEC. A clearer perspective emerges from Table 6.4 which shows changes in the trade balance on manufacturers as a proportion of trade. The worsening of the UK trade balance with the EEC on manufactured goods is part of a general, though less severe, worsening of the overall UK trade balance on manufactured goods. An adverse impact of the EEC upon UK trade in manufactured goods is also indicated by Mayes's comparisons for individual commodity groups of actual trade with projections of pre-1973 trends: increases in the EEC shares of UK imports above trend levels substantially exceed the increase in EEC shares of UK exports above trend levels.

The main trade effects of Britain's accession to the European Community are, therefore, a substantial shift in the direction of trade towards the EEC, accompanied by a worsening of the balance of trade with the EEC particularly in manufactured goods. At the same time the picture is not wholly gloomy. The improvement in the overall trade deficit since 1977 has, of course, been largely due to North Sea oil, but

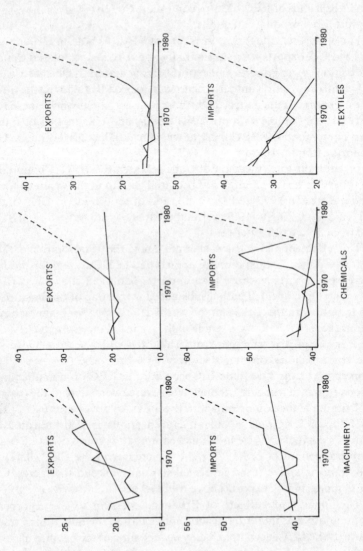

FIGURE 6.1 *The percentages of UK trade in machinery, chemicals and textiles accounted for by the EEC (6), 1963–80*

SOURCE reproduced from Mayes (1982), 'The Trade Effects of the EEC', discussion paper.

TABLE 6.3   *UK trade balances with the world and with the EEC (9) 1970–80*

	All goods		Manufactured goods	
	World *$m*	*EEC*[a] *$m*	*World* *$m*	*EEC*[a] *$m*
1970	− 2 416	− 237	+ 5 348	+ 1 020
1971	− 1 590	− 747	+ 6 853	+ 735
1972	− 2 715	− 1 619	+ 6 211	+ 41
1973	− 8 275	− 2 986	+ 3 782	− 707
1974	− 15 413	− 5 587	+ 4 200	− 1 736
1975	− 9 508	− 5 800	+ 8 645	− 1 293
1976	− 9 918	− 4 295	+ 7 944	− 4 916
1977	− 6 197	− 4 345	+ 9 626	− 1 542
1978	− 6 942	− 5 095	+ 7 541	− 2 996
1979	− 11 997	− 6 440	+ 3 585	− 6 175
1980	− 3 521	− 1 688	+ 8 933	− 3 600
1981/82[b]	− 2 838	− 5 988	+ 5 190	—

[a] Measured as: EEC reported imports from UK minus UK reported imports from EEC. This is to correct for an overstatement of UK exports to the EEC arising from the British recording of exports on a consignment rather than a destination basis (see Morgan, 1981, pp. 63–4).

[b] 1981 (Q4) to 1982 (Q1) on an annual basis.

SOURCE   OECD Foreign Trade Statistics.

even in the case of manufactured goods, the erosion of the UK trade surplus with the world and the increasing deficit with the EEC since the mid-1970s are not as dramatic as might have been expected given the combination of sluggish productivity growth, high cost inflation and an appreciating exchange rate. Indeed, Table 6.5 shows some stabilisa-

TABLE 6.4   *UK trade balance in manufactured goods as a percentage of total UK trade in manufactured goods*

	World *%*	*EEC only* *%*
1970–2	+ 19.3	+ 6.3
1973–5	+ 9.6	+ 6.3
1976–8	+ 9.6	− 8.1
1979–80	+ 4.2	− 8.6
1981 (Q4)–82 (Q1)	+ 3.6	—

SOURCE   OECD Foreign Trade Statistics.

TABLE 6.5   *The UK's share of the man-*
ufactured exports of the 12 major indus-
trialised countries

	Per cent
1955–8	19.0
1959–62	16.7
1962–5	14.7
1966–9	12.0
1970–3	10.1
1974–7	8.8
1978–80	9.2
1981(Q4)–82(Q1)	9.0

SOURCE   Mayes (1982), 'The Trade
Effects of the EEC', p.38,
updated.

tion in the UK's share of manufactured exports by the developed
countries during the late 1970s. It remains clear, however, that manufacturing trade performance has deteriorated more rapidly with the
EEC than with non-EEC countries. This may partly reflect the difficulties faced by British manufacturing industry in adjusting to the
new environment of the EEC and also the continuing high value of
sterling against the major continental currencies. Even when these
factors are taken into account, however, there remains a question
mark as to the long-term competitiveness of British manufacturers in
the sophisticated, consumer-orientated markets of the EEC.

EEC MEMBERSHIP AND THE GROWTH OF THE UK
INDUSTRIAL SECTOR

The 1970 White Paper contended that the dynamic effects of EEC
membership on UK economic growth would be far more important
than the impact effect on trade. Subsequent analyses have confirmed
this view. For example, David Mayes's survey of the trade effects of the
EEC concluded that 'even a trivial feedback effect on to the rate of
economic growth of the participant countries will tend to dominate the
welfare effects of changes in trade flows' (Mayes, 1982, p. 46).

In examining the effects of EEC membership upon the growth and
growth potential of the UK industrial sector, I shall follow the conven-
tional approach of dividing the sources of increasing real output per
employee between increases in capital per employee and increases in

output per unit of input. This chapter focuses chiefly on the latter source of growth, and in particular on the impact on input productivity which has occurred through the effect of EEC membership on the extent and direction of the structural adjustment of British industry.

INVESTMENT

The relatively minor emphasis which is given to investment in this chapter reflects, first, evidence that lack of investment in fixed capital is not the dominant source of the low rate of economic growth in the UK and, second, the apparent absence of any strong effects of EEC membership upon the volume of UK investment. Since Solow's finding that only 12.5 per cent of the increase in US output per man-hour was attributable to increased capital (Solow, 1954), considerable interest has been shown in the contribution of investment to economic growth. Denison estimated that less than one-quarter of the growth of GDP per person employed in the UK between 1950 and 1962 was due to investment (Denison, 1968, p. 235), and more recently Caves found differences in the value of capital per worker between matched US and UK industries had an insignificant effect upon the differences in labour productivity between the two countries (Caves, 1980, p. 171). The contribution of investment in industrial fixed capital to growth is extremely difficult to distinguish since investment not only increases productive capacity but also acts as an avenue for the introduction of new technology and a means of achieving the adjustment of industry structure. It has been argued by Pavitt, however, that the shift of emphasis from process to product innovation means that the linkage between capital investment and technical progress is becoming weaker in the industrialised countries (Pavitt, 1979).

While trade expansion arising from economic integration may provide a stimulus to investment, the evidence is far from clear-cut and my concern here is solely with the impact of the EEC on flows of direct investment to and from the UK. Community membership has affected these, first, by removing most legal impediments to investment between member countries and, second, through the trade effects of EEC membership. The latter are complex. The elimination of trade barriers between Britain and the Community would have tended both to reduce two-way direct investment, to the extent that trade and direct investment are substitutes, and increase direct investment, to the extent that complementary relationships exist – particularly through the establishment of overseas marketing and distribution subsidiaries by manufacturing firms.

More important for the UK is likely to have been the effect of EEC membership on inward investment from non-EEC countries – particularly from the United States. The principal argument has been that the popularity of the UK as a destination for direct investment has been increased by the ability to use the UK as a base for European manufacturing and distribution operations.

Table 6.6 shows that while there was rapid growth in the flows of both inward and outward direct investment during the 1970s, the dominant directions were between the UK and North America. There was some growth in the share of EEC countries in inward direct investment to the UK, but the share of UK direct investment going to the EEC fell over the period. As regards flows of direct investment between the UK and the non-EEC countries, there was a fall in the UK's share of total direct investment into the OECD countries (from 7.4 per cent in 1968–73 to 6.1 per cent in 1974–8), but this fall would appear to be only a continuation of a longer-term trend. It is notable that the UK's share of US overseas direct investment in manufacturing has remained steady during the later 1970s (Table 6.7) as has the UK's share of the US overseas capital stock (Table 6.8).

In recent years there has been a shift in emphasis from a lack of

TABLE 6.6   *Direct investment into and out of the UK*

	1970–2[a]	1973–5[a]	1976–8[a]	1979	1980
EEC (9)					
in the UK £m	48	95	251	270	157
% of total	12	13	22	15	6
by the UK £m	208	352	489	34	483
% of total	32	24	22	1	14
N. America					
in the UK £m	271	392	681	1 114	1 760
% of total	66	53	60	61	68
by the UK £m	167	448	761	1 801	1 896
% of total	26	31	34	64	54
Total					
in the UK £m	408	734	1 139	1 818	2 576
by the UK £m	653	1 456	2 257	2 788	3 491

[a] Annual averages.
SOURCE   The UK Balance of Payments, 1982.

TABLE 6.7 *The percentage of total overseas US manufac-turing investment in the UK*

1976	1977	1978	1979	1980	1981 (est)
12.6	13.5	13.6	14.3	15.8	15.7

SOURCE *Financial Times*, 2 December 1981, p. 4.

TABLE 6.8 *The percentage distribution of US overseas direct investment – based on end year stock values*

	1966	1970	1974	1979
Europe	31.6	33.5	40.6	42.3
UK	10.5	10.6	11.4	12.6

SOURCE *International Investment and Multi-national Enterprise* (OECD, 1981).

investment in plant and equipment towards a lack of investment in human capital as an explanation of the low level and low rate of growth of output per employee in British industry. Comparisons of levels of education and training of the British and German labour forces show clearly the high proportion of the British labour force with no educa-tional or technical qualifications as compared with the high proportion of the German labour force with intermediate qualifications (Prais, 1981). Membership of the EEC can influence the stock of human capital available to British industry through the removal of restrictions on mobility of workers within the EEC. It appears, however, that no significant labour migration has occurred between Britain and other member countries. Compared with other European countries the UK has a very small proportion of its labour force working abroad. At the same time British industry has not benefited from any significant inflow of skilled labour from elsewhere – the principal flow of labour into the UK is from the Irish Republic and largely consists of unskilled labour.

Hence, the evidence both on direct investment flows and labour movements does not give any clear indication as to EEC membership having any impact upon the stock either of physical or human capital available to British industry.

CHANGES IN OUTPUT PER UNIT OF INPUT

Increases in output per unit of input in the industrial sector arise from two main sources: technical change and structural adjustment involving the reallocation of resources from low- to high-productivity employment.

I shall not attempt any examination of the impact of the EEC on the technical progressiveness of British industry. The determinants of technical change and the role of innovation in the growth process are too poorly understood and the ways in which EEC membership might affect technical change are too many to allow any simple hypotheses to be ventured or conclusions to be drawn. Nevertheless it is likely that EEC membership has had some important effects on technical change: increased competition is likely to accelerate the diffusion of innovations and may act both as an incentive and a constraint upon investment in innovation, economic integration may enable companies to exploit economies of scale and risk spreading in R & D and may facilitate transnational technical cooperation. In addition the activities of the Community in harmonising patent law, regulating licensing agreements and promoting research may encourage technical progress.

The remainder of the chapter is concerned with the influence of EEC membership upon the structural adjustment of British industry. It is being increasingly recognised that one of the major constraints upon the economic growth of the mature economies since 1973 has been inadequate adjustment of economic structures. Not only has there been an increased need for structural adjustment as a result of oil price rises, increased competition from low-cost manufacturing countries, and other shocks to the international economy, but the capacity for adjustment has been reduced by stagnation, inflexibility of relative prices and the unresponsiveness of economic units to price incentives (OECD, 1982). Although the problem is a general one for the older industrialised countries, there is evidence to suggest that the industrial structure of Britain is specially resistant to adjustment pressures (Jones, 1980, pp. 118–21).

In examining the effect of EEC membership upon structural change in British industry it is convenient to distinguish between interindustry and intraindustry adjustment.

Interindustry structural adjustment involves the movement of factors of production from products facing declining demand to products facing expanding demand. Intraindustry structural adjustment involves changes in the size distribution of plants and firms as resources are reallocated towards the optimal sizes of plant and firm, and the reallocation of resources from inefficiently managed to efficiently managed firms. In view of the substantial growth of trade between Britain and the EEC since 1973, it is to be expected that Community membership will have exercised a powerful influence on both aspects of structural adjustment. The reduction in UK trade barriers resulting from EEC membership is conducive to the reallocation of resources between industries through specialisation on the basis of comparative advantage. The changing identity of Britain's closest trading partners is likely to influence the direction of such specialisation by altering the nature of Britain's comparative advantages. Increased specialisation also provides the potential for exploiting economies of scale within Britain's industrial specialisms. Such economies are likely to be of primary importance in industries where, due to very large minimum efficient plant size, or the very specialised nature of the market being served, or the heavy costs of research and development, the domestic market is too small to sustain commercially viable operation. Finally, the increased pressure of competition consequent upon EEC membership is likely to speed the reallocation of resources from inefficient to efficient firms within the same industry and to hasten the elimination of suboptimally-sized plants and firms.

Having outlined the ways in which EEC membership might be expected to have stimulated structural change in British industry, let us look at the evidence.

INTERINDUSTRY SPECIALISATION AND EEC MEMBERSHIP

The extent of interindustry adjustment   The view that adjustment of the structure of output of British industry to the changes in the world economy during the 1970s has been particularly slow is clearly revealed in an analysis undertaken by the UN Economic Commission for Europe (Table 6.9).

The table shows that with regard to changes in value added across eighteen manufacturing sectors the UK ranked among the lowest of nine European countries during the 1970s, although the disparity was less marked than in the previous decade. In terms of employment, UK structural change remained comparatively very low during the 1970s – probably reflecting characteristics of the UK labour market.

If EEC membership had stimulated changes in the structure of UK output by inducing increased industrial specialisation, this would be

TABLE 6.9   *Interindustry structural adjustment and growth in the manufacturing sectors of nine European countries*

	Structural change in value added at constant prices		Structural change in employment		Annual % growth of real output	
	1958/60 to 1968/70	1970 to 1978	1958/60 to 1968/70	1970 to 1978	1958/60 to 1968/70	1970 to 1978
Belgium	10.7	10.2	6.5	7.8	6.5	3.4
Finland	10.4	8.7	7.9	6.3	6.9	3.1
France	9.4	13.2	7.9	6.8	6.3	4.4
Germany	10.2	7.7	7.8	5.8	6.3	2.0
Italy	9.4	6.6	6.7	5.3	8.3	2.9
Netherlands	13.6	7.9	7.8	7.4	6.8	2.9
Norway	9.3	9.0	7.8	7.6	5.3	1.5
Sweden	11.2	6.8	6.7	7.4	6.9	0.7
UK	7.7	7.3	5.5	3.5	3.3	0.7

NOTE   The index of structural change (c) is measured $c = \sum_i (a_{i2} - a_{i1})$ for all $a_{i2} > a_{i1}$ where a_{i1} is the share of branch i of output or employment in period 1 and a_{i2} the share in period 2.

SOURCE   *Economic Survey of Europe in 1980* (New York: United Nations, 1981).

indicated by increased specialisation in Britain's trade. Government economists (Smith et al., 1982) have shown, however, that the standard deviation across MLH industries of the ratio between the trade balance and domestic sales was *less* in 1979 than in 1970 – indicating a *fall* in trade specialisation. At the same time, however, the standard deviations of both export/sales and import/sales ratios increased which was interpreted as evidence of increased intraindustry trade specialisation. This pattern of decreased interindustry specialisation and increased intraindustry specialisation was particularly evident in trade with the EEC.

The apparent failure of EEC membership to stimulate any substantial interindustry reallocation of resources during the 1970s is also indicated by the fact that, despite the rapid growth of UK trade with the EEC, the industrial composition of UK exports remained relatively stable. At the same time there was a substantial change in the composition of Britain's manufactured imports. The implication is that changes in the pattern of final demand in the UK were accomodated largely by changes in the composition of imports rather than of domestic output.

TABLE 6.10   *Structural change in the industrial composition of the exports and imports of eight European countries 1970–8*

	Exports	Imports
Belgium	16.3	9.4
France	6.0	11.1
Germany	4.2	14.1
Italy	7.6	10.7
Netherlands	8.0	9.5
Sweden	3.6	5.4
Switzerland	8.8	10.1
UK	6.5	15.3

SOURCE   *Economic Survey of Europe in 1980* (1981).

One explanation for the comparative lack of structural change of UK industry could be that the UK's manufacturing sector was already specialised in the growth industries of the 1970s. A correlation across eighteen manufacturing industries of relative specialisation for each industry in 1970 and each industry's rate of growth in Europe between 1970 and 1978 gave the following results:

France	– 0.3397
Germany	+ 0.1183
Sweden	+ 0.0795
UK	+ 0.0995

These figures show UK manufacturing industry to have been in a broadly neutral position with regard to industrial specialisms in 1970, but more favourably placed than France.

The direction of interindustry adjustment Since in advanced economies comparative advantages in manufacture are not primarily the result of exogenous factor endowments, but are created through investment in capital, innovation and human skills – the consequences of interindustry structural adjustment for economic growth depend chiefly upon the extent to which the direction of structural change is

towards industries with the highest growth potential. On the basis of
the UN Commission for Europe's eighteen-sector breakdown of manufacturing industry, it is possible to calculate the extent to which the
interindustry structural changes of 1970–8 were directed towards the
faster growing industries. Regressing the change in relative specialisation in each of the eighteen industries (ΔS_{ij}) on the growth rate of each
industry (G_i) gave the following results

	Constant	*Regression coefficient*
France	– 5.594	+ 1.338
	(– 0.8680)	(2.303)
Germany	– 2.576	– 0.06045
	(– 1.371)	(– 0.3568)
Sweden	– 0.4351	– 0.1630
	(– 1.021)	(– 0.87118)
UK	+ 3.986	– 0.7593
	(1.301)	(– 2.748)

(t-values in brackets)

The strongly negative relationship between the UK's changes in
specialisation and growth in output reflect the fact that all the industries where the UK increased its share of European output were those
with a stagnant or declining output. These included tobacco, clothing
and footwear, rubber, printing, textiles and leather. This pattern of
spcialisation reflects a tendency for the UK to maintain its output of
low-technology products whose output is increasingly shifting towards
developing countries.

To what extent, if at all, can EEC membership be held responsible
for the failure of British industry to adjust towards the growth industries of the 1970s? At the time of entry it was believed that the affluent,
sophisticated consumers of the EEC would provide a stimulus for the
development of technologically-based, high-value added industries in
the UK. An alternative view, however, would be to argue that within
the EEC the UK represents a low-wage economy with a high proportion of its labour force unskilled. To the extent that the EEC achieves
significant protection against imports from the newly-industrialising
countries through the Common External Tariff, the Multifibre Agreement and various voluntary export restraints, then the UK is encour-

aged to specialise in the production of low skill-intensity products.

An indication of the failure of EEC membership to stimulate the development of technologically-based, skill-intensive industries is provided by the analysis by Smith *et al.* (1982) of the determinants of the UK's trade specialisation. While similar studies for West Germany and Sweden have shown human capital variables to have a strong impact on trade performance of individual industries, for the UK human capital variables only had a positive impact on trade performance with less developed countries and had an insignificant impact on UK trade with the EEC. Also the R & D variable had no significant impact on UK trade performance.

The service sector and the EEC   The discussion so far has been exclusively in terms of structural adjustment within the manufacturing sector. However, probably the most fundamental long-term trend in UK industrial structure is the decline in manufacturing relative to services. Between 1970 and 1980 the contribution of manufacturing to GDP fell from 33 per cent to 23 per cent, while the contribution of the service sector (excluding the ownership of dwellings and public administration and defence) rose from 45 to 50 per cent. While this phenomenon is common to the economic development of all mature industrial economies, the disparity between the relative growth rates of manufacturing and services has been particularly large in the UK, reflecting, in comparative international terms, the inefficiency of UK manufacturing and the efficiency of many parts of the service sector. Hence there is a broad consensus that the major areas of international comparative advantage of UK industry lie chiefly in services, for example, in financial services, computer services, consultancy services and, to a lesser extent, in shipping and retail distribution.

The reduction in trade barriers consequent upon accession to the EEC would be expected to accelerate the structural adjustment from manufacturing into services and would be accompanied by an increase in the trade deficit on manufactured goods and an increase in the trade surplus on services.

The problem for the UK, however, has been that EEC trade liberalisation has been asymmetric between manufacturing and services. The elimination of tariffs and the reduction in non-tariff restrictions on manufactured goods have not been accompanied by any widespread dismantling of the multifarious regulatory requirements and restrictive practices which have hampered international trade and competition in many service industries.[4]

TABLE 6.11 – *Trade in services in total and with the EEC (9)*

Credits	1973	1974	1975	1976	1977	1978	1979	1980	1981
Total private sector and public corporation services (£ billion)	5.19	6.63	7.73	10.02	11.60	12.32	14.16	15.41	16.29
of which EEC (%)	26	26	25	24	24	23	24	24	23
transport and travel (£ billion)	3.26	4.19	4.65	6.05	6.99	7.11	8.35	8.98	9.13
of which EEC (%)	32	31	30	30	30	29	30	29	28
financial services (£ billion)[a]	0.60	0.79	1.03	1.30	1.39	1.54	1.60	1.60	1.95
of which EEC (%)	17	20	21	19	18	19	21	23	22
other services (£ billion)	1.33	1.65	2.05	2.67	3.22	3.67	4.21	4.83	5.21
of which EEC (%)	14	15	14	14	14	13	13	14	16
Balance of Service Trade									
Total private sector and public corporation services (£ billion)	1.20	1.60	2.09	3.11	3.68	4.41	4.48	4.98	4.75
of which EEC (%)	4	6	7	9	11	8	10	8	4

[a] Figures for financial services are net of debits (which are negligible).

SOURCE   The United Kingdom Balance of Payments, 1982.

Table 6.11 provides evidence of the limited effect of EEC membership on UK trade in services. Between 1973 and 1980 service receipts from the EEC have maintained a roughly constant proportion of the total from all countries and the expansion in the proportion of overseas earnings of the financial sector has been modest. The overall picture is that the EEC has remained a surprisingly small market for the UK service sector and has made a very minor contribution to the UK's surplus on service trade.

INTRAINDUSTRY STRUCTURAL CHANGE AND EEC MEMBERSHIP

Lack of research into the effects of EEC membership on the internal structure of UK industries makes it impossible to present any informed account of the impact on productivity of EEC-induced changes in the internal structures of industries. Suffice to say that even leaving aside the specific impact of EEC institutions upon individual industries (through, for example, anti-trust interventions, subsidy schemes, crisis cartels), the contribution of Community membership to the increased competitive pressure faced by most UK industries since 1973 is likely to have caused substantial reorganisation within industries, with important consequences for productivity.

An aspect of intraindustry structural change on which it is possible to offer more informed commentary concerns the impact of EEC membership on the exploitation of scale economies by British firms. Prior to entry, it will be recalled, considerable weight was given to the view that Community membership would enable UK firms and plants to lower costs and improve innovative performance by growing beyond the confines of the home market. How far has EEC membership enabled exploitation of scale economies?

Most recent research has failed to find support for this view that a limited home market had resulted in UK firms and plants being of suboptimal size. Caves's analysis of the sources of productivity differences between US and UK industries found that a variety of variables measuring the scale of firm and plant in UK industry had no significant influence on the productivity differential (Caves, 1980, p. 169). Research by Prais into plant sizes in the UK, Germany and US has shown the presumption that UK plants were of suboptimal size compared with countries serving larger markets is largely unfounded. Table 6.12 shows that across manufacturing industry, UK plant size (measured by employment) exceeded that of Germany and the US at the lower quartile and median levels.

TABLE 6.12   *Median plant sizes by numbers of employees in Britain, Germany and US, 1970–3*

	All manufacturing	Light industries	Heavy industries
Britain	440	240	820
Germany	410	140	1 080
US	380	210	810

SOURCE   Prais (1981), *Productivity and Industrial Structure*, p. 27.

In those industries where British plant size is particularly small in relation to Germany and the US – in steel and motor vehicles, for instance – this may be a reflection not of suboptimal British plant size, but a smaller optimal UK plant size because of the strike-proneness of large British plants in these industries (Prais, 1981, pp. 261–3).

Even if plant sizes are below the minimum efficient level in some UK industries, the consequences for production cost and productivity of suboptimal scale of plant are small in relation to the differential in output per employee between Britain and more advanced industrial countries. Of the thirty-seven products examined by Pratten, for twenty-seven of them, production at a plant one-half of minimum efficient size involved an increase in unit cost of 15 per cent or less (Pratten, 1971). Prais estimated that in 1975 German manufacturing output per employee exceeded that of the UK by 30 per cent, while for the United States the differential was 200 per cent (Prais, 1981, pp. 259–61).

Evidence on comparative firm sizes, though fragmentary, rejects even more strongly the notion that one source of the UK's productivity disadvantage lies in small firm size in comparison with European competitors. Of the 500 largest companies by turnover in 1972, 182 were British (*Times 1000*, 1973). Moreover, the fall since 1973 in the number of British firms in the 500 largest European firms shows no 'catching-up' by large British firms which would be implied by suboptimal size *vis-à-vis* their Continental counterparts. Comparatively large British firm size is also indicated by comparisons of seller concentration ratios between EEC countries. A survey by the EEC Commission showed that for those industries where comparisons were possible, four-firm concentration ratios were generally higher in the UK than in Germany, France or Italy during the early 1970s (HMSO, 1978, pp. 63–4).

CONCLUSIONS

The chief problem in examining the impact of the EEC upon UK industrial performance has been that a decade of Community membership has coincided with a period of unprecedented change in economic conditions both nationally and worldwide. Hence there is an acute problem of identification which is compounded by the difficulty of specifying the commercial and economic relationships with other countries which would have existed had Britain remained outside the Community. This chapter has not attempted to grapple with these problems of identification on any rigorous basis, but has simply examined some of the major trends and changes which have occurred in the 1970s in the light of some simple hypotheses as to the effects which might have been expected from an *a priori* analysis.

The most obvious consequence of Community membership has been growth in the volume of UK trade and its redirection towards the EEC. The effect of these trade changes on total manufacturing output is not easy to assess. The worsening of the UK trade balance with the EEC in manufactured goods after 1973 must be viewed in the light of the long-term deteriorating trend in British trade performance, the continuing productivity gap between Britain and much of the EEC, and the adverse initial impact effects which were forecast prior to entry. Hence, although EEC membership has clearly failed to stimulate any revival in manufacturing trade performance, it is far from apparent that British industry would have been better placed to withstand the increased international competition of the 1970s by remaining outside the Community.

The expansion of trade between Britain and the EEC appears to have done little to encourage greater change in the structure of manufacturing output. Even more serious, the changes in specialisation have been towards increasing concentration on industries which, on a European basis, are declining. There is limited evidence that EEC membership may be reinforcing the tendency of British businessmen to concentrate upon the production of goods embodying low levels of skill and technology whose production is increasingly shifting towards the newly industrialising countries. Membership of the EEC also appears to have done little to stimulate the growth of those service industries in which Britain has a significant comparative advantage in relation to the other countries of the EEC.

It was not possible to assess the impact of the EEC upon the internal structure of individual industries or their input productivity. One fact which does emerge, however, is that the scope for productivity improvement through exploiting economies of scale of plant and firm level appeared limited as a result of EEC accession.

The suggestion, therefore, is that while there have been no obviously disastrous consequences for the growth of British industry as a result of EEC accession, there is no evidence of any benefits being generated. This is not to say that Britain should not have joined the EEC in the first place, even less to imply that the prospects for industrial growth would be enhanced by leaving. The absence of significant benefits from Community membership is more likely to be a failure of the British government and British business to exploit the opportunities made available by membership, than an inevitable result of the institutions and policies of the Community.

I am reluctant on the basis of the limited evidence of this chapter to offer prescriptions for economic and industrial policies. Some of the facts speak for themselves, however. The lack of structural adjustment and the failure of industry to establish a strong export base founded on technological know-how and labour skills suggests a failure to invest in plant, innovation and training. Government must create the conditions conducive to such investment. Most fundamental, however, British governments should seek to create greater stability in their policies so as to reduce the uncertainty which encourages a short-term, risk-averse attitude among businessmen and investors. Past ambivalence of political parties towards the Community, and opposition commitments to future withdrawal have been particularly detrimental to business efforts to exploit the economic advantages of membership. Governments have also done little to encourage the exploitation of comparative advantages by British industry, particularly where this has necessitated the government taking a leading role in the shaping of Community policies. In this context, the lack of strong pressure for the more substantial liberalisation of Community trade in services may be noted.

NOTES

1. As late as 1975 the CBI stated: 'the chief argument for membership of the EEC is the opportunity it offers of sharing in the Community's rate of economic growth which has long been substantially higher than that of Britain' (CBI, 1975, p. ii).
2. The economies of scale argument attracted widespread support during the early 1970s and led to exaggerated claims being made by some of the more

ardent pro-marketeers. Sir Frederick Catherwood, former director-general of NEDO, for example, envisaged that increased specialisation would mean that the output of certain products would be increased by up to five times with savings in average cost of between 10 and 50 per cent (Catherwood, 1973).

3. The lack of perception of the EEC as a single home market for European companies is apparent from the attitudes and organisation of a sample of German and British companies. See Arthur D. Little (1979).

4. In banking, for example, it was not until 1977 that the first Council directive on the coordination of banking laws and regulations was adopted. Even though most forms of overt discrimination in national banking regulation against banks from other EEC countries have been removed, it is apparent that the seemingly uniform regulatory practices frequently operate in favour of domestic banks (see Maycock, 1981).

REFERENCES

Catherwood, Sir Frederick (1973) 'An Industrial Strategy', in Douglas Evans (ed.), *Britain in the EEC* (London: Gollancz).

Caves, R. E. (1980) 'Productivity Differences Among Industries', in R. E. Caves and L. B. Krause (eds), *Britain's Economic Performance* (Washington DC: Brookings).

CBI (1975) *British Industry and Europe. A Report by the CBI Europe Committee* (London: CBI), March.

Denison, E. F. (1968) 'Economic Growth', in R. E. Caves and associates, *Britain's Economic Prospects* (London: Kuen & Unwin).

Economic Commission For Europe (1981) *Economic Survey of Europe in 1980* (New York: United Nations).

HMSO (1978) *A Review of Monopolies and Mergers Policy. A Consultative Document*, Cmnd 7198 (London: HMSO).

HMSO (1970) *Britain and the European Communities. An Economic Assessment*, Cmnd 4289 (London: HMSO).

Jones, D. T. (1980) 'British Industrial Regeneration: the European Dimension', in William Wallace (ed.), *Britain in Europe* (London: Heinemann).

Kaldor, N. (1971) 'The Dynamic Effects of the Common Market', in D. Evans (ed.), *Destiny of Delusion?* (London: Gollancz).

Little, Arthur D. (1979) *The EEC as an Expanded Home Market for the United Kingdom and the Federal Republic of Germany* (London: Anglo German Foundation).

Maycock, J. (1981) 'Discrimination in Banking in the EEC', *The Banker* (July) pp. 29–31.

Mayes, D. G. (1982) 'The Trade Effects of the EEC', a discussion paper for the Federal Trust for Education and Science (University of Exeter).

Morgan, A. D. (1980) 'The Balance of Payments and British Membership of the European Community', in Wallace (1980), *Britain in Europe*.

OECD (1982) *Positive Adjustment Policies, Managing Structural Change. Summary and Conclusions* (Paris: OECD).

Pavitt, K. (1979) 'Technical Innovation and Industrial Development', *Futures* (December).

Prais, S. J. (1981) *Productivity and Industrial Structure. A Statistical Study of Manufacturing Industry in Britain, Germany and the United States* (Cambridge University Press).

Pratten, C. F. (1971) *Economics of Scale in Manufacturing Industry*, University of Cambridge Dept. of Applied Economics Occasional Papers 28 (Cambridge University Press).

Smith, S. R., G. M. White, N. C. Owen, M. R. Hill (1982) 'UK Trade in Manufacturing: the Pattern of Specialisation in the 1970s' (London: Departments of Trade and Industry).

Solow, R. M. (1957) 'Technical Change and the Aggregate Production Function', *Review of Economics and Statistics*, 39 (August) pp. 312–20.

Times (1973) *The Times 1000 1973–74* (London: Times Books).

7 Britain, Europe and Macroeconomic Policy

FRANCIS CRIPPS

Britain, the rest of Europe, and many countries in other parts of the world are in the grip of chronic economic depression.[1] The depression occurred and persists despite the fact that modern economists have a sophisticated understanding of national demand management policies; practical techniques of reflation, including increased government spending, tax cuts and reductions in interest rates, are readily available to any government which cares to make use of them. Some governments, including the British government, will not reflate demand because they fear that to do so would accelerate inflation. But other governments which have undertaken reflationary policies (including the present French government and past British and US governments) have found that reflation pushed their countries' trade balances into increasing deficit and destroyed confidence in the rates of exchange of their countries' currencies. There are several reasons why reflation is ineffective as a remedy for the general depression. One is the fear of inflation which makes governments cling to restrictive monetarist policies. A second is the lack of government control over international trade which leaves trade balances extremely vulnerable to reflation. Another is the volatility of international financial flows which puts exchange rates at the mercy of losses of confidence in the policies of particular governments or in the prospects of particular national economies.

The logic of reflation as a solution to the problem of economic depression is perfectly valid, and could be applied straightforwardly, in a closed economy whose government had effectively unlimited powers of credit creation. It would remain valid in an open economy provided that the government was able to regulate both the trade balance (for example, by painless devaluation or protection) and the rate of ex-

111

change of its country's currency (for example, by control of capital flows or painless interest rate adjustments). The reflationary solution ceases to be valid for a national economy when its trade balance and exchange rate cannot be regulated, or when the scale of devaluation necessary to protect its trade balance becomes large enough to have serious inflationary repercussions. Nor is reflation a valid solution for world recession because, although the world as a whole constitutes a closed economy, there is no institution which can fulfil the role of world government.[2]

The purpose of this chapter is to examine the obstacles to reflation facing Britain and other West European countries which arise because of international trade. The first section will show that the countries of Europe have a particularly high level of mutual trade and that in this respect Britain is now inextricably part of a European economic system. The second section develops a primitive algebraic model of the links between trade balances and demand management policies in different countries.[3] The third section assigns rough numerical values to the parameters of this model and draws some qualitative conclusions about the impact of reflation on trade balances in Britain, the rest of Europe and other parts of the world.

THE PATTERN OF INTERNATIONAL TRADE

Western Europe not only has a geographical identity and a juridical identity through institutions such as the European Community but is knit together as an economic system by the exceptionally high level of mutual trade between its constituent national economies. This high level of mutual trade defines the European economy more clearly than any other aspect of economic structure. Although the European countries typically have middle to high income levels and manifest a high degree of industrialisation, these characteristics are far from uniform within Europe and they are shared with a good many countries in other parts of the world.

The unique characteristic of West European countries, by which they can readily be picked out in statistical tabulations of the economic systems of the world, is the degree to which their exports are concentrated on trade with one another. Nearly 70 per cent of total exports by West European countries go to other countries in the same region. This degree of mutual interdependence is considerably higher than that of Comecon (for which the comparable figure is about 50 per cent)

and much higher than for other regions of the world (see Table 7.1).
Other trading groups can be identified in the Far East (Japan, East
Asia and Australia), North America (Canada, the USA) and Latin
America; the whole of America, North and South, together with the
Far East constitutes in some degree a giant trading bloc which rivals
Europe and its African periphery. But the degree of concentration of
trade within the vast America – Asia bloc is lower than within Western
Europe.

TABLE 7.1   *Exports of goods by destination, 1980*

	Percentage of exports identified as going to other countries in same group
Western Europe	68
Western Europe and Africa	72
Comecon	51
USA – Canada	26
Latin America	21
North and South America	46
Far East[a]	38
America and Far East	63

[a] Japan, Australia, New Zealand and developing market economies in Asia
and Oceania.

SOURCE   *UN Monthly Bulletin of Statistics* (July 1981) Special Table B.

The orientation towards intra-European trade is not only a general
characteristic of European countries but also a rather uniform one. As
Table 7.2, which gives figures for individual European countries
shows, five countries (the Netherlands, Belgium, Ireland, Norway and
Denmark) send more than three-quarters of their exports to partners
within Western Europe, most European countries send between 60
per cent and 70 per cent, and all without exception send well over 50
per cent to destinations within Western Europe. The markets of the
USA, other developed countries, OPEC and the Third World are,
from the perspective of any individual European country, of minor
significance compared with export markets within Europe itself.

If the destination of exports is taken as the criterion, the European
economic system does not end strictly at the geographical frontiers of
Western Europe itself. Developing Africa as a whole sends 50 per cent

TABLE 7.2 *Exports of goods from West European countries by destination, 1980 (% of total exports from each country)*

Destinations:	Western Europe	Other developed economies[a]	OPEC	Other developing economies
Origins:				
Netherlands	81	6	6	8
Belgium[b]	81	7	5	7
Ireland	80	9	4	6
Norway[c]	80	9	2	9
Denmark	76	12	5	7
Portugal	73	11	2	15
Austria	72	16	6	6
Sweden	72	13	5	9
W. Germany	69	15	7	9
France	64	11	9	15
Finland	64	26	4	6
Switzerland	63	16	7	13
Italy	62	12	13	14
Spain	57	11	13	19
UK	56	17	9	18
Greece	53	18	16	14

Rows may not sum to 100 because of rounding.
[a] Including Comecon.
[b] Including Luxemburg.
[c] Data for 1979.

SOURCE Calculated from tape supplied by European Commission (DG II).

of its exports to Western Europe; the proportions for some individual African countries must be as high as for some individual European countries. But other parts of the world are much less specialised in exporting to Western Europe. The proportions for other major blocs in 1980 were as follows: Middle East 39 per cent, Comecon 29 per cent, USA–Canada 27 per cent, Latin America 23 per cent and Far East 18 per cent.

Britain, although slightly less European than most continental countries, is by the criterion of its trade definitely and unambiguously part of the European economic system, sending well over half its exports to other countries in Western Europe. This state of affairs seems certain to persist for a long time into the future since, if it were possible at all, it would take decades for Britain to replace European export markets with new outlets in other parts of the world.

Many European countries are not only specialised in trade with one another but have open economies in the sense that the value of their trade is high relative to GDP. However the ratio of exports to GDP varies widely, from over 60 per cent in the case of Belgium to around 25 per cent in the largest countries (Germany, France, Italy and the UK) and down to as little as 15 per cent in the case of Spain. These ratios (see Table 7.3) indicate that the economies of individual European countries including Britain are more open than those of the USA and Japan, but they are not so different in this respect from the economies of developing countries in the Middle East and Africa or of developed countries such as Canada or New Zealand.

TABLE 7.3   *Exports of goods and services as a percentage of GDP, 1980 (per cent)*

Western Europe		Other OECD	
Belgium	63	New Zealand	30
Ireland	54	Canada	29
Netherlands	53	Australia	18
Norway	48	Japan	14
Austria	39	USA	10
Switzerland	37	Turkey	7
Finland	34		
Denmark	33		
Sweden	30		
UK	28		
Portugal	28		
W. Germany	27		
Italy	25		
France	22		
Greece	20		
Spain	15		

SOURCE   *OECD Economic Outlook, Historical Statistics 1960–1980*, Table 6.10.

The scale of exports relative to GDP and the specialisation of exports in the intra-European market provide a *prima facie* case for supposing that the level of economic activity in individual European countries is considerably influenced by market conditions in Europe as a whole. The extreme example would be Belgium whose exports are equal to over 60 per cent of its GDP, with 80 per cent of exports going to other European countries. The value of Belgian exports to the rest of Western Europe is equal to about half of the country's GDP. The more typical figure for most individual countries including the UK is much lower than this, at 15–20 per cent, while the value of exports from Greece or Spain to the rest of Europe is only equal to about 10 per cent of their GDP.

More important, the value of exports to particular destinations does not in itself reveal how trade flows and balances are likely to respond to changes in demand when the entire system of trade, production, income and government policies is an interdependent one. It is necessary to try to take account of feedbacks between the expansion or contraction of markets, changes in trade flows and adjustments of government budgets and interest rates throughout the international system. This is the task undertaken, albeit in a highly-simplified manner, in the remainder of this chapter.

TRADE BALANCES AND DEMAND MANAGEMENT

In order to investigate links between changes in demand management policies and trade flows in an international context, an elementary algebraic model will now be developed which focuses on a few crucial aspects of the interactions involved. The particular and limited question which the model seeks to answer is how changes in national demand management policies are likely to affect, and to be affected by, changes in trade balances and levels of economic activity. In concentrating on this question, the model ignores many important related issues such as the repercussions for inflation and for stocks of financial assets. Conceptually, all quantities are to be regarded as being measured after adjustment for inflation in units of constant real value or purchasing power. To keep the analysis simple the model is linearised, being confined to a consideration of small or marginal changes relative to an actual or potential baseline state of affairs. The changes under consideration are hypothetical displacements in an imaginary short- to medium-term period of, say, two to four years without any analytic consideration of the dynamics of the adjustments. The only justification for these limitations is that they make it possible to focus attention closely on the main question which the model seeks to address.

CHANGES IN TRADE BALANCES

Suppose that there is some change in demand management policies in one or more countries of an international system which induces changes, y, in levels of real income in the different countries and further induces changes, b, in the trade balances of individual countries. The first issue to be examined is the nature of the relationship between changes in trade balances, b, and real income changes, y, with which they are associated.

A very simple characterisation of this relationship is given by the following traditional model:

(i)   changes in the real value of imports, m, are related to changes in real income by marginal propensities to import, μ:

$$m = \mu y$$

(ii)   changes in the real value of exports, x, are related to changes in imports by marginal export market shares, S:

$$x = Sm$$

(iii)   changes in the real value of trade balances are the difference between changes in exports and changes in imports:

$$b = x - m$$

It can be inferred that the relationship between changes in trade balances and changes in real income levels is given by

$$b = (S - 1)m = (S - 1)\mu y$$

$$\text{or} \qquad b = Ry \tag{1}$$

$$\text{where} \quad R = (S - 1)\mu \tag{2}$$

Quantities written in small roman letters are vectors whose elements correspond to individual countries; capital letters denote matrices of linkages between pairs of countries; and Greek letters denote diagonal matrices of effects within individual countries. The symbol 1 denotes the diagonal unit matrix.

As a matter of accounting, it is desirable in the above model that exports and imports should be measured on a consistent basis so that trade balances sum to zero for the world as a whole and marginal export market shares sum to one for each destination. This can be achieved, for example, by measuring trade flows as they are valued at the moment of shipment and by using a single price deflator to adjust trade denominated in common currency units for inflation measured in terms of the same common unit.

The model may readily be extended to incorporate the effects of changes in trade independent of income which we may also want to consider – for example, shifts achieved by commercial or sectoral policies. Denoting the effects of such changes at given levels of real income by s, equation (1) above may be rewritten as

$$b = Ry + s \qquad (3)$$

Note that if the accounting rules just discussed are observed, independent shifts in trade balances, s, must sum to zero for the world as a whole: in other words they can benefit the trade balances of some countries only at the expense of the trade balances of others. But as will be seen later this does not imply that they will have nil effect on the aggregate level of world income.

A more serious defect of the traditional model set out above is that it assumes that the real value of imports to any one country is not affected in any way by changes in income levels in other countries. This might be the case if the relative prices of traded goods and services were insensitive to the level of world demand, or if the elasticities of import demand in each country with respect to relative price shifts were −1. But neither of those assumptions is sustainable in the modern world where the prices of raw materials and oil may be quite sensitive to the level of world demand and the price elasticity of demand for imports (at least in the case of oil) seems in many countries to be too weak to prevent a rise in the real value of imports when the price goes up.

To take account of the effects of relative price changes induced by changes in demand in other countries, it is necessary to modify the strict identification of imports with the level of income within the importing country and exports with levels of income in other countries. We can still write the effects of changes in income levels and trade balances in terms of a set of linkages denoted by a matrix of coefficients, R, whose columns sum to zero. But countries whose import bill for oil or raw materials rises in real terms when there is an increase in demand elsewhere must now be thought of as having an additional vulnerability, equivalent in its effects on the trade balance to a negative marginal export share. The empirical problem of determining plausible values for the matrix of linkage coefficients, R, is rendered more difficult. It is necessary to consider not only how import propensities and export shares are likely to differ at the margin from the average coefficients which are directly observed, but also how relative price shifts induced by changes in demand are likely to impact on the trade balances of different countries, depending on their degree of self-sufficiency in energy and other raw materials and on the elasticities of their internal demand and supply with respect to changes in world market prices.

CHANGES IN DEMAND MANAGEMENT POLICY

So far we have examined how changes in levels of real income may influence the trade balances of different countries. It remains to consider possible feedbacks from trade to levels of real income. This matter may be considered from two rather different points of view. On the one hand, it may be regarded as a question of policy priorities of national governments which are at least potentially in the position of adjusting the level of economic activity in their own country through demand management policies. On the other hand, it may be considered in a more mechanistic way as a question of the interaction of flows of expenditure and income in which governments may or may not choose to intervene. The two approaches are ultimately equivalent in the sense that an analysis of the mechanics of demand will show what specific government actions would be compatible with any assumed policy priorities.

Here we shall first examine the question of policy priorities and then briefly consider the mechanics.

National governments adjust their budgetary and monetary policies in accordance with a variety of criteria and in response to a range of different, often inconsistent pressures. The state of a country's trade balance and the level of its real income are clearly relevant. Some governments have explicit targets for their country's trade balance or for the current account balance of payments (of which the trade balance is generally a major constituent). Even when governments pay little attention to the trade balance as such, the latter still has important effects on the market for their country's currency and hence on the exchange rate and prices or inflation; the trade balance may also influence domestic processes of credit creation and the size of the government's budget deficit.

A fully-specified model would have to trace through the links between the variables with which we are directly concerned, real income y and the trade balance b, and the various pressures and implicit or explicit criteria according to which governments regulate fiscal and monetary policies. In this chapter I shall adopt an extreme simplification and proceed as if the objectives of government policy could be expressed directly in terms of a real income target, y^*, for each country and a target trade balance, b^*. Very broadly we may think of the real income target as being defined by the government's aims in respect of domestic economic development, capacity utilisation and employment as well as by its perceptions of internal inflationary pressures. The target trade balance will be defined, implicitly, mainly by financial considerations including the country's foreign assets and debts, the stability of its exchange rate and government objectives for budget balance.

In our simple model the two targets, y^* and b^*, represent what governments would like to happen, measured relative to the baseline. Let us assume that if it were possible for both targets to be achieved simultaneously, governments would arrange their demand management policies accordingly and that the targets would be broadly, if not in practice precisely, fulfilled. But whenever the two targets cannot be achieved simultaneously the government is faced by the need to make a choice. The choice will be described here by the formulation.

$$y - y^* = \beta(b - b^*) \qquad (4)$$

where β is a quantitative trade-off between the two targets. If the trade balance is worse than the government explicitly or implicitly wishes, the government is assumed to accept a level of national income below the target, which will help to cushion the balance of trade. If the trade balance is stronger than the government desires, it is assumed to accept an excessive level of internal demand and income, judged by other criteria, as the counterpart of the strong trade balance (the high level of demand will keep the trade surplus within bounds and may ease upward pressure on the country's exchange rate).

Note that the formulation given in equation (4) implies that in the baseline situation, government targets and trade-offs must satisfy the relation

$$y^* = \beta b^*$$

since in the baseline situation y and b are both zero by construction.

As observed earlier, government policy objectives are in practice determined by a wide range of pressures and perceptions of what is possible, which may themselves be mutually conflicting or inconsistent. To make a realistic analysis it would be necessary to determine the relevance of such pressures and perceptions in different countries to policy choice defined in terms of the parameters set out above. Within Europe, for example, the German, French, Italian and British governments typically have different attitudes to demand management and trade balances, conditioned by views about internal inflation and income distribution and about the conditions under which their countries could achieve or maintain strong positions in international trade in the long run. It is far beyond the scope of this chapter to provide a usable model of the determinants of government policy choice in different countries; the conceivable perceptions and pressures will be illustrated by a short discussion of stances which might be adopted by hypothetical 'monetarist' and 'reflationary' governments.

The logic of monetarism, at least in its political manifestations in Europe, is that the government should avoid stimulating demand and rely instead on natural forces to engender competitive production. At the extreme, a monetarist government would be content to allow the level of economic activity, y, to follow its own course. But in so far as the government is subject to social and business pressures it will pay at least some attention to the level of economic activity. It may also take the view that expansionary fiscal and monetary policies which might, at least in the short run, stimulate higher economic activity will simultaneously accelerate inflation. In this case the government's policy will tend to be such as to hold real demand and income down unless inflation is very low, but with misgivings on account of social and business consequences.

The state of the trade balance may have a strong influence on the level of demand which a monetarist government regards as prudent. If the trade balance is heavily in deficit, the country's currency will be weak in foreign exchange markets and the government's budget will tend to be in deficit as tax revenues are depressed by the country's losses in trade. A monetarist government will in such circumstances tighten its own budget and restrain domestic credit creation, thereby correcting the trade deficit and strengthening the national currency at the expense of a depression of domestic demand and activity. In terms of our parameters, a monetarist government may not only favour a cautious real income target, y*, but also give considerable weight to a relatively ambitious trade target, b*, even if this implies that real income has to fall below the level which the government would prefer.

A reflationary government will have a more ambitious real income target and may have a different trade-off between real income and other objectives. It may implicitly prefer a weak trade balance as the counterpart of high internal borrowing. But just as a monetarist government is subject to pressures if its policies lead to recession, so also a reflationary government is exposed to pressures from financial markets if its policies lead to large deficits.

THE MECHANICS OF DEMAND MANAGEMENT

The following simple model serves to illustrate the mechanics involved in implementing government policy choices.

Denoting changes in domestic final expenditure (public and private, consumption and investment) by d, the flow of real income in each country is given by

$$y = d + x - m \qquad \text{or} \qquad y = d + b \tag{5}$$

Now let g denote changes in domestic expenditure deliberately engineered by the government – for example, changes in government spending itself, or changes in private spending directly induced by adjustment of tax rates or interest rates and credit conditions. The induced change in domestic spending, allowing for multiplier–accelerator effects, may be written as

$$d = g + (1 - \theta)y \tag{6}$$

where θ denotes leakages in the form of changes in tax payments and in net private acquisition of financial assets.

The demand management policy consistent with any combination of real income, y, and trade balance, b, is given by equations (5) and (6) as

$$g = \theta y - b \tag{7}$$

To enforce the policy trade-off discussed earlier, the government will have to vary its budgetary and monetary actions in line with changes in the outturn for the trade balance. The adjustment rule implied by equations (4) and (7) is

$$g = (\theta\beta - 1)(b - b^*) + (\theta y^* - b^*)$$

This expression suggests that in practice the weighting β in favour of trade balance objectives must normally be at least as large as $1/\theta$, where θ is the income leakage parameter defined in equation (6). Any autonomous change in the trade balance will tend to alter real income and government tax receipts in the same direction as the shift in the trade balance itself. It would nowadays be regarded as extreme

Keynesianism if the government made no accommodation at all to changes in its own revenues; if it does respond so as to cushion in some degree the impact of shifts in trade on its budget deficit the implicit weighting, β, must at least be larger than $1/\theta$.

The relevant range of values for the trade-off, β, might in contemporary circumstances be characterised as running broadly from $1/\theta$ (Keynesian) towards infinity (ultra-monetarism). As β tends to infinity, the trade balance becomes locked onto its target value as the government undertakes demand management policies with increasing determination to correct deviations of the trade balance and domestic financial balances from their targets.

SOLUTIONS OF A CLOSED WORLD MODEL

Combining the model of trade

$$b = Ry + s \tag{3}$$

and the model of demand management policy

$$y - y^* = \beta(b - b^*) \tag{4}$$

the following general solution is obtained for a closed world system: levels of real income in all countries are given by

$$y = (1 - \beta R)^{-1}(y^* + \beta(s - b^*)) \tag{8}$$

with resulting trade balances obtained by substituting this solution in equation (3) above.

Some general observations can be made about the outcome. First, if u' denotes the unit row vector by which columns of vectors and matrices may be premultiplied to obtain their sums, and recalling that with appropriate accounting rules trade balances sum to zero for the world as a whole, it follows directly from (4) that

$$u'\beta^{-1}(y - y^*) = -u'b^* \tag{9}$$

This equation implies that there is a non-negative weighting of deviations of income from target levels whose sum is proportionate to the sum of target trade balances, but with the opposite sign. Thus if target trade balances sum to zero, the income levels of individual countries will in some cases exceed, and in some cases fall short of, their governments' targets. If target trade balances, added together, are positive it is possible that *all* countries may have income levels below their governments' targets. If the weighting, β, is uniform across countries the proposition can be made stronger: the level of real income in the world as a whole will exceed, be equal to or fall short of the sum of national targets according as the sum of target trade balances represents a collective target deficit, exact balance or surplus. It is clear from the equation that the level of world income may also rise on account of a shift from monetarist to reflationary policy priorities, increasing the levels of income targets or reducing target trade balances.

The trade model has some further general implications. First, note that at least in the case of the simple, traditional model with marginal import propensities and export market shares, a shift towards reflationary policy priorities in any one country unambiguously raises income levels in all countries of the world. (This result may not hold if some countries are highly vulnerable to increases in the price of oil or raw materials.) Another implication is that there is always some pattern of income changes that would have nil effects on trade balances (in the simple linear model such income changes could be upwards or downwards and of any magnitude). This possibility is what lies behind the concept of a 'locomotive' approach to recovery from world recession which envisages reflation coordinated in such a manner as to avoid increased financial strains. The problem is that a very particular pattern of government priorities would have to hold in order for 'locomotive' reflation to occur in practice. In the absence of autonomous shifts in trade balances (i.e. with $s = 0$), it follows from equation (3) that a 'locomotive' pattern of changes in income levels, y_o, must satisfy

$$Ry_o = b = 0$$

If y_o satisfies this condition, so in our linear model does any scalar multiple (positive or negative) of y_o. Premultiplying equation (4) by the matrix R, it follows that policy priorities must satisfy

$$R(y^* - \beta b^*) = 0$$

in order to satisfy the preceding condition. The vector

$$y^* - \beta b^*$$

represents the direct reflationary contribution of changes in government policy priorities relative to the baseline situation. Denoting this by c^*, the general solution of the model may be rewritten as

$$(1 - \beta R)y = c^* + \beta s$$

In the 'locomotive' case (with $s = 0$) the reflation achieved will simply be

$$y = c^*$$

The conditions which c^* must satisfy in order to achieve reflation with nil changes in trade balances are unlikely to hold in practice because they imply that policy priorities in all countries (more accurately, in all but one) should be dictated by the matrix of trade linkages, R, which has little to do with the domestic priorities that reflation would normally be concerned to satisfy.

Coordinated shifts of trading advantage between countries could, at least logically, overcome obstacles to locomotive reflation. Assume any pattern, c^*, of reflationary initiatives and suppose it is accompanied by a shift in trading advantages

$$s = Rc^*$$

(the shift will always sum to zero for the world as a whole because the columns of R sum to zero). The solution of the model will then be given by

$$(1 - \beta R)y = (1 - \beta R)c^*$$
$$\text{or } y = c^*$$
$$\text{with} \quad b = Ry + s = 0$$

Thus there always exists a pattern of trade shifts which will logically be capable of validating any pattern of reflationary initiatives with nil changes in *ex post* trade balances. Unfortunately this, like the logic of pure locomotive reflation, does not tell us anything about how the necessary adjustments might be procured in practice. The merit of trade shifts as an adjunct to reflationary initiatives is in principle that they would imply interventions more or less directly related to the problem at hand.

It may be noted, finally, that even in the absence of changes in demand management priorities, trade shifts may alter the level of aggregate world income. The pattern of income levels will adjust by

$$y = (1 - \beta R)^{-1} \beta s$$

and it has been shown earlier that unless β is uniform across countries, changes in the pattern of income distribution between countries, even with given policy targets, will in general alter the aggregate level of world income.

REFLATION IN BRITAIN AND EUROPE

It remains to apply the general model developed in the preceding section to the actual situation confronting Britain and other European countries. Some rough and somewhat arbitrary quantitative estimates will be provided here. These could be refined in a more elaborate empirical exercise but such refinement would be unlikely to alter the character of the results.

Let us apply the model to a world comprising three blocs – Britain, the rest of Europe and the rest of the world. To calculate the consequences of reflationary initiatives, it is first necessary to assign values to the matrix of marginal trade linkages, R. Table 7.4 shows the actual matrix of market shares for exports of goods by the three blocs in 1980, together with estimates of actual ratios of imports of goods and services to GDP.

TABLE 7.4   *Export shares and import propensities, 1980 (per cent)*

	Shares of world exports[a] to			Ratio of imports to GDP[b]
	UK	Rest of Europe	Rest of world	
UK	—	8	5	25
Rest of Europe	51	56	19	30
Rest of world	49	36	76	17

[a] Exports of goods.
[b] Approximate figures for goods and services.

SOURCE   Estimates from *UN Monthly Bulletin of Statistics* (July 1981) and *OECD Economic Outlook*.

There are reasons for supposing that marginal import propensities are considerably higher than average import ratios. This is strongly suggested by time-series evidence. Trade in manufactures (especially prominent in UK imports) appears to have a particularly high income elasticity. As a working assumption let us put marginal propensities to import at 50 per cent for Britain and other European countries and 30 per cent for the rest of the world.

Marginal export market shares (with correction for oil price effects) are probably not too different from the average shares shown in Table 7.4. The UK appears to have a rather inelastic response to fluctuations in demand in its export markets but its strong position in oil should compensate for this. The rest of Western Europe, taken as a whole, might be supposed to have comparatively high marginal export shares but these must be offset by its heavy deficit in oil.

The pattern of trade linkages which will be assumed to hold here, calculated from the formula

$$R = (S - 1)\mu$$

with S given by Table 7.4 and μ as described above, comes out as follows:

Effects on trade balance of:	Increase of 100 units in real income in		
	UK	Rest of Europe	Rest of world
UK	− 50	4	2
Rest of Europe	26	− 22	6
Rest of world	24	18	− 8

To adjust for differences in the size of our three blocs we shall from now on measure changes in income and trade balances as percentages of baseline GDP. This requires rows and columns of the trade linkage matrix to be scaled, yielding the following:

Effects on trade balance as % of GNP in:	Increase of 10% in real income in		
	UK	Rest of Europe	Rest of world
UK	−5.0	+ 1.7	+ 2.2
Rest of Europe	+ 0.6	− 2.2	+ 1.9
Rest of world	+ 0.2	+ 0.5	−0.7

Since a deterioration in the trade balance amounting to several percentage points would be more than enough to provoke a major financial crisis, it is clear that a rise in income in the UK, not accompanied by changes in income elsewhere, could not go very far. The same would be true of other individual countries in Europe and indeed in the rest of the world. If income rose simultaneously in Britain and the rest of Europe, costs to trade balances would be reduced. Adding the first two columns of the table together, the estimated effects on trade balances of a 10 per cent rise in income throughout Western Europe, in the absence of any income change in the rest of the world, would be

UK   − 3.3%
Rest of Europe − 1.6%
Rest of world   + 0.7%

These effects of independent changes in income levels are purely hypothetical because in practice income levels will change simultaneously in all three blocs. To proceed further, assumptions must be made about policy initiatives and responses which will be described here in terms of the variable

c^* denoting reflationary initiatives, and the parameter
β denoting the strength of priorities in government responses to changes in trade flows.

In the previous section it was argued that the parameter β is nowadays likely to be not less than $1/\theta$ where θ is the income leakage attributable to tax systems and changes in private financial balances. In Britain and the rest of Europe the leakage is probably of the order of at least 50 per cent although in much of the rest of the world it may be lower. Values of β are therefore likely at a minimum to be around 2 and may be considerably higher if governments voluntarily, or because of pressures on them, give high priority to financial adjustments. For illustrative purposes let us assume that the normal value of β is 4, implying that for each 1 per cent by which a country's trade balance deteriorates or improves, its government will in the short to medium term procure, or accept, a 4 per cent deterioration or improvement in the level of real income (relative to the baseline).

The solution of our model, allowing for induced policy responses, may be as expressed as follows:

Percentage effects on real income in	Reflationary initiative achieving a 10% rise in real income in		
	UK	Rest of Europe	Rest of world
UK	10.0	2.8	4.0
Rest of Europe	1.5	10.0	4.6
Rest of world	0.8	1.8	10.0

Effects on trade balance as % of GNP in			
UK	− 4.6	+ 0.7	+ 1.0
Rest of Europe	+ 0.4	− 1.7	+ 1.2
Rest of world	+ 0.2	+ 0.4	− 0.4

If the priority given to adjustments were relatively weak ($\beta = 2$), the induced income changes in other blocs would be smaller and the trade balance effects would be

UK	− 4.8	+ 1.0	+ 1.4
Rest of Europe	+ 0.5	− 1.9	+ 1.4
Rest of world	+ 0.2	+ 0.5	− 0.5

The results are clearly not all that sensitive to the precise value assumed for β.

Looking at the results from the point of view of the UK (or any other single European country), it still remains the case that a unilateral reflationary initiative is likely to have a very high cost in terms of deterioration of the trade balance. A general reflation in the rest of Europe would afford some benefit to the UK, but not so much as a general reflation in the rest of the world outside Europe. This latter result is at first sight surprising when, as emphasised in the first section of this chapter, more than half of the UK's exports go to other countries within Europe. The reason for the result is that a general reflation outside Europe would produce strong indirect benefits for the UK by raising the level of income in other European countries. Europe, although quite large in the world economy, is not large enough for the same to be true in reverse.

A joint reflation in Britain and the rest of Europe, designed to achieve a 10 per cent rise in the real income of both, would be considerably less damaging to the UK's trade balance than a unilateral reflation. But the estimated cost, at nearly 3 per cent of GNP, is still high enough to look impractical, even if the political conditions for joint reflation could be met. More realistically in the context of a joint reflation the UK might have to accept being a laggard, achieving a smaller income gain than other European countries, in order to cushion the effect on its trade balance.

The problem which Britain and other European countries face is that unilateral reflationary initiatives are extremely prejudicial to the trade balances of countries undertaking them. In principle a partial solution could be provided by coordinated reflation but, as suggested in the previous section, a full solution requires mechanisms for shifting the balance of advantage between countries to accommodate their otherwise incompatible domestic objectives. Present institutions in Europe are not favourable to either possibility. If this could be changed, Britain and other European countries would have better opportunities for reflation, although they might still be left with significant obstacles deriving from Europe's dependence on trade with the rest of the world.

NOTES

1. For details of the situation across Western Europe see *OECD Economic Outlook*, 31 (Paris, July 1982).
2. The premises for this argument are set out more fully in an article, 'What is Wrong with Monetarism', to be published in K. Jansen (ed.), *Monetarism, Economic Crisis and the Third World* (London: Frank Cass, 1983).
3. Versions of this model applied to problems of Europe in the world economy have been published in *Cambridge Economic Policy Reviews*, notably vol. 6, no. 3 (Gower, December 1980) and vol. 7, no. 2 (Gower, December 1981).

8 The European Monetary System – Past Developments, Future Prospects and Economic Rationale

GEOFFREY E. WOOD

There have been several proposals to develop a European Monetary Union, parallel to the political integration and freeing of trade within the EEC which has so far taken place. This is generally seen as the logical third component of greater European integration. There is a European Parliament; goods and labour mobility is intended to be as free within Europe as it is within one country; should there not also, then, be a common monetary system? The latest attempt to achieve this is the European Monetary System (EMS), launched on 13 March 1979, following planning and discussion initiated by Roy Jenkins in his 1977 Jean Monnet Lecture. The system has thus been in place for a little over three years.

That provides sufficient data for a preliminary appraisal of how the system has performed. Such an appraisal comprises the first part of this chapter. That in turn prepares the way for analysis of why the system has behaved as it has, and of how it is likely to behave in the future. The analysis of likely future behaviour lays the foundation for the final part of this chapter, an examination of whether the goal of a European Monetary System is a sensible objective from an economic point of view.

A major initial point is that there are two quite distinct perspectives from which the EMS can be appraised. One is economic, the other political. From the political perspective, the EMS is judged by whether it will further movement to European unity. Many of the arguments about whether Britain should join concern that issue. The discussion thus parallels the earlier discussion of whether Britain should join the EEC, a debate partly conducted on economic grounds the substance of which was hard to evaluate, and in which the protaganists were clearly, and usually admittedly, influenced by their views on the desirability of European political integration.[1]

The perspective of this chapter is as far as possible the economic one. Has the EMS contributed to achieving goals which can be justified by economic arguments? Will it continue to do so? Are there better ways of achieving those goals? It is also, however, pointed out that major political issues, as yet largely unconsidered in the debate about the European Monetary System, must be resolved if a durable European Monetary Union is to be achieved.

THE SYSTEM IN OUTLINE

The EMS has three aspects. These are an arrangement for pegging exchange rates, a system of credit facilities to help defend these pegged rates, and a proposed 'European Monetary Fund'.[2]

Two exchange-rate pegging arrangements were initially considered – the 'party grid' and the 'basket'. The first ties every currency to every other currency in a system of mutually agreed (and consistent) cross rates. The second ties each currency to a 'European Currency Unit' (ECU), equal to a somehow-weighted average of all the member countries' currencies. The system ultimately adopted was the parity grid. This choice was based on perceptions of where it would lay responsibility for responding to exchange-rate pressure. Under the parity grid system, whenever one currency moved, all other exchange rates would also diverge from their agreed level, thus creating an apparent obligation for all countries to respond. Under the 'basket' system, it was possible for one currency to move relative to the rest without creating any divergence, apart from its own, among the mutually agreed set of rates.

The parity grid system was chosen, but with features of the 'basket' added to it. The central rates of the parity grid were defined in terms of the ECU, and the ECU served as a 'divergence indicator' – a movement by any currency away from its 'central rate' measured in terms of the ECU, when it was greater than an agreed amount, created a 'presumption' that the country which issued that currency should act to correct the divergence.

Turning now to the credit facilities, it is still the case that loans to enable exchange rate intervention are made directly from one country to another. These loans are in three categories: short-term loans, repayable within forty-five days; medium-term loans, repayable within nine months; and loans repayable within five years. The reason for dividing these facilities by maturity was that different amounts were made available at each maturity. Fourteen billion ECUs were available in the second facility, and eleven billion ECUs under the third (approximately speaking, US$ 18 billion, and US$ 14 billion respectively). The amount available under the first facility was supposedly unlimited.

In addition, loans were made available at subsidised rates to certain member countries from the European Investment Bank and certain other Community institutions. These loans were not, however, a part of the workings of the scheme, but rather were an inducement to join it.

The European Monetary Fund (EMF) is intended to have pooled under its authority a portion of the gold and dollar reserves of member countries. In return, members of the EMS will receive deposits in the EMF. These deposits are denominated in ECUs, and to be used in settlement of intra-EEC debt. The ECU is thus intended to develop a role identical (within Europe) to that of the SDR for the (worldwide) members of the IMF. Pending final establishment of the EMF, reserve pooling was carried out in the form of revolving three-month 'swaps' among the separate national monetary authorities. That avoided any question of transfer of ownership of these assets in the absence of enabling national legislation.

Two points clearly emerge from that outline of the system. First, it is manifestly intended to operate as a pegged exchange rate regime, a European version of the Bretton Woods system of the 1950s and 1960s.

Second, it lacks provision for the replacement of national currencies in private hands by the ECU or some other supranational currency unit, and thus lacks provision for the development of a 'European Money'.

How well it has functioned as a 'mini Bretton Woods' is considered in the following sections of this chapter, and reasons for the above-noted omission are considered subsequently.

PERFORMANCE TO DATE

When the EMS was established, and even while it was being discussed, there were predictions that it would collapse – Brittan (1978), for example. In fact, the system has held together.

Fluctuations in exchange rates among member countries have been modest relative to the experience of the preceding decade. (Remember that the UK is not a member.) For example, in 1979, the initial year of the system, the annual average fluctuation against the ECU was 1.9 per cent as compared to 2.7 per cent in 1978, and was in fact the least since 1972. This relative stability continued in 1980 and throughout most of 1981.

Currency movements against the US dollar illustrate this. Measured against that currency as a convenient unit of account, the currencies have moved together. No dramatic divergence, such as was predicted by those who anticipated the breakdown of the scheme, is apparent.

This apparent stability does conceal certain tensions. There have been periods of substantial intervention, notably in the first few months after the inception of the system. But in general, borrowing under the credit arrangements has been modest, and entirely short term. There was, however, fairly early in the system's history, a modest realignment of some rates; the DM was revalued by 2 per cent, and Danish Krona devalued by 3 per cent, against all member countries in September 1979, and there was a further devaluation of the Krona in November 1979.

To date, then, the system, while not being a zone of 'perfect monetary stability', has certainly not appeared to be in danger of imminent collapse, and has been associated with greater stability of member countries' exchange rates than before the system, and greater stability than rates outside the system.

Why is this? Was it the outcome of special factors, either peculiar to the time or associated with the establishment of the EMS? Or does it result from more long-lasting changes, either in the conduct of economic policy by member states or in the structures of their economies, which will make exchange-rate fixity in Europe more long lasting?

SPECIAL FACTORS

There appear to have been four factors which particularly contributed to this exchange rate stability. First, when the system was established, exchange rates were set so as to offset already discernible inflation differences. Some price level divergence was allowed for. Second, there has been some deliberate manipulation of interest rates to keep exchange rates together. Third, a certain amount of demand management was engaged in to preserve the exchange rate structure. Fourth, the US dollar has been fairly strong.

None of these can be expected to persist in its influence. Exchange rates were set to offset some price level divergences already in prospect. But unless after that there is no further price level divergence, exchange rates will become inappropriate. This inappropriateness will emerge when, converted into a common currency at existing exchange rates, national price levels are no longer aligned.[3] Has anything been done to keep price levels in line? Price levels are affected by two quite distinct types of influence. One is money growth, and the other is exogenous cost shocks resulting from factors such as bad harvests or Middle East War. If divergent money growth is not to produce diverging price levels there must be agreement, and *binding* commitment, to prevent this happening. There are declarations of intent in plenty; but, to quote de Grauwe and Peters (1979): 'As in the past, the great drawback is the absence of binding commitments.'

Hence there is nothing to prevent diverging inflation rates resulting from inconsistent money growth rates. For that reason alone, except by chance, there will be long-term inflation differences. Indeed, the situation is worse than that. An exogenous shock such as an oil price increase will have different price level effects in different countries. If this were not to require exchange-rate changes, there would have to be offsetting money stock adjustments. Aside from the problems of implementation, there is not even agreement in principle to attempt such policies. Hence the basic condition for a *durable* pegged rate system has not been fulfilled.

The second and third factors, interest rate and demand manipulation, cannot be expected to have persistent effects in the presence of sustained inflation rate divergences; they can certainly offset transitory pressures, but if longer-term monetary trends produce sustained price level divergence, they will ultimately fail.[4]

What of the fourth factor, a period of dollar strength? Should the dollar come under pressure, the EMS would inevitably come under great strain. The basic reason for this is that some, but not all, EMS currencies are natural alternative investments to the dollar. Hence any portfolio adjustment into or out of dollars such as occurred in 1977–8 (see Wood, 1979) would impose strains not only on the EMS rate relative to the dollar, but within the EMS. The latter could only be avoided if the monetary authorities of the potential reserve currencies (mainly the DM) were clearly willing passively to accommodate international portfolio flows – and there is no trace of such willingness. Divergent exchange rate behaviour was, indeed, for that reason apparent during the dollar weakness of 1977–8, and no action has been taken or proposed since then to prevent the same happening again.

In summary, then, certain special factors have contributed to the stability of EMS currencies since the formation of the EMS. There is good reason to believe that these influences will not persist and further, that some measures taken to preserve the system have imposed costs on the member countries' economies.

This assessment of the future of the EMS does of course depend (in part) on a view of the long-run determinants of exchange-rate behaviour. It is necessary to set out and defend that view.

EXCHANGE-RATE BEHAVIOUR

A basic, and very long-established, theory of exchange rate behaviour is Purchasing Power Parity (PPP).[5] This theory says that exchange rates will move around so as to keep national price levels, when calculated in any one unit of account, in line. The factors which are said to produce this are *commodity arbitrage* and *factor mobility*.

Commodity arbitrage occurs when some good cost less in one country than it does in another (aside from tariffs and transport costs). It will under those conditions be profitable to buy the good where it is cheap, to sell or use it where it is dear. This process will continue until the good has the same price (apart from tariffs and transport costs) everywhere. And this process will continue for all goods, hence tending to equalise national price levels.

Of course, not all goods can very readily be traded across long distances. None the less, their prices will also tend to be equalised, as the prices of the raw materials and other productive resources embodied in traded goods are drawn together by trade. This process is accelerated and facilitated by the movement of factors of production – labour and capital – to where the rewards are highest.[6] Hence profit-seeking behaviour in goods and factor markets leads to the prediction that exchange rates will stand at purchasing power parity, and by doing so will offset movements in national price levels.

How does this theory perform in practice?

The chart of exchange rate and price level behaviour (Frenkel,

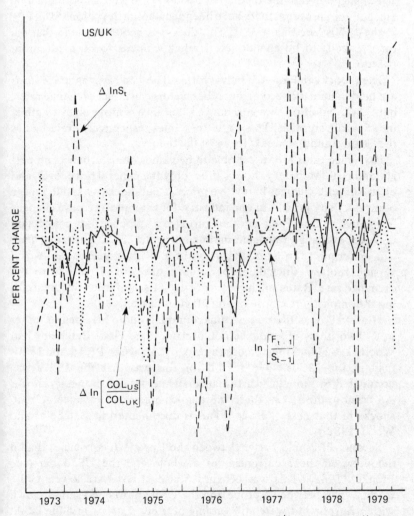

Monthly percentage changes of the US/UK consumer price indices $[\Delta(\ln COL_{US}/COL_{UK})]$ of the $/£ exchange rate, $(\Delta \ln S_t)$, and the monthly forward premium; $\ln (F_{t-1}/S_{t-1})$ July 1973—July 1979.

FIGURE 8.1   *Exchange rate and price level volatility*

SOURCE   'Turbulence in the Foreign Exchange Markets and Macroeconomic Policies', by Jacob A. Frenkel. Third Henry Thornton Lecture, April 1982. Copyright The City University, London.

1982) suggests that the theory has not done too well. In both the long run and the short run, there have been substantial deviations from PPP in the 1970s (see Figure 8.1). This does not, however, mean that the theory needs to be abandoned. Rather it needs to be made more precise.

The theory can be stated in two forms. The first says that *price levels* are held in line; the second that other factors can affect exchange rates, but that in addition these exchange rates always move so as to offset inflation differentials. These are sometimes respectively described as the 'strong' and the 'weak' forms of the theory.

Exchange rates are susceptible to two kinds of disturbance, monetary and real. Monetary shocks affect only the general price level, and do not require changes in relative prices. Real shocks – a sudden surge of productivity growth in one industry, for example – require changes in relative prices. They can thus produce a rather looser connection between exchange rates and national price levels. In particular they can undermine the 'strong' version of PPP theory. But the 'weak' version remains unchallenged by such once-for-all shocks to the exchange rate. Rates still have to move to offset inflation differentials, but they move in response to other factors as well.

How well does the theory, thus refined, hold up? It does so rather well. Two items of evidence demonstrate this. First, Batchelor and Wood (1982) find much more rapid convergence to PPP in the 1920s than in the 1970s. One reason for this was that the 1920s was dominated by monetary disturbances, while, though monetary shocks did occur in the 1970s, there was a much greater abundance of 'real' shocks in that latter decade. (This is documented in Batchelor and Wood, 1982.)

Second, PPP held better between the European currencies than it did between those currencies as a whole and the US dollar (see Frenkel, 1982). This was because transport costs are lower within Europe than between Europe and the USA; tariffs had settled down within Europe but were still varying between Europe and the USA; and changing portfolio preferences at the end of the decade (see Wood, 1979) affected the relationship.

Hence it can be concluded that PPP theory is a reliable long-run guide to the trend movements of exchange rates; although how long is the long run is somewhat variable. (An excellent demonstration of the theory's long-run robustness is provided by Friedman, 1980.)

What of the extensive short-run variability of exchange rates about the PPP prediction? Here it is necessary to recollect that there is a fundamental difference between exchange rates and national price levels. Exchange rates are the prices of national moneys – of one asset in terms of another. Asset markets display two characteristics vital to explaining the record of exchange-rate behaviour. Prices on these markets are highly flexible, and reflect expectations about the future. Hence exchange rates will change whenever some item of information appears, or some event occurs, which may affect relative national price levels *in the future*. Volatility is in some measure intrinsic to asset markets, as they are continually affected by a flow of new information.[7] Some of that information will later be offset by other items of information, but it is possible to know which items these will be at the time they occur only for a very few items. It is in general not possible to know which effects are permanent and which transitory.

The record of exchange-rate behaviour, then, is consistent with a PPP view of the long-run behaviour of exchange rates. This implies in turn that, whatever fortunate combination of events occurs to sustain the EMS, without agreement on mutually consistent monetary policies diverging rates of price change within its member states will ultimately bring about the collapse of the system. It is not a truly fixed rate system.

The conclusion of this analysis is that as presently constructed the EMS is flawed. EMS exchange rates will not stay as they are for ever. The Bretton Woods system, the characteristics of which the EMS does to a certain extent embody, provides a precedent for this conclusion. So long as countries were willing to pursue a common monetary policy, exchange rates were not under pressure. But any country which systematically diverged from the average inflation rate (to which that of the USA was a close approximation) had to revalue or devalue. Germany exemplifies the former course, and the UK the latter.[8]

Does that conclusion imply that efforts to form an EMS should be abandoned? The answer to that is, not necessarily. All that has so far been shown is that the present system is not a durable fixed rate system. That does not answer whether the best way forward is to let it break down, and return to floating rates, to strengthen it further, perhaps moving to a common currency, or to continue with it as an adjustable peg system. All these routes are possible. Which should be sought depends on the costs and benefits.

THE COSTS AND BENEFITS OF BREAKDOWN

For clarity, 'complete' breakdown is considered. By that is meant that every individual European currency rejoins the international float and that the float is free of official intervention.[9] What would be lost if we had that outcome?

As was observed above, agreement on long-run harmonised monetary policies is necessary for a pegged exchange rate system to survive, but it is not sufficient. Exchange rates will still be subject to shocks, from developments in the real economy and from monetary innovations which produce shifts in money demand or supply functions. These impart an inevitable degree of exchange rate volatility – or, if exchange rates are pegged, impart volatility elsewhere.

Suppose all countries announce target inflation paths, and implement monetary policies to achieve these targets on average. Under those conditions, in a floating rate world all exchange rate movements will be fluctuations about anticipatable trends. Does such a minimum – minimum in the sense that no volatility is induced by monetary uncertainty, not in the sense that it is technically impossible to reduce it further – degree of fluctuation matter? There is little evidence that international trade has been affected by the system of floating exchange rates we have had for some ten years now. This finding may be the result of the difficulty of constructing such evidence; for what is necessary is to predict trade in the absence of exchange rate volatility, and then compare that prediction with actual trade flows. None the less, there is reason to have confidence in the finding. The reason for this confidence is that foreign traders have available to them ways of protecting themselves against exchange risk at little cost, and have been using them for some years.[10]

Hence breakdown would appear to be of little significance for trade flows.

A second issue is the effect of breakdown on investment decisions. The problem facing firms making investment decisions in a world where exchange rates can move has been well summarised by Malcolm Crawford (1982).

A company can lay down millions in plant and equipment on calculations that it will be competitive against foreign firms and find, when the plant goes into production, that its calculations have been knocked miles off course by a change in the exchange rate, which has not been compensated by offsetting changes in its costs or those of its competitors. The risk cannot, in general, be hedged.

Crawford has identified a genuine problem – but not really one which can be solved by pegging exchange rates. The problem can have two sources. Divergent money growth can produce it since, as noted above, exchange markets are asset markets, and move *in anticipation* of the price level consequences of monetary policies. This can be prevented by monetary policy harmonisation without an agreement to peg exchange rates. The problem can also arise because of exogenous shocks – the first oil price increase, for example – impacting differently on different economies. These shocks, whether of real or monetary origin, can affect national price levels (although not rates of inflation). They can thereby produce the deviations from PPP to which Crawford draws attention. These would emerge under any exchange rate regime, for by their nature they often cannot be anticipated, and, that being so, monetary policy could not be conducted so as to offset them. They can be reduced to a minimum by pre-announced monetary policy irrespective of exchange rate regime, but they can never be prevented. If exchange rates are to remain pegged in the face of them, then the burden of adjustment would have to be borne elsewhere. The world is an intrinsically uncertain place.

Hence, from the points of view of international trade and the planning of long-term investments, a pegged rate system would seem to bring few benefits that would not be brought by preannounced monetary policies in combination with a freely floating exchange rate.

So far, then, the choice between free float and a pegged rate (as opposed to a *fixed* one, i.e. in effect a common currency) seems rather evenly balanced.

Other benefits are, however, claimed for pegged exchange rates, and other vices attributed to floating ones. It is necessary to consider these.

PRICE LEVEL STABILITY

It is sometimes suggested that a country can best achieve price level stability by pegging its exchange rate to that of some other country, or to some 'basket' of currencies. This can be either because a country does not have a developed money market in which monetary policy can be conducted or, more often, because so large a part of what is consumed and produced in that country is involved in trade with some other country or group of countries (see, e.g. Connolly, forthcoming 1983).

No member of the EMS lacks the technical ability to conduct its own monetary policy – at any rate in principle. Indeed, it should be noted that absence of a market in government debt does not necessitate pegging the currency – Switzerland sometimes conducts its monetary policy via the foreign exchange markets without such a peg (see Schiltknecht, 1981). Nor is any member of the EMS as yet so open to foreign trade as to justify pegging on these grounds.

Countries may, however, choose an exchange rate target as a substitute for control over their own monetary policy. The UK, for example, might choose to peg to the DM, so as to import a superior monetary policy. That is clearly better than choosing to conduct an incompetent home-made policy. The interesting question, though, is whether, if both monetary policies are equally competent, there is anything to be gained by pegging? Can greater price level predictability be attained by that route? In general, the answer is no. Only the special case where countries consistently receive offsetting shocks appears to present a case for pegging the exchange rate, so as to import the shocks of the other. And even here, there are qualifications. One country must peg its money stock, or the price level of both will be indeterminate. Secondly, if both countries adopt a monetary rule, then the long-run predictability of the exchange rate will allow the importing of transitory offsetting shocks. Even in this special case, a monetary rule is as good as an exchange rate peg.

DISADVANTAGES OF FLOATING

The case for a pegged exchange rate system may rest not on the virtues of that system, but on the vices of the alternative. If floating is unsatisfactory, the EMS may, although not as good as Bretton Woods, be better than the available alternative. What are the vices of floating? One sometimes claimed is that exchange rate volatility is 'excessive'. In Alexander Lamfalussy's words (1982),

> It is quite obvious, however, that a substantial part of the variation in the dollar price of the main floating currencies since 1973 has been unnecessary from the point of view of balance of payments adjustment.

That is a more precise version of the common complaint that exchange rates are 'too volatile'. As argued by Frenkel (1982), exchange rates are not 'too volatile', when compared with how other asset prices have behaved in a similarly uncertain environment. This does not refute Lamfalussy's contention, however. Indeed, since these rate movements to which Lamfalussy refers have generally reversed, he is clearly correct. *But the judgement can only be made with hindsight.* No one could know at the time of the fluctuation that it would reverse. If that information had been available, then, in an efficient asset market such as the foreign exchange market, the fluctuation would not have occurred. The information would have been used to prevent the fluctuation, for it would have been profitable to do so. We can look back and say that one exchange rate movement or another was unnecessary; but we cannot make that judgement at the time the exchange rate movement actually takes place. If we could, the movement would not occur.

A second complaint is that foreign exchange markets 'overshoot' – that is to say, that exchange rates overreact to news. This can have two meanings. One is that they move immediately to their long-run equilibrium while other prices move more slowly. The second is that they move beyond that equilibrium. The first complaint is true – it is a characteristic of asset markets. The second is false. Models can be constructed which display that property, but they have other properties which just do not fit the world.[11] The first property is a problem, but it is an inevitable feature of the world. Suppose a rule were adopted which asked central banks to intervene so that exchange rates were continually at PPP. As Frenkel (1982) wrote,

> An intervention rule which links changes in exchange rates rigidly to changes in domestic and foreign prices in accord with purchasing power parity ignores the occasional need for equilibrating changes in relative prices.

Since it cannot be known at the time whether such a change has occurred, and if so whether it is permanent or temporary, the rule would be operational only with hindsight. It could not guide policy.

Hence the 'disadvantages' of floating are really a consequence of the nature of the world. They will not go away if exchange rates are pegged. Rather, they will be shifted to other markets. The case for doing so has yet to be made.[12]

TO FLOAT OR TO PEG?

What conclusion can be reached on the question of whether the EMS should stay as it is or be replaced by a floating exchange rate system? First, not discussed so far but worth emphasising, whatever system is adopted should have clear rules. If pegged rates are chosen, there should be a clear rule for exchange rate policy, and if a floating rate is chosen, it should be a free float, not one with occasional, discretionary, intervention. The reason for this is that such discretionary policy increases uncertainty – uncertainty about the actions of a large market transactor. The net effect of such discretionary policy need not be stabilising; indeed, on the basis of past experience, it would *increase* rate volatility (see Batchelor and Wood, 1982).

The choice between pegging and floating can be summarised in Figure 8.2.

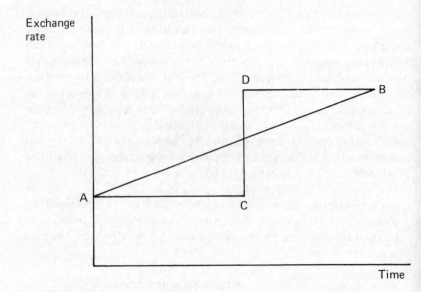

FIGURE 8.2

With a floating rate, an exchange rate would oscillate along a path such as AB. With an adjustable peg, it would oscillate along AC, then jump to oscillating along DB. Which path is preferable?

Would the oscillations about one path be smaller than they were about the other? Suppose they were smaller about AC DB than about AB. This could be produced by *interest rate policy* or by the use of *foreign exchange reserves*. The former would simply shift volatility to another market – there is no reason to believe there is any gain from doing so. Pursuit of the second course implies that there is some positive rate of return from doing so – but since trade is not hampered by floating, and such short-term fluctuations do not matter for long-term investment, it is hard to identify the return.

It should therefore be presumed that these fluctuations, the result of random shocks shifting the rate to and fro, would be the same under both regimes. There is no case for reducing fluctuations further.[13]

How, then, can we choose between the paths? Two considerations seem to point, albeit not conclusively, to the gradual rather than the step path. The step path involves alternately squeezing and assisting the tradeable goods sector of the economy. In the long run this would not matter – by C, in the diagram, the effects would have evened out. But why impose it? Second, once an exchange rate is pegged, adjusting it tends to be delayed by all sorts of harmful devices – tariffs, exchange controls, and so forth. After all, it is hard to tell when it really is time to adjust.

On balance then, floating with a preannounced monetary policy is better than an 'adjustable peg' with a preannounced monetary policy. It is therefore also clearly better, *a fortiori*, than the present EMS, which is a pegged exchange rate system *without* a set of preannounced monetary policies.[14]

Where does this conclusion lead us?

WHITHER THE EMS?

So far it has been argued that few benefits accrue from exchange rate pegging. Once unnecessary exchange rate volatility has been removed by having an announced policy for money growth, the additional step of pegging the exchange rate brings costs but not identifiable benefits.

That in a sense seems to prove too much, in that it leads to the question of why countries use only one currency. Why does London not have one currency and Birmingham another, for example? The answer is that there are advantages in having a common currency. It makes trade and factor movement easier. It is like a common language.

Over what area should there be a common currency? Should Europe move not towards floating exchange rates, but towards a common currency? Here economics has little to say. There is a small literature on 'optimal currency ideas', but it has never succeeded in providing more than qualitative guidance (see Wood, 1973).

What then should be done in Europe? The alternative to floating is one not envisaged under the current system, but which has occasionally been envisaged before – in 'Monetary Integration in Europe' (1972), for example. This is to develop a European Currency, in competition with national currencies and defined as a somehow weighted average of the currencies. This would be available for private as well as government transactors, and consumer choice would determine whether it survived.

The advantages of this procedure is that it recognises that the present system of national currencies may not be efficient, and recognises also that as trade and factor mobility increase within Europe so the nations of Europe will have become increasingly like one economy, a United States of Europe, and thereby become more suited to having one currency. It also, however, recognises that economics can offer little guidance on *when* that has occurred. Leaving the adoption – or abandoning – of the currency to consumer choice means that it will be adopted only if it actually is desirable.

Europe may or may not be an optimal currency area. The only way to find out is to try. Why has this not been done? There is certainly one clear reason. The power to print money brings with it the power to tax. Whoever issues money gains control over real resources by so doing. There would have to be agreement on the distribution of revenue from the creation of the European Money.[15] This has not been considered by any of Europe's political institutions.

SUMMARY AND CONCLUSIONS

The EMS as at present established is not viable. It will not be a zone of monetary stability. The basic reason for this is that the necessary commitments on monetary policy have not been made. Until these are made and implemented, exchange rate changes will be a regular feature of the EMS, and so will exchange rate crises.

What could be done in Europe is for there to be agreement to announce and stick to national rates of monetary expansion. These would determine the trend of prices, and the trend of exchange rates. There would be fluctuations about these trends but pegging rates would not abolish these fluctuations. Rather, it would only shift them to other markets. The benefits of doing so are not clear.

Steps could, however, also be taken to launch a European Money. If it caught on, it would be because it brought benefits – and if it did not, it would be because there were no benefits. That step, however, must await a considerable degree of fiscal harmonisation, since the power to issue money carries with it, automatically, the power to tax. There is a way open to monetary union in Europe, if it should turn out to be economically desirable. But that way requires greater political harmony than we have at present. Under present conditions the best European Monetary System would be one of floating exchange rates, stabilised by preannounced rates of monetary growth in every member country of the EEC. Such a system might have drawbacks; but it is better than any currently available alternative.

ACKNOWLEDGEMENTS

This chapter was prepared at the invitation of the British Association for the Advancement of Science for presentation at the 1982 meetings of that Society. I am indebted for extensive discussion of the issues considered here to Roy Batchelor, Allan Meltzer and, particularly, John Williamson (who has also commented extensively on this chapter); of course, none of these carries any responsibility for either the analysis or the views expressed. This chapter was written before the currency realignments of 13–14 June 1982. These realignments provide further evidence in support of the assessment of the EMS on pp. 134–6, and in the concluding section.

NOTES

1. An excellent example of the work of this era, in which there is thorough examination of the economic arguments together with open admission of political preference, is Williamson (1971).
2. A good account of the details of those arrangements can be found in the *Bank of England Quarterly Bulletin*, June (1979).
3. This implies a view of exchange rate determination. This view is explicitly set out and defended below.
4. It is worth noting that unpredictable interest rate variability (calculated in the same way as was unpredictable exchange rate volatility in Batchelor and Wood, 1982) has increased in three member countries, most strikingly in Germany, where it has increased tenfold, and remained unchanged in the other countries, except Eire where it declined, if we compare 1979–81 with 1976–8. This suggests that the interest rate manipulations were not costless; they added to the uncertainty of the economic environment.
5. For an exposition of the history of this approach, see Thomas M. Humphrey (1979).
6. Under certain assumptions goods price equalisation implies factor price

equalisation across nations. This does not, however, preclude factor movements. First, goods price equalisation may not be instantaneous. Second, tariffs may prevent the equalisation of market prices of goods, thus making it profitable, because of the gap created by the tariff, for factors to move even although prices free of tariffs are equal. A clear and thorough exposition of the conditions under which factor prices are fully equalised by trade in goods can be found in Samuelson (1948 and 1949).

7. In fact exchange rates in the 1970s were made unnecessarily volatile by certain official policies. See Batchelor and Wood (1982).

8. As Triffin frequently pointed out (e.g. 'Gold and the Dollar Problem', 1960), Bretton Woods was also lacking in a satisfactory mechanism for supplying international reserves. This produced the ultimate collapse of the *system* as opposed to the frequent lapses from it by individual countries. No serious thought has been given to this issue by proponents of the EMS; so one can only say that no reserve supply mechanism is in place or proposed.

9. This does not of course mean that governments do not enter the exchange market. It means only that they behave like any other transactor, entering it when trading or investing overseas. In principle they should also be encouraged to speculate. But in practical terms this is a slippery slope, for while private speculators who lose money by making mistakes leave the market, there is no guarantee that similar 'official' speculators would do so.

10. These ways include practices such as exporters invoicing in their home currency. There is detailed analysis of these procedures in Carse, Williamson and Wood (1980).

11. See Phylaktis and Wood (1982) for analysis of the models and testing of them against the evidence. The main evidence against the existence of overshooting in the second sense is provided by comparison of the behaviour of spot and forward exchange rates. If spot exchange rates overshot, then while forward rates moved to their long-run value, spot rates would move beyond that value and then return to it. Hence spot rates would be more variable than forward rates. There is no evidence that they are.

12. Floating does, of course, solve the problem of the method and speed of reserve creation. With a floating rate system, any country that wants more reserves simply acquires them in the foreign exchange market. This would raise the price of the acquired currency relative to other currencies, and increase the purchasing power of reserves held in that currency. The real quantity of international reserves would be demand determined, as is the *real* quantity of money in any one country.

13. The intervention rule guiding the central banks would therefore prescribe free floating until some boundary was reached, and at that boundary the rate would then be rigidly defended. The boundary would be chosen on the basis of previous experience of rate volatility. This rule would produce exchange rate behaviour approximating to that described in the text.

14. It has been suggested by John Williamson, in correspondence with the author, that the EMS has in fact been a kind of 'crawling peg' system, which has allowed 'the distribution of the money supply between the EMS

member countries to vary in accordance with variations in demand, and thus reduced total instability in the system'. An initial point is that if that is how the system has operated, it is certainly not how it was intended to operate by its founders. Neither exchange rate changes nor exchange market intervention have been guided by any preannounced rule. The system thus lacks most of the virtues of the 'crawling peg', as described in John Williamson's Princeton Paper of that name (Williamson, 1965). This may be why interest rate volatility as noted earlier was increased in some EMS member countries. Were the system reconstructed as an explicit 'crawling peg' regime, then its future *could* be more promising than that of the present system. Whether it actually was so would depend on the rules adopted. It is, of course, still vulnerable to the criticism (quoted above) which Frenkel makes of a PPP intervention rule; the information to decide on when to start crawling is not always present. In this regard, it is noteworthy that the crawling peg system has had its notable successes in countries where inflation has been very high relative to a country's trading partners', and has thus dominated any real effect on its exchange rate.

15. This point was first made in 'The Proposed New European Monetary System', evidence submitted to the General Subcommittee of the Expenditure Committee, the House of Commons, November 1978, by the Centre for Banking and International Finance, the City University, London.

REFERENCES

Bank of England (1979) 'Intervention Arrangements in the European Monetary System', *Quarterly Bulletin* (June) pp. 190–4.

Batchelor, R. A. and Wood, Geoffrey E. (1982) 'Exchange Rate Behaviour in Historical Perspective', in *Exchange Rate Policy: UK Options for the 1980s*, ed. R. A. Batchelor and G. E. Wood (London: Macmillan).

Brittan, Samuel (1978) 'European Monetary System', privately circulated (London: Hederwick, Sterling, Grumbar).

Carse, Stephen, Williamson, John and Wood, Geoffrey E. (1980) *Financing Procedures of UK Foreign Trade* (Cambridge University Press).

Connolly, Michael (1983 forthcoming) 'Optimal Currency Pegs for Latin America', *Journal of Money, Credit and Banking*.

Crawford, Malcolm (1982) 'No EMS for Britain', *The Banker* (April) pp. 51–5.

de Grauwe, Paul and Peters, Theo (1979) 'The EMS, Europe, and the Dollar', *The Banker* (April).

Frenkel, Jacob A. (1982) 'Turbulence in the Foreign Exchange Markets and Macroeconomic Policies', Henry Thornton Lecture, City University, London.

Friedman, Milton (1980) 'Prices of Money and Goods Across Frontiers', Harry G. Johnson Memorial Lecture no. 1, Trade Policy Research Centre, London.

Humphrey, Thomas M. (1979) 'The Purchasing Power Parity Doctrine', *Federal Reserve Bank of Richmond Economic Review* (May/June).

Lamfalussy, Alexander (1982) 'A Plea for International Commitment to Exchange Rate Stability', in *Economic Interests in the 1980s: Convergence or Divergence*, ed. Gregory Flynn (Paris: Atlantic Institute for Economic Affairs).

'Monetary Integration in Europe' (1972) Report of a Federal Trust Study Group, Federal Trust for Education and Research, February 1972.

Phylaktis, Kate, and Wood, Geoffrey E. (1982) 'Exchange Rate Overshooting: A Survey', *Annual Monetary Review*, no. 3 (London: Centre for Banking and International Finance, City University).

Samuelson, P. A. (1948) 'International Trade and the Equalisation of Factor Prices', *Economic Journal* (June) pp. 163–84.

Samuelson, P. A. (1949) 'International Factor Price Equalisation Once Again', *Economic Journal* (June) pp. 181–97.

Schiltknecht, Kurt (1981) 'Targeting the Base – The Swiss Experience' in *Monetary Targets*, ed. Brian Griffiths and Geoffrey E. Wood (London: Macmillan).

Triffin, Robert A. (1969) *Gold and the Dollar Crisis* (New Haven: Yale University Press).

Williamson, John (1965) 'The Crawling Peg', *Princeton Paper in International Finance*, no. 50.

Williamson, John (1971) 'On Estimating the Income Effects of British Entry to the EEC', *Surrey Economic Paper*, no. 6.

Wood, Geoffrey E. (1973) 'European Monetary Union and the UK: A Cost-Benefit Analysis', *Surrey Economic Paper*, no. 9.

Wood, Geoffrey E. (1979) 'The Dollar Rollercoaster', *Annual Monetary Review*, no. 1 (London: Centre for Banking and International Finance, City University).

9 The European Community's Trade Policy[1]

MARTIN WOLF

'The European Community and the United States of America are today the two principal pillars of the Western political and economic system.'[2] This is a proud but justified boast. Being such a pillar does, however, entail responsibilities, among the most important of which are those for the maintenance of the open, multilateral trading system. Indeed, the European Community began as an attempt, at a regional level, to take economic integration further than was possible on a global scale. It is, therefore, the most complete expression of the ideas that did, in the late 1940s and 1950s, bring about the successful recreation of an open world economy.[3]

Not for the European Community is the luxury of myopic mercantilism. The members of the Community accounted for 23 per cent of gross world product in 1979 and a third of world exports and no less than 45 per cent of world exports of manufactures in 1980.[4] Even if intra-Community trade were excluded, the Community would still account for 19 per cent of all world exports and 29 per cent of world exports of manufactures in the latter year. By way of contrast, the United States accounted for only 13 per cent of world exports (excluding intra-Community trade) and 16 per cent of world exports of manufactures, while Japan accounted for 8 and 14 per cent respectively.[5] Thus, the Community does not only have a moral responsibility for the functioning of the world trading system but, equally inescapably and more practically, it must assume that its actions will reflect back upon itself, both directly, because of their effect on the world economy, and indirectly, because of the likelihood that they will be imitated.

How well is the European Community living up to its responsibilities? One answer may be obtained by examining the state of the Community's trade relations. It will be noted that the Community as a whole is in conflict with the United States over the effects of subsidies to production of steel and to exports of agricultural products, as well as over its import restrictions in agriculture, while key members are in conflict over export credit subsidies and over the oil pipeline from Siberia. The Community is in conflict with developing countries over market access for textiles, over its responsiveness to complaints against it in the General Agreement on Tariffs and Trade (GATT) and over the issue of selectivity in actions for emergency protection against imports of a particular product. It is in conflict with Japan over the latter's bilateral trade surplus. Finally, it is in almost permanent conflict with traditional agricultural exporters like New Zealand, Canada and Australia. To paraphrase Oscar Wilde, to be involved in one dispute may be thought a misfortune, to be involved in disputes with everyone looks very much like carelessness.

The discussion below begins with an analysis of the international economic order and shows that the conception of the European Community was fully compatible with it. It then proceeds to consider the evolution of the Community and, in particular, the implications of the growing economic difficulties of member countries. This leads to a discussion of the disturbing elements in the Community's external policies, which are shown to reflect the adjustment problems and defensive interventions of its members. Finally, the extent of the current danger both to the Community and to the international trading system is considered.

Certain *caveats* are in order. The subject of this chapter, the European Community's external trade policies, is large. Indeed, it is virtually coterminous with that of the Community itself. Selection is inevitable. For this reason, there is a danger that the discussion will appear unbalanced, at best, and biased, at worst. Mention needs to be made of points that are omitted, in order to preclude misunderstanding.

In the first place, while it is evident that rising unemployment and slow growth exacerbate protectionism, the source of these underlying difficulties is not examined. The approach to the link between overall economic performance and trade policy is a simpler one, namely, to suggest that the malfunctioning of European economies has deep roots, which protectionist attitudes and policies exacerbate and further doses of protection will not cure. One implication is that it is unwise to wait for a sustained recovery before winding protection back. On the contrary, winding it back may be one, although certainly not the only, condition for such a recovery.

In the second place, nothing is said about policies required to help those adversely affected by economic change in general, and import competition in particular. The reason is that this is a general problem, to which a general solution is required. The starting-points for the discussion below are two: first, that there is no reason for compensating or assisting people on the basis of the industry they happen to have been in rather than of the losses they have experienced.[6] Second, policy to help those affected by change should not consist of inefficient interventions, like protection, which lower aggregate income.

In the third place, criticism of the Community's present policies should not be taken to imply that the world as a whole, still less the members themselves, would be better off if it were to disappear. On the contrary the collapse of the European Economic Community in mutual recrimination would probably prove a disaster. Yet it is such a collapse that is threatened, if members of the Community persist with policies that are inimical to its nature.

Finally, while this chapter focuses on the Community, it should not be taken to imply that the Community's trade policies are dramatically more illiberal than those of others. Since part of the concern is with the Community's own prospects, the fact that others pursue wasteful and inefficient policies is, of course, not a reason for the Community to do the same. At the same time, from the point of view of the world economy as a whole, the Community's policies are more disruptive than those of others not because they are worse, but because they are more important. The Community shares with the United States and – increasingly – Japan a responsibility which others can ignore.

Again, it is clear that neither of these great powers is blameless. The United States, in particular, has been playing a game of protectionist leapfrog with the Community in sectors like agriculture, textiles, steel and automobiles as well as in bilateral relations with Japan and the newly industrialising countries. Thus, while this chapter seeks to show that the Community is a crumbling 'pillar' of the international trading system, this does not mean that the other principal 'pillar', the United States of America, is necessarily in much better state.

UNDERLYING CONCEPTS OF THE EUROPEAN COMMUNITY AND OF THE WORLD TRADING SYSTEM

Rules of the international economic order exist to bind governments and restrict their actions, in order to allow economic agents, wherever located, to make long-term plans in a stable policy environment and so participate fully in an integrated world economy. In this way, extensive economic specialisation across national frontiers is made possible. It will be seen, therefore, that international rules help to ensure the survival of an international economic system based on market principles.

In order to achieve their desired goal in international trade, those who framed the General Agreement on Tariffs and Trade (GATT) decided that the commercial policies of participating states should have three fundamental attributes: liberalism, stability and transparency.[7] The tariff was selected as the sole instrument of commercial policy because it is intrinsically transparent, easy to negotiate, and fully compatible with the market. Tariff bindings were agreed in order to give economic agents the security to invest on the assumption of long-term market access. Restrictions on the circumstances and ways in which protection could be increased (including articles and codes on non-tariff measures) were also intended to ensure stability and transparency. Finally, it was agreed that trade policies would not retain the desired attributes without acceptance of the principle of non-discrimination. In this view the authors of the GATT were influenced by the experiences of the 1930s.

The rules of the international trading system were not designed to achieve free trade. It was accepted that individual countries were bound to differ on this issue and that many would wish to reserve the right to protect. At the same time, since it is politically difficult to sustain greater liberalism in one democratic country than in another, when they are in apparently similar circumstances, and since mercantilist prejudices were strong, reciprocal bargaining over trade barriers became, in practice, a principal instrument of general trade liberalisation.

Adherence to the rules by major market economies is much more important than adherence by smaller countries. If Sri Lanka were to pursue free trade one year and autarky the next, the upheaval would be a legitimate concern for its own citizens, but would be of little importance to the rest of the world. The same is not true for the European Community or the United States. They face consequences and, therefore, constraints – fortunately, entirely beneficial ones from the point of view of their own long-term interests – which do not affect others to the same degree.

The most important responsibility of large market economies derives from their role as global markets of last resort. If a major market is suddenly cut off from the rest of the world, especially by quantitative controls, the impact of global supply and demand fluctuations will be felt more sharply in the remaining open markets. Partly for this reason such protection tends, in practice, to spread rapidly. If, however, all major markets are controlled, no exporter can enjoy predictable market access. Potentially efficient investments will then be curtailed. Thus, adherence by major economies to the rules makes possible a global public good: a reasonably stable, yet dynamic, world economy.

It is possible, therefore, to consider a country's trade policies from two perspectives. For the country, looked at in isolation, the question is whether the government's policies allow for efficient international specialisation. This is the classic problem in international trade theory and the current view is that except where the aim is to exploit monopoly power – a dangerous game – the best trade policy is simply free trade.[8] From the point of view of outsiders, however, the question is whether the country's policies contribute to an harmoniously functioning international economy. From this standpoint free trade is unnecessary. What are required, especially in the case of large economies, are simply the stable, transparent and liberal policies that the GATT attempted to ensure. Thus, the first question is the *domestic* costs of deviations from free trade; the second is whether *international* disruption is created by such deviations.

THE GATT AND THE TREATY OF ROME

The relation between the General Agreement and the Treaty of Rome as sets of rules governing the policies of their members is fairly simple. The rules of the latter are generally compatible with those of the former and significantly tighter in their restrictions on governments. The differences reflect those in the membership. The GATT was an agreement among diverse nations who lacked full confidence both in one another and in the advisability of liberal trade, and consequently insisted both upon the right to maintain protection and upon the preservation of several means of escape from their commitments. The Treaty of Rome, by way of contrast, was an agreement of a more binding kind, because the nations concerned had a much stronger mutual commitment and a greater confidence in the wisdom of competition at least *vis-à-vis* one another.

The contrasts are illuminating: the GATT said nothing about the structure of tariffs and did not propose their elimination (although it did propose the progressive liberalisation of trade), while the Treaty of Rome led to the complete abolition of tariffs among members.[9] The GATT allowed for emergency protection against particularly competitive imports, which the Treaty of Rome did not, except during the transition to free trade. The GATT was concerned only with trade in goods, while the Treaty of Rome insisted upon free trade in services and free movement of labour and capital. Finally, and perhaps most important, the GATT provided for no supranational judicial authority, while the development of European law, interpreted by central bodies and providing for private rights, is a unique element in the European idea.

The one fundamental respect in which the European Community appears to violate basic GATT principles was that its existence necessitated discrimination. Article 24 of the GATT had, however, already allowed for discrimination in the case of common markets and free trade areas. There were two reasons for this exception: first, if nations decide to treat one another as if they are part of a single economy, nothing can be done to prevent them; second, such an agreement usually has a strong impulse towards liberalisation, and, in this case, liberalisation should be regarded as more important than the principle of non-discrimination. Moreover, in the case of the Community, liberalisation was not just internal. The creation of the Community was the principal impetus for the Kennedy Round negotiations in the GATT, the sixth since the Second World War, which resulted in substantial global liberalisation, namely a 40 per cent average tariff reduction in major industrial countries on a most-favoured-nation (MFN) basis.[10]

EARLY CONFLICTS BETWEEN THE GATT AND THE EUROPEAN COMMUNITY

At the same time, there were two important respects in which the European Community did create difficulties for the international trading order from its inception:

1. In the first place, the Community completed agreements allowing for various degrees of preferential trade, but not completely free

trade, with many countries. While the result was trade liberalisation, the principle of non-discrimination was eroded. This erosion threatened subsequent growth of more malign forms of discrimination.[11]

2. In the second place, the Community proceeded to construct a virtually watertight system of protection for agriculture. Apart from the costs for the Community itself, the policy had two other important consequences: first, since prices facing Community producers are not responsive to changing market conditions, producers who sell in the residual world markets experience increased price instability; and, second, because of high Community prices, world prices are generally lower than they would otherwise be.[12] In consequence, the Common Agricultural Policy (CAP) was, is and will continue to be a source of international bitterness and conflict.[13]

EVOLUTION OF THE COMMUNITY

In an important paper on the Community, Dr Jan Tumlir, Director of Economic Analysis and Research at the GATT, distinguishes the 'strong and weak elements' of the European Community's constitution, the former consisting of the entrenched individual rights and economic liberalisation, the latter consisting of 'the range of provisions for coordination, progressive approximation and harmonisation of economic policies, culminating in the three mandated common policies (for agriculture, foreign commerce and transport)'.[14] One element of the Community's history consists, then, of a transition from the 'strong', liberal, to the 'weak', more interventionist, concept. A second major element is the battle for power, especially over the more interventionist policies, between Community organs and the member states. The attempt to control national policies and the consequent negotiation not only between Community organs and the members but also among members is a permanent element of Community trade policy.

FROM LIBERALISM TO INTERVENTIONISM

At no time did everyone in Europe embrace economic liberalism and at no time did everyone turn towards governmental activism (or 'positive' policies, as they are sometimes called).[15] On the contrary, the institutions and practices of the post-war world, both international and national, show an uneasy compromise between the two viewpoints. Nevertheless, there has also been an evolution. From the end of the war to about the middle of the 1960s, the main thrust of policy, both in product markets and in international financial arrangements, was towards liberalisation, but in the 1960s and especially the late 1960s there was a change of emphasis and an associated change of direction. There were two distinct forces that combined to bring about this result.

1. The first was euphoria. Governments had promised full employment and it had been delivered. Now they were increasingly tempted to promise accelerated growth and control over industrial structure as well. They were encouraged to take this more interventionist path by the spectacular successes of such apparently interventionist countries as France and Japan, who were putting in the shade the liberal models, the United States and Germany.[16]
2. The second was anxiety. Evidence of the arteriosclerosis of the market process was mounting in one country after another, the problem apparently originating in labour markets, the most important markets that had not been subject to the general liberalisation. As witness to this arteriosclerosis, by the late 1960s or early 1970s, there was an upward drift in inflation, a deterioration in corporate profitability and a rise in the ratio of unemployment to vacancies in one member country after the other.[17] Governments were then tempted to achieve in product markets what they could not achieve in factor markets or, more dangerously, to tackle in the former the symptoms of rigidities in the latter.

The changing emphasis was soon reflected at the Community level. Thus the ruling idea of the agricultural policy, management of a sector by permanent negotiation among member governments, was extended to industry in 1970. Given the conflicts the agricultural policy created, both within the European Community and with those outside, the example should perhaps have served as a warning rather than an inducement, but this did not turn out to be the case. We find:

Simply removing customs duties is not enough: the difficulties being experienced in certain industrial sectors and the need to develop new high technology industries require the Community to develop and implement a coordinated industrial policy. In 1970, the Commission announced that 'the customs union, though it is the basis of all the rest, should be complemented as much as possible by new common instruments of action'.[18]

INTERVENTIONISM DURING THE ECONOMIC CRISIS

It can be argued that in a generally propitious environment government policy to accelerate microeconomic change might have succeeded. The environment rapidly ceased to be propitious, however.
Moreover, the lasting impact on European economies of the oil price
rises of 1973 and 1979 showed that anxiety about economic arteriosclerosis had been justified. As the Commission itself remarked in 1982,
'over the past 10 years the number of available jobs has increased by
only 2 million in the European Community compared to 5 million in
Japan and 19 million in the USA ...'[19] What the oil price rise revealed,
therefore, was the loss of flexibility, especially in the labour markets of
European economies, but – still worse – this rigidity was not equally
prevalent in member countries.

Slow growth, inflation and unemployment moved governments
towards increasingly defensive intervention.[20] In some cases, governments had become identified with the success or failure of particular
sectors or firms. Where policies of constant consultation with firms
were followed, it was discovered, to nobody's surprise, that the latter
agreed most readily on the need to keep out disruptive foreign
competition. It was this stage of national policy-making that most
clearly deserves the stricture of Ludwig M. Lachmann, of New York
University, that '"public policy decisions" are largely a euphemism for
incoherent sequences of desperate expedients'.[21]

With member countries struggling with the problems that made
selective intervention attractive, the Commission again followed the
intellectual trend. Thus, the anxiety about competition and the hopes
of salvation by government action are perfectly revealed in a 1981
Commission document: 'In a world of increasingly fierce competition,
change becomes at once more necessary yet more difficult and the
authorities have to intervene more and more in order to bring it
about.'[22]

Unfortunately, the increased willingness to intervene, especially
given its defensive orientation, has not improved economic performance. This is perhaps not surprising. It is difficult to see why
sustaining loss-making industries should be expected to increase the
flexibility or improve the efficiency of any economy.

CHALLENGE TO THE COMMUNITY

The move towards defensive interventionism both posed a threat and
offered an opportunity to the Community and its organs, but it was the

threat that predominated. The more interventionist a state, the more unitary it tends to be, since there can be room for independent super- or subordinate levels of government only at the price of confusion among those directed. Since the relevant powers were almost all in the hands of national governments, the Community as a whole was in danger of being rendered irrelevant.

More threatening still, the new policy direction put at risk the two main achievements of the Community, the freedom of internal trade and the common commercial policy. Members of the Community generally avoided border measures, when attempting to curb the effects of competition from other members, but there were other instruments available. Indeed, one of the reasons that direct subsidisation became particularly common within the Community was that it was the most effective way of fending off internal competition. While economists tend to view subsidisation as a relatively efficient method of intervention, the form it often took, tailor-made assistance to particular firms, rendered it undesirable, except for the single merit of visibility.[23] Moreover, many of these subsidies to production and investment provoked hostile reactions from other members. Meanwhile, where outsiders were concerned, bilateral agreements to restrain exports were often reached between governments or even by industries with the connivance of governments.

The attempt by the Community to control national policies was not new. In the area of commercial policy, for example, national governments maintained throughout a number of barriers to imports, often of a discriminatory kind, which they were reluctant either to abandon or to hand over to the Community. In this respect, therefore, a common commercial policy was never achieved. In the 1960s, however, it was plausible to see such deviations as a modest and, above all, temporary problem, so long as general liberalisation proceeded. In the 1970s, by way of contrast, national barriers to imports and industrial subsidisation bid fair to become cancerous growths.

As the Commission remarks, 'public interventions in the economy – which have tended to multiply during the economic crisis – fragment the industrial market-place, give rise to the permanent risk of protectionism and lead to a waste of public funds ...'[24] While it is not generally true that policies within a common market need to be harmonised, if by that is meant made similar to one another, they do need to be compatible.[25] There was every likelihood that independently pursued sectoral policies would both be incompatible with one another within the European market and threaten the common external front of the members. As a favourably disposed observer has remarked of internal trade in textiles, 'the issue that confronted the Commission was ... how to make legitimate needs for intervention compatible with the maintenance of competition'.[26]

The Commission's response was to attempt to get involved. Many of those responsible were, in any case, willing to act, especially as some parts of the bureaucracy perceived an opportunity for increased influence. That opportunity arose because the members of the Community wished to preserve the common market and the common external policy. The solution, the Commission suggested, was to 'concert' their industrial and commercial policies at the Community level. As inducements, the Commission could insist upon its power to make commercial policy as a lever for collective agreement on the new protectionist instruments; could propose a cartel directly in the case of steel, for which the treaty of the European Coal and Steel Community appeared to give authority; and could effectively waive the Competition Law in order to make more or less tacit provision for other cartels.[27]

What the Commission offers is attractive. So long as there remains free trade within a common market it is useful for protectionist countries to obtain the cooperation of other members of the Community in imposing barriers to imports. Furthermore, the collective weight of the Community provides some help in coercing recalcitrant outsiders. Meanwhile, cartel agreements, which curtail the activities of the most competitive internal producers, reduce the direct budgetary cost of maintaining inefficient firms, as does protection. For all these reasons the more activist policies of individual members offered an opportunity for at least a part of the Community's bureaucracy both to attempt to manage the interventionist policies and to participate in the control over internal and external trade, which those policies necessitate.

PROBLEMS OF COMMUNITY TRADE POLICIES

The principal elements of Community trade policy reflect the forces that are working both on the Community as a whole and on its members. These are: (i) a steadily deteriorating economic performance; (ii) pressures to help industries that have proved most vulnerable to international competition; (iii) growing hostility towards the world's most successful exporters; and (iv) a wish to limit the direct

budgetary costs of intervention. These pressures come up against two
principal constraints: (i) an overriding desire to preserve the Community itself and, therefore, to control internal conflicts, even if this
involves agreements likely to increase conflict with outsiders; and (ii)
an unwillingness to attack directly the network of international agreements to liberalise trade.

The principal current problems of Community trade policy may then
best be seen as the consequence of the conflict between the desire to
conserve habitual economic structures, on the one hand, and the desire
to conserve arrangements like the GATT and the Community itself,
which, being based on market principles, have radical and uncontrolla-
ble implications for those traditional structures. This conflict has been
resolved by the cumulation of *ad hoc* compromises.

In practice, saving vulnerable industries, while limiting the damage
to free internal competition, is the priority. The attempt is then made
to externalise problems. The pressure to externalise is strong. One
reason is the impulse to replace mutual historic enmities with an
external enemy, who, since this is a trading community, tends frequently to be another trade power. There are also political forces at
work. Thus, in deciding what to do about a particular sector, the
members of the Community are under great temptation to come to
agreements which appear to penalise those who are not represented at
the meetings, namely outsiders and politically weak, if economically
competitive, outsiders, in particular.

The conclusion of this process is the attempt to manage 'disruptive'
trade. As Tumlir remarks, 'the voluntary export restraint and orderly
marketing agreements developed in the illusion that the quiet life and
benefits of liberal trade could be combined and preserved for the
advanced industrial countries if they could control and limit imports
from the developing ones'.[28] In practice, in order to manage disruptive
outsiders, especially where a Community sectoral arrangement is
involved, the European Community finds it necessary to liberate itself
from the international constraints to which its members had previously
agreed. The result is conflict not merely between the Community and
its suppliers but between the Community and the GATT, the Community's conservatism showing itself as a desire to achieve the GATT's
tacit renegotiation rather than its outright repudiation.

THE EUROPEAN COMMUNITY AND GATT LAW

Before considering the Community's specific problems with the
GATT framework, a general point should be made. All along the

Community has left to the United States the role of developing or protecting the global institutions, especially the GATT. One reason for this is, no doubt, the pouring of energy into the regional structure of the Community and its associate arrangements. Another is the difficulty of reaching agreement within the Community on the features of a desirable world order. The result has been that, while the Community has responded to initiatives, it initiates itself only when it feels threatened. Given the weight of the Community, this failure to take direct responsibility for the global institutions is undoubtedly troublesome.[29]

On a more specific level, two interrelated problems emerge: the lack of responsiveness to complaints against it under the GATT, and the desire to change GATT principles when they prove inconvenient.

The Community seems all along to have been happier with the idea of the GATT as a venue for negotiation than as either a body of settled principles or a set of detailed rules. This has shown itself in its attitude towards the settlement of trade disputes. The Community creates two kinds of problem. The first results simply from its creation. As a large economic bloc, the Community is inclined to settle issues on the basis of power. Influential countries, like the United States, can be dealt with directly. The associated states can also be managed in an informal manner, while unimportant outsiders can be ignored. Thus, unlike its individual members, when on their own before the Community's birth, the Community as a whole is not very interested in the concept of general trade law.[30]

The second problem is created by Community actions. The Community has been essentially uncooperative and unresponsive when complaints have been made against it.[31] At the same time, the Community has not been very interested in using the procedures itself. One exception was the case against the United States' DISC scheme for postponing taxes on exporter's income. Another exception that tends almost to prove the rule is the currently proposed case against Japan under Article 23, which deals with 'nullification or impairment' of benefits under the GATT. By suggesting that Japan's culture is frustrating the Community's expectations from trade liberalisation, the Community is proposing a case that can only bring the GATT into disrepute.[32] Trade law cannot plausibly be used in order to change a country's entire culture.

Attempts to change GATT rules are another aspect of the Community's role that bears attention. The most important example is the Community's proposal to legalise selective action against the exports of particularly 'disruptive' suppliers under the emergency protection provisions of the GATT. This proposal, made initially by the United Kingdom and supported by France, was rejected by the developing countries. In consequence, a code on emergency protection under Article 19 of the GATT was not agreed during the Tokyo Round. An important justification for the proposal from the Community's point of view is that it would make it easier to achieve a common commercial policy, the problem for the Community being the survival and even growth of a large number of selective restrictions at the national level. This is not an adequate justification from an international point of view, however. Thus, the proposal has two essential features: it liberates protectionist governments from a constraint and at the same time strikes at the heart of the GATT by authorising discrimination at what amounts to the importer's discretion. As such, it represents the logical conclusion of Community efforts to make protection easier and to increase discrimination in world trade. If achieved, political conflict and economic uncertainty can only increase.

NATURE OF CURRENT CONFLICTS

While the Community attempts to weaken the GATT, it also continues with policies that violate its underlying principles. Management of 'disruptive' outsiders takes the form of sectoralism, especially for agriculture, steel and textiles; bilateralism, especially *vis-à-vis* Japan and newly industrialising countries; or – frequently – both together. Restrictions usually originate at national levels, but the discussion below focuses on what is already sanctioned as Community policy. Thus, automobiles, consumer electronics and other industries subject to national restrictions are not discussed, because there is as yet no common policy. Shipbuilding, a heavily subsidised sector with problems that are *sui generis*, is also not considered.

The Common Agricultural Policy (CAP) began as an attempt to improve farmers' incomes by raising internal prices. In consequence, it was necessary to control imports as well, which was done through the device of the Variable Levy, a charge on imports designed to bring import prices up to European Community levels. Member countries that are relatively large importers from outside the Community pay relatively large sums on these levies. Meanwhile, for a number of commodities, the internal prices have been sufficiently high to generate surpluses, which are either stored or exported at prices below those paid by Community consumers.[33]

The rationale for the policy, with all its complexities and economic inefficiencies, was the creation of a common market for agricultural produce. This was not achieved, however. From the late 1960s governments have frequently been unwilling to allow domestic producer prices to move in line with exchange rate adjustments, which has led to the system of 'green' currency exchange rates. In consequence, prices are not uniform throughout the Community and import taxes and subsidies have to be paid at the internal borders (giving copious opportunities for profitable smuggling).

The full tale of the objections to this extraordinary system cannot be told in a short space but the salient points for the themes of the present chapter can be stated; first, the CAP has become increasingly comprehensive over time, as more and more products are brought into the system; second, it is a source of major internal conflicts over the determination of 'just' prices and – still worse – over the large reassignments of income within and between member countries that it generates; thirdly, it is economically costly for the Community itself; and, finally, by imposing adjustment to changes in market conditions on external markets the CAP increases uncertainty elsewhere, and is, in consequence, a source of world economic disorder. These related internal and external difficulties are ultimately the consequence of the long-standing refusal of many continental European countries to adjust to the force of comparative advantage in agriculture.

The salient characteristics of the steel industry are a deterioration in demand which is more than just cyclical; the small number of firms; the industry's capital intensity; and, as with such sectors as synthetic fibres and plastics, the role of indiscriminate subsidies to investment and output by some member countries in creating and sustaining excess capacity. These subsidies threaten the common market, since member governments are under pressure from their industries to prevent imports of subsidised steel from other members.[34]

While these features of the industry led to a unique policy system, namely an enforced cartel, the fundamental issues are quite similar to those in agriculture. As with agriculture, higher domestic prices were the chosen policy instrument and these could not be achieved without control over imports. Accordingly, bilateral export restraint agreements were reached with the principal suppliers. Since funds were not available to purchase steel, prices could be raised in the face of excess capacity only by reducing output, with the result that the enforcement of production cutbacks became the principal policy problem. (Paradoxically, therefore, a policy aimed at reducing excess capacity inevitably increased it.) Again, as with agriculture, the maintenance of internal discipline in a subsidised and protected sector was made easier by an export pressure valve and this led to the charge of export subsidisation by the United States' steel industry.

The steel cartel was started on a voluntary basis in 1977 as a provisional step and has since become compulsory and more restrictive. In the process the Community's authorities are involved in the impossible task of agreeing upon production cutbacks and, therefore, a 'just' allocation of production within the Community. As with agriculture, an underlying problem is the unwillingness of some member governments to accept an orderly internal solution; immediate and simultaneous problems for the common market itself and for the Community's external trade relations are the inevitable result.

In the case of textiles and clothing, direct cartelisation or another form of direct management is impossible, because of the number of producers. At the same time, price guarantees were never considered. The chosen policies were, therefore, protection and subsidisation. The latter led to substantial conflict within the Community with the result that protection and, therefore, higher prices were preferred.

The framework for protection of textiles and clothing is the Multifibre Arrangement (MFA), which is itself the progeny of arrangements going back to 1961. The United States was the progenitor of those arrangements but in 1977 the Community led the renegotiation of the MFA in a protectionist direction and brought about the erosion of the guarantees previously granted to developing countries.[35] As with steel, *c'est le provisoire qui dure*: a supposedly temporary hardening of terms in 1977 was a preliminary to still tougher terms in the renegotiations of 1981.

The MFA authorises bilateral restraint agreements with 'low cost' producers while leaving developed country producers restricted by tariffs alone. The original feature of the Community policy of 1977 was the setting of global limits to the imports under bilateral agreements. In the process the Community even separated the internal market for imports of textiles and clothing into seven regions. As with most discriminatory arrangements, the export restraints on steel being another example, the tendency of Community import policy is conservative, namely, to freeze world trade shares.

While the textile policy differs in detail from those for other sectors, there is the same underlying dynamic: the tendency to increased restrictiveness over time; the refusal to adjust to the force of comparative advantage, this time that of developing countries in clothing; and the desire to use protection as a means of mitigating, although it cannot preclude, the internal conflicts that the unwillingness of member countries to adjust brings about. That internal conflict cannot be precluded is shown, in the case of clothing, by the success of Italy in taking advantage of export opportunities created by restrictions on outsiders. This success is a source of some resentment in other member countries.

Concentration on the problems of single sectors like textiles is not conducive to economic rationality, as is revealed by Community literature on the subject. Thus, the Commission remarks:

Despite the difficulties caused by the comparative advantages that low-cost countries enjoy, particularly for products at the lower end of the market, the Community must keep all essential types of production in its own territory. If not, the trend towards specialization and interdependence of the different links in the textiles/clothing chain risks exporting entire sections of the industry.[36]

In the same paper, one finds 'European exports [of textile products] must be boosted ... The aim here must be to offset any increase in imports with a corresponding increase in exports.'[37]

Given the precedents, any major sector which is in difficulty, in which there is copious government intervention, over which there is internal conflict, and against which there appears an external threat, is ripe for a Community sectoral arrangement. There are already several branches of the chemical, electronics, computer, telecommunications and transport goods producing industries which are potentially exposed to this treatment. Unfortunately, given present policies in several member countries, the consequences of failure to agree to such a Community-wide sectoral policy may be still worse: the disintegration of the common market itself. What is most striking is that these dangers are being run for policies that, as elementary economic analysis suggests, impose greater losses than gains within the Community itself.

Just as concern with sectoral trade balances is a symptom of the focus upon problems of particular industries, so distress over bilateral trade balances is a symptom of the equally unjustifiable concern with exports from particular countries. The latter is, however, a reflection of a deeper mercantilism (or belief that exports are the benefit of trade and imports the cost). The Commission shows mercantilist reasoning when it defines the Community's industrial problems in the following terms: 'The Community's share of world exports in manufactured goods is declining while the USA's share remains steady and Japan's is increasing. Europe is just managing to keep a trade surplus, excluding energy products, while the USA and Japan are increasing theirs.'[38]

Such mercantilist attitudes are a prominent feature of the debate about Japan's bilateral surplus, but the emotions roused by that debate conceal its intrinsic unimportance. Thus, the hysterical tone of the discussion of the Japanese bilateral surplus in manufactures hides the fact that that surplus is less than 1 per cent of the Community's gross output of manufactured goods. The complaint is also intellectually incoherent. In a multilateral trading system, bilateral balances are irrelevant: the real issue is that of the overall balance of payments and its adjustment. Moreover, contrary to popular impression, Japan has not had a chronic overall current account surplus.

The Community's suggested remedy for the fictitious bilateral problem is that Japan import more. This is not in itself an objectionable goal but it is unlikely to resolve the issue that concerns the Community and is actually likely to make it worse. Unless Japan reduces its overall current account surplus at the same time (an independent issue from that of the level of imports, since the surplus depends on the relation between national income and expenditure), increased imports into Japan imply increased exports from Japan.[39] Moreover, in Japan, the adjustment of exports to changes in imports is rapid, because of the economy's flexibility. Such increased export levels will, however, demand from its trading partners even more of the sorts of adjustment that they consider so painful. It would actually be more logical for the Community to insist that Japan import (and so export) less.

Underlying the Community's attitudes towards Japan and the East Asian newly industrialising countries, as well as its sectoral problems, is its inability to resolve the internal conflicts, both within and between member countries, that make it difficult to profit from growth in other parts of the world. Thus, trade conflicts are, like Janus, two-faced: external and internal frictions go together. Meanwhile, a succession of *ad hoc* compromises has served as no more than a palliative. Being unable or unwilling, therefore, to engage in positive-sum games with the forces of the future, the Community is committed to negative-sum games, in order to protect the past. As a result, the Community is an increasingly disruptive force in world trade. Its policies make impossible the predictability and sustained openness that the trade rules were intended to achieve.

EUROPEAN COMMUNITY AS DECISION-MAKER

The problems for the world outside are exacerbated by the nature of the European Community. It is a troublesome entity to deal with, largely because its common external front is reached only after strenuous internal bargaining. There are three aspects: (i) decisions are usually reached on the basis of the lowest, that is most protectionist, common denominator; (ii) dealings with the Community are complex and time-consuming; and (iii) the Community is an inflexible negotiator.

The tendency of the Community to agree on the most protectionist of the national positions is clear, as is the reason. The obligation to agree on a common commercial policy allows the most recalcitrant government to determine it, except when strongly and violently opposed by the greater part of the membership. In the case of sectoral arrangements, the producer interests directly involved will agree on protection against outsiders. That the sector is considered to be in crisis indicates that at least some member governments will share the industry's views. In consequence any liberally-inclined government will find itself facing a combined European producer lobby *plus* other members' governments. If that government is not prepared to prevent the Community from reaching a decision altogether, it will yield. Moreover, it enjoys the added bonuses of yielding to the noble cause of unity, while providing what its own producer lobby wants, without having explicitly betrayed its liberal principles. It can simply claim *force majeure*. The result in the sectors where there is a common policy, namely agriculture, textiles and steel, is one that tends to conform to the desires of the most protectionist members.[40]

The second problem is that of the complexities and delays involved in dealing with the Community. Thus, the Community takes a long time to agree on any position, since the Commission proposes, but the member governments dispose. As many of them do not fully trust the Commission, the ultimate result is not only delay but a tightly-written brief for the negotiators. At the same time, there are aspects of commercial policy that are still *de facto* in the hands of national governments.[41] Thus, outsiders often have to negotiate simultaneously with the Commission and the member states. While this is possible for the United States or Japan (which is particularly adept at playing one off against the other), it is beyond the resources of smaller nations.[42]

Once internal agreement has been reached, including agreement on measures to control imports, the Community is inflexible. One reason is procedural: it is very tedious to renegotiate a tightly-written brief and the Commission would rather not have to try. The more important reason is that the agreed position represents the result of a complex set of compromises. One element cannot be reopened without threatening all of it. Thus, the Community tends rather to try to ram its approach down the throats of its negotiating partners, which it usually has the power to do. When it fails, negotiations are likely to break down.

In sum, quite apart from the often protectionist objectives of particular members, the very nature of the Community creates problems for outsiders. This is especially true as a more interventionist and flexible policy is pursued, which requires exactly the administrative suppleness that the Community lacks. At the same time, protectionist log-rolling among members tends to make the substance of those policies particularly restrictive.

The administrative difficulties of the Community are not, of course, entirely unlike those of any democracy and, above all, a federal democracy like the United States. Nevertheless, there are important differences. Thus, the Community lacks a central figure like the President able to explain the European interest as a whole; and the Community also has to obtain the consent of each 'region' to any policy. Particularism and delay are inevitably increased by this diffusion of authority.

LESSONS OF COMMUNITY TRADE POLICY

There are certain lessons to be learned from the evolution of Community commercial policy:

1. The Community has found itself tempted by a form of conservatism that can only be disruptive. The failure to see how problems are linked leads to tackling them one by one in a crisis atmosphere. The result is economic inefficiency and political conflicts.
2. Nibbling at the framework of rules, in order to preserve the historic agreements that liberalised trade, threatens what the rules were intended to achieve: predictability and sustained openness in trade policy.
3. A principal element of Community sectoral policies is the attempt to raise internal prices. The aim is to help Community producers, who readily agree among themselves on 'more for all'. For governments, raising prices is an alternative to subsidisation. Subsidies are anathema because they are visible, a clear drain on budgets, and

objectionable to members who do not wish to subsidise their own producers. Policies to raise prices entail protection and often demand cartels and export subsidies as well.

4. In externalising its problems the Community has shown a tendency to take protectionist devices to their logical conclusion. Examples are the policies on agriculture and textiles. In both of these cases it was the United States that first went formally outside the GATT rules but it was the Community that took more complete advantage of the exceptions.

5. Both the steel cartel and the textile restraints were supposed to be temporary devices but both have endured and become more restrictive over time, as appears to be the inherent tendency of sectoral policies.

6. Precedents for the spread of protection are well established and exert force. The Community's efforts to modify the GATT will make it still more difficult in future to resist such pressures.

In sum, it is not excessive to talk of a cumulative breakdown of rational policy-making. The inability of the Community to make and implement efficient sectoral policies threatens its internal cohesion and renders it a disruptive force in international relations.

CURRENT DANGERS

For the Community and its members the flirtation with activist sectoral policy has led to far from satisfactory results. For the international economic order the prospects are still more threatening:

1. Trade has become thoroughly politicised and trade conflicts are, in consequence, putting at risk the ability of the major Western powers to cooperate with one another.

2. The Community and the United States are imitating each other's protectionism, as well as conflicting directly over agriculture, steel and other trade issues, in the process attempting to separate themselves from the world economy in one sector after another and threatening its progressive disintegration.

3. The evolution from a trading order characterised by general rules to one characterised by permanent negotiation over market access increases uncertainty for private decision-makers and reduces willingness to make efficient, trade-expanding investments.

4. Negotiation over market access entails bilateralism, but a world of

bilateral bargaining over trade could not be expected to sustain the present level of commercial exchange, let alone expand it. Indeed, in a world in which every country controlled its imports (and, therefore, every country's exports were controlled *ipso facto*), it would be virtually impossible to coordinate world economic activity.

5. If it were to become clear that world trade will cease to grow, a chain of defaults would be probable, since debt obligations are of little value if the foreign exchange cannot be obtained to service them.

In sum, the tendencies inherent in the European Community's current ideas about commercial policy cannot continue indefinitely without breakdown of the world economy.

Such a breakdown is clearly not in the Community's interests. Yet there are now those who suggest that there should be controlled market access for all competitive imports. The reasons advanced are that in this way painful adjustment can be avoided and the free internal market be maintained.[43] There are three fundamental errors in these arguments:

1. Adjustments to changes in the world will occur in one form or another. All that a country can do is to attempt to shift adjustment from one sector or one group of people to another. Thus, determined protection of industries with a comparative disadvantage taxes those with a comparative advantage thus damaging the economy's exports and future growth.

2. The adjustment that would be required in the event of the establishment of a Community protectionist wall would far exceed that necessitated by the continuous changes characteristic of an integrated world economy. The reason is evident: such policies make probable the breakdown of the world economy with catastrophic effects on Community export industries.

3. All the external conflicts are a reflection of the inability to resolve internal difficulties, both at sectoral and overall levels. In consequence, determined protection cannot ensure internal harmony. It is true that protection against outsiders has somewhat reduced direct internal conflict over subsidies, but this success is short term and partial. The basic internal problem remains. Contrary to impressions abroad in Europe, protectionist policies do not increase incomes. On the contrary, they reduce them in aggregate and reassign them within and among Community members. There can be no 'just' way to assign such income, any more than there can be a 'just'

way of allocating production of steel. Given the differences in the adjustment capacity and economic strength of Community members, there is little reason to expect that all will be prepared to bear the costs of trade diversion in favour of the weaker members or to tolerate the Community decisions that determine their industrial structures.

It was the original conception of the Community, characterised by general commercial policies fully compatible with world economic order, that makes sense. Its essential notion, it should be remembered, was that 'positive' action was the right and duty not of the state but of individuals operating under predictable rules. The 'positive' concept of government has, by contrast, contributed to economic malaise and led to conflict among members of the Community and, simultaneously, with outsiders. Taken to its logical limit, the concept precludes world economic order and threatens the Community itself. Thus, conflicts over the Community's evolving trade policy are a symptom of a deeper crisis that can be resolved only by a reconsideration of the proper responsibilities of government in an open world economy. Failing that, the Community will cease to be one of the two 'pillars' of the Western economic system and the structure as a whole will collapse.

NOTES AND REFERENCES

1. The author's principal intellectual debt is to Dr Jan Tumlir, Director of Economic Analysis and Research at the GATT, and especially to his paper 'Strong and Weak Elements in the Concept of European Integration', Chapter 2 in Fritz Machlup, Gerhard Fels and Hubertus Mueller-Groeling (eds), *Reflections on a Troubled World Economy: Essays in Honour of Herbert Giersch* (London: Macmillan for the Trade Policy Research Centre, 1983). Detailed and particularly helpful comments on an earlier draft of the paper were received from Dr J. Michael Finger of the World Bank and Professor David Henderson of University College, London. The author also acknowledges the useful comments of Mr Sidney Golt, Professor Oli Havrylyshyn of George Washington University, Messrs Stanley Please and Ernest Stern of the World Bank and Professor Jean Waelbroeck of the Université Libre, Brussels. Responsibility for remaining errors of fact and interpretation rests solely with the author.
2. See 'The European Community and the United States', *Europe Information*, vol. 39, no. 80 (Brussels: Commission of the European Community, 1980) p. 1.

3. On the endeavours to recreate an open international trading system see, in particular, Richard N. Gardner, *Sterling-Dollar Diplomacy: the Origins and Prospects of Our International Economic Order*, 3rd edn (New York: Columbia University Press, 1981); Gerard Curzon, *Multilateral Commercial Diplomacy: the General Agreement on Tariffs and Trade and its Impact on National Commercial Policies and Techniques* (London: Michael Joseph, 1965); and Robert E. Hudec, *The GATT Legal System and World Trade Diplomacy* (New York: Praeger, 1975).

4. Data on the Community's share of gross world product are derived from World Bank, *World Development Report 1981* (New York: Oxford University Press, 1981) Annex Table 1. Data on the Community's share of world trade are from *International Trade 1980/81* (Geneva: GATT Secretariat, 1981) Tables A20, A22 and A23.

5. Data are from *International Trade 1980/81*, Tables A17, A19, A22 and A23.

6. For a discussion of the issue of adjustment policy as an alternative to protection see Wolf, *Adjustment Policies and Problems in Developed Countries*, World Bank Staff Working Paper no. 349 (Washington: World Bank, 1979).

7. Liberalism cannot be defined precisely. In this context what is meant is, first, permitting markets – rather than discretionary, administrative intervention – to allocate resources and, second, setting protectionist instruments at levels that permit a steady expansion of world trade.

8. The case for free trade, while allowing for other interventions, is set out in W. M. Corden, *Trade Policy and Economic Welfare* (Oxford: Clarendon Press, 1974).

9. The abolition of all customs duties among the six original members was completed eighteen months ahead of schedule on 1 July 1968.

10. See Hudec, *The GATT Legal System*, pp. 198–9. The Commission of the European Community remarks: 'Following the establishment of the EEC, the industrialised nations – and amongst them particularly Europe and the United States – agreed to mutual reductions in trade barriers, within still modest limits in the Dillon round, but on an unprecedented scale after the United States Congress passed the Trade Expansion Act (Kennedy Round). The Community emerged from these negotiations with the lowest customs tariff of any of the major trading powers, amounting to hardly more than half the average of the original tariffs of its Member States.' See 'Development of an Overall Approach to Trade in View of the Coming Multilateral Negotiations in GATT', *Bulletin of the European Communities*, Supplement 2/73 (1973) p. 5.

11. See Hudec, *The GATT Legal System*, pp. 204–8.

12. It can be shown quite easily that, under normal assumptions, if prices in one segment of a market are fixed, the clearing prices in the remaining segment will, *ceteris paribus*, fluctuate more than before. Moreover, if the price level in that segment is set at levels higher than the clearing level for the world (when there is no protection), prices in the rest of the world will fall.

13. See Hudec, *The GATT Legal System*, pp. 200–3.

14. From Tumlir, 'Strong and Weak Elements in the Concept of European Integration'.

15. See *A Community Strategy to Develop Europe's Industry*, COM (81) 639 final/2, Communication from the Commission to the Council (Brussels: Commission of the European Community, 1981) p. 4.

16. On European industrial policies see Lawrence G. Franko, 'Industrial Policies in Western Europe – Solution or Problem', *The World Economy*, vol. II (January 1979) pp. 31–50. The force of the French and Japanese examples is considered on pp. 33–6. A more sceptical view than Professor Franko's is in Victoria Curzon Price, *Industrial Policies in the European Community* (London: Macmillan for the Trade Policy Research Centre, 1981).

17. The rates of inflation of the four largest present members, France, Germany, Italy and the United Kingdom, went above their respective averages for 1961 to 1970, never to return below them in any year during the 1970s, in 1968 for France and the United Kingdom and in 1970 for Italy and West Germany (except that the latter did manage to achieve a rate of inflation in 1978 equal to its average for 1961 to 1970). See *Main Economic Indicators: Historical Statistics 1960–75* (Paris: OECD Secretariat, 1976) and *OECD Economic Outlook* (Paris: OECD Secretariat, July 1982) Table R10. On real wages, productivity and profits in developed countries see Paul McCracken, Guido Carli, Herbert Giersch, Attila Karaosmanoglu, Ryutaro Komiya, Assar Lindbeck, Robert Marjolin and Robin Matthews, *Towards Full Employment and Price Stability* (Paris: OECD Secretariat, 1977) especially pp. 161–4, and *OECD Economic Outlook* (Paris: OECD Secretariat, July 1977). Declining trends in the industrial profitability of several major OECD countries including Germany, Italy and the United Kingdom, are shown in T. P. Hill, *Profits and Rates of Return* (Paris: OECD Secretariat, 1979) Table 6.6. On the rising rates of unemployment at successive cyclical peaks in the 1960s and 1970s and the deteriorating relationship between vacancies and unemployment over the same period see *A Medium Term Strategy for Employment and Manpower Policies* (Paris: OECD Secretariat, 1978) Table 1 and Diagram 4.

18. From 'The Community's Industrial Policy', *European File*, 3/79 (Brussels: Commission of the European Community, 1979) p. 2.

19. From 'Relaunching Europe: A New Community for Industry and Employment', *European File*, 3/82 (Brussels: Commission of the European Community, 1982) p. 1.

20. See, for example, *Industrial Policies in the Community: State Intervention and Structural Adjustment*, Report of a Study Group, II/419/80–EN Final (Brussels: Commission of the European Community, 1981) pp. 58–62.

21. From Ludwig M. Lachmann, 'From Mises to Schackle: An Essay on Austrian Economics and the Kaleidic Society', *Journal of Economic Literature*, vol. XIV (March 1976) p. 61.

22. From *A Community Strategy to Develop Europe's Industry*, p. 4.

23. On the theoretical case for subsidies see Corden, *Trade Policy and Economic Welfare*, chap. 2. On the argument that subsidies have been extremely costly in practice see, for example, Helen Hughes and Jean Waelbroeck, 'Can Developing-country Exports Keep Growing in the 1980s?', *The World Economy*, vol. IV (June 1981) p. 142 and on the view that subsidies are trade policy by another name see Richard Blackhurst,

'The Twilight of Domestic Policies', *The World Economy*, vol IV (December 1981) pp. 357–73.

24. From 'Relaunching Europe', p. 2.
25. For a clear discussion of the economics of policy harmonisation in a free trade area see Harry G. Johnson, 'The Implications of Free or Freer Trade for the Harmonization of Other Policies' in Johnson, Paul Wonnacott and Hirofumi Shibata, *Harmonization of National Economic Policies under Free Trade* (University of Toronto Press for the Private Planning Association of Canada, 1968).
26. From José de la Torré and Michel Bacchetta, 'The Uncommon Market: European Policies towards the Clothing Industry in the 1970s', *Journal of Common Market Studies*, vol. XIX (December 1980) p. 100.
27. See on the issue of competition law and crisis sectors René Joliet, 'Cartelisation, Dirigism and Crisis in the European Community', *The World Economy*, vol III (January 1981) pp. 403–45.
28. From Tumlir, 'Salvation through Cartels? On the Revival of a Myth', *The World Economy*, vol. I (October 1978) p. 386.
29. The problem is pervasive. Kenneth W. Dam, currently Deputy Secretary of State, refers to the fact that in the debates on the international monetary system of the 1970s only the United States developed a comprehensive position. He cites Marcus Fleming, a high official of the IMF, as saying 'The Europeans handicapped themselves by trying to agree issue by issue on a joint EEC position.' See Dam, *The Rules of the Game: Reform and Evolution in the International Monetary System* (University of Chicago Press, 1982) p. 222.
30. On the European Community in dispute settlement see, in particular, Hudec, *Adjudication of International Trade Disputes*, Thames Essay no. 16 (London: Trade Policy Research Centre, 1978) especially pp. 21–3. See also a paper by Gardner Patterson, a former senior official at the GATT, 'The European Community as a Threat to the System', presented at a conference on 'Trade Policy in the Eighties' organised by the Institute for International Economics in Washington DC, 23–25 June 1982.
31. Ibid. See also C. F. Teese, 'A View from the Dress Circle in the Theatre of Trade Disputes', *The World Economy*, vol. IV (March 1982) especially pp. 43–6.
32. On 25 March 1982 the Commission's Head of Delegation in Geneva sent a letter to the Japanese representative, informing him of the Community's desire to enter into consultations with Japan under Article 23 of the GATT. The Community suggested that, because of factors particular to the Japanese economy, Japan imports negligible quantities of manufactured goods. The resulting surplus in manufactures, especially *vis-à-vis* the European Community, has nullified the GATT objective of 'reciprocal and mutually advantageous arrangements'. The Community's suggestion is that the Japanese government adopt a programme to expand imports.
33. A lucid recent discussion of the CAP is in T. E. Josling, Mark Langworthy and Scott Pearson, *Options for Farm Policy in the European Community*, Thames Essay no. 27 (London: Trade Policy Research Centre, 1981).

34. On the genesis of the Community's steel policies see Ingo Walter, 'Protection of Industries in Trouble: the Case of Iron and Steel', *The World Economy*, vol. II (May 1979) pp. 171–6. On Community dumping see ibid., p. 180.

35. On the genesis of the textile protection system and the Community's role in 1977, see Donald B. Keesing and Wolf, *Textile Quotas against Developing Countries*, Thames Essay no. 23 (London: Trade Policy Research Centre, 1980). On the variety of government policies to subsidise textiles and clothing see de la Torré and Bacchetta, 'The Uncommon Market: European Policies towards the Clothing Industry in the 1970s'.

36. 'The European Community Textile Industry', *European File*, 7/82 (Brussels: Commission of the European Community, 1982) p. 5.

37. Ibid., p. 7.

38. From *A Community Strategy to Develop Europe's Industry*, p. 2.

39. It is a basic proposition in balance of payments theory that the current account surplus depends on the relation between real national income and expenditure. (For a discussion of this relationship see Rudiger Dornbusch, *Open Economy Macroeconomics* (New York: Basic Books, 1980).) In the case of Japan the relevant behavioural hypothesis is that resources will not be allowed to rest idle. Thus, if the Japanese switch to purchasing more imports, those who produced the goods that are no longer purchased domestically will produce exports instead. The consequence of the increased propensity to import will then be an increase in the share of both imports and exports in GNP (from what are still rather modest levels by international standards), but no change in the structure of the balance of payments.

40. It is interesting to note that in the case of agriculture, when prices of wheat were unified in 1964, the West German price was above the French and the agreement raised the Community price to the German level. See A. E. Walsh and John Paxton, *Into Europe: the Structure and Development of the Common Market*, 2nd edn (London: Hutchinson, 1972) p. 79. In industry, the Germans have been on the liberal side and have generally lost. On textiles, for example, see Chris Farrands, 'Textile Diplomacy: the Making and Implementation of European Textile Policy 1974–1978', *Journal of Common Market Studies*, vol. XVIII (September 1979) especially pp. 28–9.

41. Many bilateral agreements with outsiders are national. An important example is automobile restraints on Japan.

42. An excellent account of the Community as a decision-maker in commercial policy is given in the paper by Gardner Patterson, 'The European Community as a Threat to the System'.

43. For these arguments see Wolfgang Hager, 'Protectionism and Autonomy: How to Preserve Free Trade in Europe', *International Affairs*, vol. LVIII (Summer 1982) pp. 413–28.

10 Britain, the EEC and the Third World

DAVID WALL

In the debate over whether or not Britain should join the EEC, the development lobby was split into pro-entry and anti-entry factions. Both factions included groups with widely divergent positions. A common theme of the anti-entry faction, however, was that the EEC was an inward-looking 'rich man's' club, and that the logic of its existence was a self-serving one, which would naturally be expected to lead to the subordination of the interests of inhabitants of non-member countries to those of its own citizens. It was argued that by joining such a community Britain would be reneging on the liberal trade relations embodied in the Commonwealth Preference System and also cease to be able to maintain its traditionally liberal stance in global trade, and aid, negotiations. The common theme of the pro-entry faction was that only by joining the Community could Britain's economy be strengthened to give sufficient weight to its political status in its role in international affairs. It was believed that this enhanced status could and would be used effectively from within the EEC to liberalise the Community's economic relations with developing countries. In addition the pro-entry faction of the development lobby argued that the British government would seek safeguards for Commonwealth interests threatened by the necessary abolition of the Commonwealth Preference System.

Alongside this general conflict of opinion, there was a series of more specific arguments as to the effects on British/Third World relations of the harmonisation of British economic policies with those of the enlarged Community. Several more important arguments concerned the effects of Britain adopting the Common Agricultural Policy on its agricultural imports, especially sugar, from Third World suppliers; the effect on the quantity and quality of the UK's aid flows of their partial diversion through the European Development Fund; and the effect on trade in industrial products of Britain adopting the type of non-tariff barriers to trade favoured by existing member countries. In addition, fears were expressed by the anti-entry faction that political relations with Third World countries would suffer. The arrangements between Commonwealth members were seen as a partnership of equals. A move towards the neo-colonialist arrangements between the Community and its members' colonies and ex-colonies, as embodied in the Yaoundé Convention of Association and other treaties, was thought to entail a step backwards.

Sufficient time has now passed for Britain to have made its mark in Europe and the question of whether or not Britain has had a liberalising effect on the EEC's relations with Third World countries can now be investigated.

THE CRITERIA FOR EVALUATING LIBERALITY

In the fifteen years which have passed since the peak of the debate over British entry, the criteria used to define liberality and to evaluate the welfare consequences of liberal trade and aid policies have changed. On the one hand the inflamed, idealist rhetoric of the professional leaders of the development lobby has inflated the quantitative specification of liberality, and generated a rate of growth of aspirations for resource flows which has outrun the growth rate of the capacity and willingness of the industrialised Western democracies to provide them. On the other hand, concern over the competence of those officials and politicians charged with advising on the selection and implementation of development orientated economic policies in both rich and poor countries, has led to doubts about the ability and even willingness of such people to select and apply policies which are truly liberal in their effects. The combination of the growing gap between the demand for and supply of resources, and doubts about the effectiveness of the delivery mechanism, has led to a crisis of confidence in the ability of leaders to provide guidance on how to move towards the attainment of the development targets supposed to be the objective of truly liberal policies. It would be desirable if there were a harmonious cooperative movement of the politicians, officials and citizens of rich countries working together with their counterparts in poor countries on a programme for the removal of poverty from our midst. In practice a battleground has developed where self-serving interest groups, power-hungry individuals and eclectic and schismatic ideological groupings are in constant conflict. In this situation resource flows to poor countries consisting of food aid, private capital, official capital, technical assistance and expanded access to rich country markets, can be and are simultaneously described as liberal and illiberal, supportive and exploitative.

The last fifteen years have taught us that the different participants in the development debate have no common objective and consequently can have no common criterion by which to judge the relative merits of policy proposals. In a world where many countries have fascist, totalitarian, militaristic or simply self-centred corrupt governments, transfers of resources as aid or through the market may at best have no effect, and at worst may harm the welfare of the poorer citizens of those countries. It is, then, necessary to be careful in evaluating the impact of British entry into the EEC on the Community's economic relations with the Third World. While policies designed to increase resource flows to developing countries are commonly described as 'liberal', it has to be recognised that these are neither a sufficient nor even a necessary condition for achieving improvements in the welfare of the poor.

Aside from the issue of whether or not increased resource flows to less developed countries benefit their poor, it has to be recognised also that policies described as liberal in this way may not actually lead to increased aid or trade. For example, the removal of tariffs on a range of imports into the EEC from developing countries need not lead to any increase in such imports, and could reduce the total value of developing country exports. Non-tariff barriers of many forms may continue to prevent growth in trade, or the developing countries may not have the technical competence to produce the items competitively. For primary or intermediate products, the removal of tariffs may lead to a reduction in imports of the processed or manufactured products which embody those items.[1] Similarly a claim that 100 per cent of imports enter a market tariff-free may simply mean that all potential imports which would threaten domestic interests have been successfully excluded by other means. In the case of aid, an increase in the amount of funds potentially available may be described as liberal, even though actual flows might be reduced if the costs or conditions attached to such aid are changed in ways which reduce the attractiveness or availability of the funds to recipients. Also some so-called aid is sometimes purely welfare augmenting for nationals of the donor country.

In sum, in addition to the problem of attributing welfare values to the effects of British entry on the EEC's trade and aid policies there is the problem of assessing whether or not such effects are actually liberal in the sense of generating increased resource flows or only cosmetic and unlikely to have any real impact. These problems are particularly acute in the evaluation of changes in aid policies. Consequently, attention in this brief chapter is focused on trade policies. The next two sections describe first the changes in the EEC's trade relations with Third World countries at the time of British entry and second, subsequent developments in these relations. The final section discusses the problems of identifying and quantifying the direct and indirect effects of British membership.

THE INSTITUTIONAL IMPACTS OF BRITISH ENTRY

British entry to the EEC necessitated institutional changes which would accommodate British membership within the existing, complex structure of EEC's economic relationships with the Third World. Britain's pre-entry relations with Third World countries therefore underwent a metamorphosis, the institutional aspect of which is clearly visible. Prior to entry, Britain's relations with non-Commonwealth developing countries were, broadly speaking, based on non-discriminatory application of its international obligations under the General Agreement on Tariffs and Trade (GATT) and support of non-discriminatory multilateral organisations such as the International Monetary Fund (IMF) and the World Bank (IBRD). Discriminatory treatment for Commonwealth countries was provided through the bilateral aid programme, and for trade through the Commonwealth Preference System. Most raw materials and agricultural products, and almost all manufactured imports from developing Commonwealth countries, entered the British market on a tariff-free basis with no quantitative restrictions (other than a few quotas on specific items such as cotton textiles). In addition, during the negotiations but prior to accession Britain introduced its version of the Generalised System of Preferences (GSP), parallel to the Commonwealth scheme, under which all developing countries gained entry to the British market on the same preferential terms, but subject to a safeguard clause. Britain also provided protected markets to Commonwealth producers of sugar under a special purchasing agreement.

The EEC's economic relations with poor countries were much more complicated. In addition to the individual members' bilateral aid programmes and their individual membership of the Economic Community they had their own collective aid programme, channelled largely to their colonies and ex-colonies through the European Development Fund (EDF). This collective aid programme was embodied in the Yaoundé Convention of Association between the EEC and eighteen ex-colonies in Africa (including Madagascar). The convention also established reciprocal preferential trading arrangements between the EEC and the eighteen. (A parallel agreement extended similar trade preferences to the East African Community from 1971 to 1975.) These trade preferences assured free access into the EEC for exports from the eighteen, with the exception of some agricultural products covered by the Common Agricultural Policy (CAP). Various regulations, for example those defining the origins of exports and excise duties on some tropical products such as tea and coffee, did however limit the value of such free access. Free access for industrial goods, except for some sensitive products, and preferential access for some selected agricultural products, was afforded to various Mediterranean countries (such as those of the Magreb) under different bilateral trade agreements. Finally, all poor countries were to be afforded preferential access (mostly tariff free) within well-defined quantitative limits for almost all industrial products and some agricultural products under the EEC's own scheme for the GSP.

Before examining the changes in these institutional arrangements brought about by British entry, it should be noted that the significance of free or preferential access to the EEC and UK markets was in any case limited by the degree of free access they accorded to developed countries. EEC members afforded to each other free access to their markets. Similarly, the UK market was freely accessible to fellow members of the European Free Trade Association (EFTA). So poor country exporters were limited at best to competing on an equal footing with producers in the EEC and EFTA. And at the time of the negotiations, the value of preferential access for poor countries was being further eroded. General tariff levels, and therefore their protective effect, were being negotiated down in the GATT at first under the Kennedy Round and later the Tokyo Round of Multilateral Tariff Negotiations. This meant that developing countries faced increased competition from developed non-members of EEC and EFTA within EEC markets. In addition a free trade area in industrial products among the members of EEC (enlarged) and EFTA (reduced) was proposed.

During the negotiations for British entry to the EEC the government stated that the terms of agreement would 'safeguard the interests of Commonwealth developing countries'. In practice this meant seeking, first, trade arrangements which would compensate them for having to share preferential access to the UK market with EEC countries, and secondly, arrangements designed to ensure that diversion of UK aid away from Commonwealth recipients did not occur.

The EEC's original offer of accommodation for Commonwealth developing countries was the very limited one of extending Yaoundé Convention treatment to Commonwealth African countries, and UK dependent territories other than Hong Kong and Gibraltar. No special arrangements were offered for other Commonwealth developing countries and the offer of Yaoundé status implied a considerable restriction of market access for sugar producers, and also for producers of processed agricultural commodities. Britain negotiated an extension of the offer of Yaoundé-type association to cover Mauritius and Commonwealth developing countries in the Caribbean and Pacific. These arrangements were incorporated in the Lomé Convention between the EEC and the African, Caribbean and Pacific states (ACP). As the ACP included the Commonwealth developing country sugar and banana producers it was possible to negotiate protocols to cover their interests within the Lomé Convention.

Commonwealth countries in Asia, including Hong Kong – the Seven Outside as they came to be known – were offered nothing except a concession to extend to Hong Kong[2] the preferential access of the harmonised GSP scheme, and a commitment (embodied in an answer to Britain's Treaty of Accession) to examine the problems of the other six countries, with a view to devising bilateral commercial cooperation agreements. Four such commercial cooperation agreements were subsequently signed – by India in 1974, Pakistan and Sri Lanka in 1975 and Bangladesh in 1976. Very little of any significance in terms of market access was achieved within the framework of these agreements. The agreement to discuss their establishment did, however, provide a forum for bilateral talks to discuss ways in which the GSP, for example, could be adjusted to limit the restrictions on market access threatened by UK entry. In this way a few *ad hoc* adjustments to EEC GSP and other trade policies covering coir, jute, tobacco, plywood and pineapple slices were negotiated. Such minor measures had little impact on the overall trading relations of the enlarged EEC with the six Asian Commonwealth countries.

The nature of the EEC's GSP created further consequences for Britain's trade relations with the Third World. At the time of Britain's entry to the EEC, the orginal United Nations plan, to have one global system, had failed. The various OECD countries were operating or planning to introduce widely differing schemes. As the British scheme varied significantly in its arrangements from that of the EEC it was necessary to find a way to harmonise the two schemes. The British scheme proposed unlimited duty-free entry for almost all industrial products, although a safeguard clause was written in so that specific preferences could be reduced or suspended if domestic interests were 'injured'. No such clause existed in the Commonwealth Preference System, which continued to operate, nor was there one in the EEC GSP. The EEC GSP was, however, more restricted in that, while tariffs were removed on almost all industrial products, this tariff-free treatment was limited by strict quotas – for entry into both the EEC member's market and that of the Community as a whole. In addition a wider range of processed agricultural products was excluded from the EEC scheme, or granted only minor tariff reductions. The UK agreed to harmonise by adopting the EEC's GSP mechanisms, as amended during the review of the scheme timed for 1973. The grounds on which the agreement was made were (i) that most Commonwealth developing countries would continue to receive tariff- and quota-free entry into the UK market and to the EEC market under the agreed extensions of Yaoundé Convention arrangements, and (ii) that a commitment had been negotiated to examine the problems of the Asian members of the Commonwealth before the Commonwealth Preference System was abolished (by the gradual adoption by the UK of the Common External Tariff (CET)).

Although the 1973 review of the EEC's GSP came after the UK had joined the Community, it was seen as an occasion on which some of Britain's entry commitments to the Commonwealth could be made good, rather as the negotiations for the replacement of the Yaoundé Convention by the Lomé Convention were used to accommodate the interests of eligible ACP states. When trying to identify the impact of UK entry on the EEC's stance towards developing countries, once Britain had become a member it became increasingly difficult to single out individual country positions and the effectiveness of their negotiators in 'selling' them. Given the pre-entry commitments of the UK, it was clear that it would be attempting to liberalise the EEC's GSP scheme in order to accommodate Commonwealth interests. But the development lobbies of the original six members and officials in the Commission were also pressing for similar reforms. It is probable, given the internal and external political pressures present in 1973, that the enlargement of the tariff-free quotas and ceilings, and the reclassification from sensitive to semi-sensitive of twelve products (although three were added to the sensitive group), would in any case have been implemented by the original six members. British pressure was concentrated on processed agricultural goods. The resulting liberalisation was very limited, and fell far short of Britain's requests. It consisted of doubling the preference margin from 20 to 40 per cent for most items, and adding Commonwealth products such as packaged tea, coconut oil, cocoa butter, canned pineapples and instant coffee to the list of products accorded preferences. However, even this probably would not have occurred without Britain's insistence.

In the case of cotton textiles, it was the British position that was liberalised by entry to the EEC. Cotton textiles were excluded from the British GSP scheme and were subject to tariffs in the Commonwealth scheme. In the EEC scheme they were included on a tariff-free basis, within quota limits, for countries who were signatories to the GATT Long-term Arrangement on Cotton Textiles (LTA). Other textiles (and footwear) were included in both the Commonwealth and EEC schemes, but dependent territories (such as Hong Kong) were excluded from the EEC scheme, which also imposed tight quotas. These arrangements were continued in the 1973 revision, although the LTA had been replaced by the Multifibre Textile Agreement (MFA) – which thus constrained the GSP treatment of textiles other than cotton.

In sum, then, those who argued that British entry liberalised the EEC's trade relations with the Third World by improving market access do have valid arguments to support their view. The continental EEC countries extended free access to their markets, under the Lomé Convention, for industrial products and for most agricultural products, to Commonwealth ACP countries. Similarly, access was extended by the improved offers on preferential margins for the limited range of processed agricultural goods mentioned earlier. But against these liberalisations must be set the restrictions on access to the UK market for the six Commonwealth countries in Asia. This restriction was a result of introducing quota restrictions where previously access had been free under the Commonwealth Preference System, and of introducing tariffs on processed agricultural goods, under the EEC GSP scheme adopted by Britain. The *ad hoc* modifications negotiated by the six only partly reduced this restriction of access although the removal of tariffs on their cotton textile exports to the UK does also have to be put into the balance.

Those who argued that British entry led to an overall worsening in Third World access to markets maintained that the adoption by the UK of the EEC GSP scheme was itself a major illiberal move. Even as modified in 1973, the restrictions on access to the UK for agricultural products, and the replacement of (escape clause protected) free access under the UK's GSP scheme, by quota-bound access, was claimed to restrict access significantly. The freedom from quotas (which might have restricted tariff-free access), negotiated under the Lomé Convention, was dismissed as irrelevant for industrial products, given the limited industrial production facilities in the beneficiary countries. Such industrial exports as ACP could send to the EEC were unlikely to approach the quota limits of the GSP scheme. The limited concessions negotiated on processed agricultural products were also dismissed as too small to be of any real significance. Possibly the most telling argument, among the many advanced by those concerned that UK entry worsened the trade position of the Third World, centred on the increased preferences afforded to each other by the EEC members, and by them collectively to the rump of EFTA. These preferences effectively eroded the protection afforded to the Third World. With preferential margins already reduced by the Kennedy Round of tariff cuts, GSP and Lomé preferences offered beneficiaries only limited protection against competition from the USA and Canada, South Africa, the socialist countries and Japan.

With respect to the effects of British entry into the EEC on access to European markets for imports from Third World countries, it is, then, relatively easy to identify the issues. The negotiating positions were well publicised and the debate was reasonably open to public scrutiny. It is relatively simple to associate cause and effect. The economist trying to establish the significance of those effects for trade flows faces two problems, however: first, to isolate their influence from all other forces affecting those flows; and second, to estimate their quantitative significance. Neither problem has an easy solution. They are complicated for the period subsequent to the completion of entry negotiations (taken to include the 1973 renegotiations on the GSP and those establishing the Lomé Convention) by the difficulty of identifying the impact of UK membership on the evolution of EEC policy.

UK INFLUENCE IN THE EEC SINCE ENTRY

The entry negotiations (and the Labour government's renegotiations) took place in the full glare of national and international publicity. The objectives of the UK government were constantly enunciated by politicians and officials and disseminated in a variety of documents. Successes in the negotiations were well publicised. Once Britain became a full member, however, statements of position and subsequent manoeuvring on EEC policy towards the Third World move behind the closed doors of the bureaucratic world of EEC committees and councils. Attributable documentation on national positions taken in those committees and councils is non-existent and the only evidence available to researchers is the opinions of those participants to which they have access. This normally means officials of the Commission of the European Communities deputed to respond to enquiries, and government officials.

Participants in closed-door negotiations, often taking place late into the night in smoke-filled rooms, are usually partisan and tend to have conflicting memories. Thus, while it is possible to relate the actual evolution of policy over the period since UK entry, it is not possible to ascribe any element in that evolving policy with scientific precision to any national source.

During the period 1973 to 1980, the Commission took much of the lead in proposing to liberalise the GSP. Its proposals ran ahead of the willingness of the member states to adopt them. The moves on improved treatment for least developed countries, the reduction in the number of quota-bound sensitive items, and the movement of the base years, are generally considered to have been led by the North European countries, especially Germany and Holland. They would have been adopted even if Britain had not been a member. The only liberalising initiative generally recognised to have been taken by Britain was again that on processed agricultural products.

Only when substantial controversy breaks out – as it did in 1982 over the agreements for textiles and sugar imports – does a national position become publicly exposed. Before examining specific issues, the broad lines of evolution of EEC policy will be described.

CHANGES IN THE EEC'S ORIGINAL GSP SCHEME

The EEC's GSP scheme underwent a series of changes over its original span of life, from 1971 to 1981. Apart from the changes in 1973 already mentioned, a number of modifications were introduced which could be described as liberalising in the sense of expanding potential market access. The most significant modifications were in the area of processed agricultural products. Each year's annual review has tended to increase the number of such products on which preferences were granted, from 147 in 1974 to 310 in 1979. In addition while most of these items were still subject to an average tariff of 12 per cent, giving a preferential margin of four percentage points, the number of items allowed duty-free treatment was 73 in 1979. No quantitative limits were imposed on the imports which could benefit from those improved preferences except for six products – soluble coffee, cocoa butter, Virginia tobacco, cigar wrapper tobacco and canned pineapples in cubes or slices – where quotas were imposed to protect ACP states' benefits under the Lomé Convention.

Quantitative limitations were also eased in two ways. First, the base year on which the quotas were based was changed,[3] as were the regulations on country shares. Secondly, some products were moved off the sensitive list, where the quotas were rigidly enforced, to the semi-sensitive and non-sensitive lists, where they were applied on a discretionary basis or not at all. In addition, for eight least developed countries not benefiting from Lomé Convention preferences, all quantitative limitations on semi-sensitive and non-sensitive items were abolished, thus removing the uncertainty over their imposition should future growth in such trade take place. For members of the ASEAN, Central American Common Market and Andean Group associations of states, another liberalisation was introduced in 1975: the highly restrictive rules of origin for benefiting from the GSP were modified to allow a product to undergo a series of cumulative processes in different members of a group before being exported to the EEC.

THE RENEWAL OF THE GSP SCHEME

On 1 January 1981, a new GSP was introduced, replacing the old one whose ten-year life had expired. In the negotiation of this new scheme, the UK is universally acknowledged to have taken an illiberal protectionist line. The basic changes in the new scheme concerned industrial products. These were split into two groups: non-sensitive items were afforded duty-free access subject only to statistical surveillance, an escape clause, and the rules of origin. The other group of 128 products consisted of two categories: a semi-sensitive category, of products which were subject to ceilings on duty-free imports from each beneficiary country but with no overall quota; and a sensitive list. The sensitive category includes chemicals, leather goods, footwear, rubber goods, miscellaneous metal products, electronic goods and a variety of manufactured consumer products. For these sensitive items certain beneficiary countries were designated as 'competitive' on the basis of their previous exports to the EEC, and subjected to a tariff quota limiting duty-free imports and also to limits on the share of that quota which could be sent to any one EEC market. For less competitive suppliers the restriction was only a ceiling on total duty-free exports to the Community as a whole; if a country hits this ceiling three years in a row it is classified as competitive and made subject to the more restrictive tariff quota. According to officials participating in the negotiation, this criterion for defining competitiveness was insisted on by Britain, and was more restrictive than criteria suggested by other members and the Commission itself. It led to a larger number of countries being subjected to tariff quotas than would have resulted from the application of any of the other criteria. Britain also pressed, apparently successfully, for reductions in the size of some of the quotas, and, following representations from ICI, insisted on a range of chemical products being classified as sensitive, and having tariff quotas imposed on GSP imports from Libya, Venezuela, Romania, China, Brazil and South Korea.

THE RENEGOTIATION OF THE LOMÉ CONVENTION

The other major internal issue concerning EEC trade relations with Third World countries after the completion of British entry negotiations was the renegotiation in 1979 of the Lomé Convention. Imports of industrial products from ACP states were afforded duty-free entry into the EEC under Lomé I, subject only to an escape clause and the rules of origin. The only scope for liberalisation in the negotiations for Lomé II therefore covered these restrictions and the treatment of agricultural products. In the event, the range of preference margins on agricultural products was extended to cover tomatoes, carrots, onions, asparagus, arrowroot, mushrooms and guava and passion fruit juices and preserves; there was a 9 per cent increase in the amount of beef and veal allowed in with a 90 per cent cut in import levies; and the annual increase in the quota for duty-free imports of rum was augmented slightly. Neither the escape clause nor the rules of origin were liberalised, although the EEC declared that the escape clause would not be invoked for 'protectionist purposes or to hamper structural development'. There is no evidence available to suggest that Britain took any lead in pressing for the acceptance of even these meagre concessions. There is evidence, however, that Britain almost sabotaged the whole negotiation process by pressing for the insertion of a clause preventing ACP states from benefiting from the provisions of the Convention if they had unacceptable records on human rights. This pressure apparently arose from the humiliation Prime Minister Callaghan felt he had suffered at the hands of President Amin of Uganda.

The sugar protocol attached to the Lomé Convention was negotiated as part of British entry arrangements, to compensate Commonwealth sugar producers for the abolition of the Commonwealth Sugar Agreement. Although attached to the Lomé Convention it has an indefinite timescale of operation. It contains the proviso that amendments could be negotiated from 1981. In 1981 the UK attempted to amend the protocol with a view to reducing the value of access. The British attack was not on the guarantees on access or the price but on the equality of treatment as to increases in the guaranteed prices. In the 1981/2 negotiations, Britain attempted to restrict the price increase for ACP sugar to 7.5 per cent while that being offered to EEC producers was 8.5 per cent. The British argument, that the margin was required to cover higher refining costs for cane sugar, was repudiated by the British refining industry. The British position held up agreement for several months before it was forced to retract. In the meantime a great deal of damage was done to UK/ACP relations.

THE RENEGOTIATION OF THE MULTIFIBRE AGREEMENT

The only other specifically EEC/Third World trade negotiations which have taken place since British entry concerned the bilateral deals on textiles negotiated in the context of the GATT Multifibre Agreement (MFA). Here Britain and France led the protectionist lobby which succeeded eventually in forcing an agreement which reduces potential access for textiles from the Third World to EEC markets. The product and country coverage of the MFA was extended and the annual growth allowed in the quotas was reduced, in some cases almost to zero. The coverage extensions reduce the absolute size of potential access for Third World textiles into the EEC, while the growth rate restrictions will almost certainly ensure that the Third World share of the EEC market in many products will fall once economic activity redevelops after the recession.

THE BRITISH POSITION IN TRADE POLICY NEGOTIATIONS

The negotiations on sugar and textiles took place partly, in both cases, in contexts where both EEC and Third World delegations participated: the ACP/EEC Council for sugar and the GATT for textiles. As a result, the parties threatened by the illiberal position being taken by Britain had the information and the interest to expose Britain publicly in order to muster support from the development lobbies in the EEC's member states. This publicity makes the identification of the British position easier than it can be when the negotiations are 'private' and internal to the EEC, when participants have to be identified and approached directly, and may be reluctant to identify national positions. However, the evidence that is available from these sources indicates that, subsequent to the negotiation and implementation of arrangements for Commonwealth countries at the time of British entry to the EEC, and the harmonisation of the GSP schemes, Britain has on no occasion taken a position which could be described as liberal, in terms of improved potential market access. On the contrary, on the occasions when it has been possible to identify national positions, those of the UK have been illiberal both in absolute terms and relative to those of other members of the EEC.

This statement needs qualification, however, if its significance is to be interpreted correctly. As has been explained, focusing attention solely on potential market access can give distorted pictures of the situation, with the direction of bias going either way. For while a country may remove visible trade barriers on imports from a given country, it may remove a more extensive range of barriers on imports from other countries on a more liberal basis (giving wider preferential margins) so that relatively, the position of the first country has worsened. As has already been indicated, this was the case when, following entry to the EEC, the UK liberalised its trade policy towards the other eight members of the EEC and the remaining countries of EFTA more than it did for Third World countries under the GSP and Lomé Convention. In addition to their worsened relative position, in terms of trade policy effects on market access, the absolute position of the Third World worsened as preferential margins were eroded through GATT negotiated reductions in MFN tariffs. Therefore the change by the UK to an illiberal approach was within the context of an EEC trade policy frame, which was itself becoming, comparatively speaking, increasingly illiberal. Thus while direct commercial policy was apparently offering increased potential access, actual conditions were worsening in relative terms. And as the EEC proceeded to offer a series of special preferential arrangements for Mediterranean basin countries under various associations (as part of prospective membership arrangements in the case of Greece) this relative position continued to worsen. The special arrangements on textiles with Portugal and East European countries (the latter under the outward processing arrangements) have, in addition, worsened the relative and absolute access position of Third World textile exporters to the EEC, who are constrained by the MFA.

The second qualification needed to help evaluate the UK's position on trade relations with Third World countries is based on a comparison of changes in the policy frame of these relations with changes in the domestic policy treatment of domestic producers, who are in competition with potential beneficiaries of liberalised trade policies *vis-à-vis* the Third World. In other words, the significance of any reduction of trade barriers on imports is reduced to the extent that domestic policies are changed to improve artificially the competitive position of domestic producers of substitutes for these imports. Even a casual observer of domestic British economic policy, as influenced by EEC membership, cannot have failed to notice the increasingly extensive and intensive protective involvement of government in agriculture and industry. In some cases the motive has been purely protective, as subsidies and other support measures have been granted to companies to allow them to survive competition from increased imports following trade liberalisation. In other cases the motive has been more local, aimed at restricting the socioeconomic decline of regions. In both cases the outcome is the same – the potential growth in imports, which the trade liberalisation moves alone could have been expected to generate, is reduced.[4]

These two qualifications show how it is possible for the UK to proclaim a stance of increased liberality in trade relations with the Third World while ensuring that the ability of beneficiaries to increase exports to the UK is reduced. In the EEC context it is as if the members of the Community are walking up a downward moving escalator, but the UK is walking more slowly so that the gap between it and the others is widening, while all are moving backwards.

Before turning to the difficulties involved in attempting to quantify the effects of changes in trade policy, the actual level of UK imports should be considered in order to put the trends in perspective. In terms of actual imports the UK still imports more from the Third World than all fellow members of the EEC except West Germany and more than Germany too in terms of shares of total expenditure. The ratio of West German income to UK income in 1980 was roughly 3.5 to 1 while the ratio of total imports from the Third World (IMF definition) was only about 1.41 to 1. In terms of shares of imports, the UK share of its total imports in 1980 which it obtained from the Third World (again using the IMF definition) was 14.2 per cent compared to 12.8 per cent for West Germany and 11.3 per cent for France. Only in the cases of Greece (19.7 per cent) and Italy (15.4 per cent) was this ratio higher and in both cases trade with Balkan and Mediterranean countries – classified by the IMF as developing – made up a significant part of this figure. In terms of the metaphor of the earlier paragraph, the UK starting position is in fact higher up the escalator than its EEC partners so that its relative illiberality in recent years is only narrowing the lead that exists between it and its partners (again as they all move backwards).

So far the analysis of this (and the preceding) section has been concerned with the evolution of policy positions over a relatively brief period. It has pointed out the conceptual and practical difficulties to be faced in attempts to identify changes in positions on trade policy towards the Third World, and in assessing the liberality of those changes in terms of their effect on potential market access. It has shown that a liberal trade position does not necessarily imply any improvement in the welfare of the poorer sections of society in beneficiary countries. Similarly what appears to be an illiberal stance, or a move to a less liberal position in trade policy, may not truly reflect the disposition of the government but only the compromise it has had to reach between its own liberal position and the illiberal position of powerful domestic interest groups pressing for even more protectionist measures. In the case of the UK, at least, there is the added twist that some apparently illiberal measures are designed to protect immigrant groups against competition from imports from their countries of origin: measures on cotton textiles and Indian processed foodstuffs fall into this category.

We must now conclude, therefore, that even when we can overcome research problems and identify country positions in trade negotiations, and can select an unambiguous criterion of liberality, there will still be serious problems of evaluation. First, an apparently liberal bilateral position may be illiberal when evaluated in its multilateral trade policy context. Second, a liberal trade policy position may be dominated by the overriding influence of domestic economic policies which limit the effect of the trade policies. Third, illiberal moves on its trade policy may still leave a country's overall trade involvement with Third World countries on a more liberal footing than those of other countries. Fourth, an apparently illiberal move on trade policy may represent a major victory, for liberal forces in the government, over protectionist lobbies. Fifth, and finally, there is no unequivocal measure of liberality in trade policy and the usual criterion of potential market access can be dismissed as irrelevant by those factions of the development lobby which place priority on measures which have a direct impact on the welfare of the poor.

EEC IMPORTS: THE TRADE DATA

Whether or not it is possible to identify a government's position on trade policy it seems reasonable to argue that its position will be exposed by 'the facts'. In other words, the overall effect of changes in a country's trade policy (and other policies which impinge on trade flows) should be 'visible' in trade statistics.

TABLE 9.1   *EEC impor*

Imports to (1)	From total world (2)	From all developed countries (3)	EEC(6) (4)	EEC(9) (5)	Rump EFTA (6)	Other developed countries (7)	All developm countri (8)
EEC(6)	556 290	396 087	233 031	277 474	41 474	79 859	142 91
EEC(9)	714 625	502 156	281 353	340 411	55 568	109 020	168 37:
UK	117 902	80 337	39 194	45 717	9 817	24 901	22 31
Denmark	19 302	15 830	6 971	9 327	3 913	2 611	2 12
Eire	11 132	9 902	2 157	7 893	364	1 649	1 01
							Percenta
EEC(6)	99.2ᵃ	69.9	41.2	49.0	7.3	14.1	2!
EEC(9)	97.4	70.3	39.4	47.6	7.8	15.3	2:
UK	88.8	68.1	33.2	38.8	8.3	21.1	1!
Denmark	97.3	82.0	36.1	48.3	20.3	13.5	1
Eire	99.4	89.0	19.4	70.9	3.3	14.8	!

NOTES
Column 3:   All DD–OECD – (Turkey + Yugoslavia). Includes Greece and Portugal.
Column 6:   Rump EFTA is Austria, Iceland, Norway, Portugal, Sweden and Switzerland.
Column 7:   Canada, US, Japan, Australia, New Zealand, Finland, Greece and Spain.
Column 8:   All DVG = all non OECD + Turkey – Comecon.
Column 9:   Yaoundé + Commonwealth ACP + Others. (ACP = African, Caribbean and Pacific group of states as in 1980).
Column 10: Yaoundé states are Benin, Burundi, Cameroon, Central African Republic, Chad, Congo, Gabon, Ivory Coast, Madagascar, Mali, Mauritania, Niger, Rwanda, Senegal, Somalia, Togo, U. Volta, Zaire.
Column 12: Commonwealth ACP are Gambia, Sierra Leone, Ghana, Nigeria, Uganda, Kenya, Tanzania, Zambia, Malawi, Mauritius, Seychelles, Botswana, Lesotho, Swaziland, Jamaica, Bahamas, Barbados, Dominica, St Lucia, Grenada, Trinidad, Guyana, PNG, Solomon Is., Fiji, Tonga.

Tables 9.1 and 9.2 give data on total imports by the EEC broken down into the original six members and the nine, and also into individual country data for the new members. The import data are further broken down for a variety of sources, and are for the post-enlargement year 1980 and the pre-enlargement year 1970. These data show that the original EEC's imports from developing countries increased significantly, their share increasing from 20.7 per cent to 25.2 per cent of total imports. The ACP share of the EEC (6) market also rose, from 3.8 per cent to 4.0 per cent, and here the expectation that Commonwealth countries would benefit at the expense of Yaoundé countries appears to be corroborated as the former increased their shares from 1.3 per cent to 2.4 per cent in the case of those given Lomé status and from 0.7 per cent to 1.0 per cent for Asian Commonwealth countries; the share of the Yaoundé countries meanwhile fell

80 ($ million)

ACP (9)	Yaoundé (10)	Other ACP (11)	Commonwealth developing countries (ACP) (12)	Asian Commonwealth countries (13)	Hong Kong (14)	Other developing countries (15)	COMECON centrally planned (16)
2 604	7 506	1 356	13 742	5 618	2 986	111 711	23 215
5 836	7 899	1 473	16 454	7 714	4 862	129 973	26 326
2 789	303	98	2 388	1 824	1 739	15 959	2 133
277	59	19	199	186	97	1 569	832
155	30	0	125	86	40	735	147
ares							
4.0	1.3	0.2	2.4	1.0	0.5	19.7	4.1
3.6	1.1	0.2	2.3	1.1	0.7	18.2	3.7
2.4	0.3	0.1	2.0	1.5	1.5	13.5	1.8
1.4	0.3	0.1	1.0	0.1	0.1	8.1	4.3
1.4	0.3	0	1.1	0.8	0.4	6.6	1.3

N.B. Kiribati and Tuvalu are not specified independently in OECD figures (total pop. 66 000).

Column 11: Other ACP are Sudan, Guinea–Bissau, Cape Verde Is., Guinea, Liberia, Sao Tome Principe, Equatorial Guinea, Ethiopia, Comore Is., Surinam, W. Samoa. N.B. Djibouti is not given by OECD.

Column 13: Pakistan, Bangladesh, India, Sri Lanka, Malaysia, Singapore.

Column 15: Column 6 – Columns 7, 11 and 12.

a The failure of % to sum to 100 may be explained by the large items in the row 'secret' at end of OECD table, and rounding errors.

SOURCE Prepared by Nancy Wall from OECD Commodity Trade Statistics, Series C, 1971 and 1981.

from 2.1 per cent to 1.3 per cent. An overall shift to more liberal access following the introduction of the GSP and the GATT negotiations appears to be substantiated by the growth in the share of other developing countries from 15.8 per cent to 19.7 per cent. UK imports from Commonwealth developing countries, however, fell – from 4.9 per cent to 2.0 per cent of total UK imports in the case of the Commonwealth members of the ACP and from 2.8 per cent to 1.5 per cent in the case of the Asian Commonwealth countries; at the same time UK imports from the EEC (6) increased, the share rising from 19.7 per cent to 33.2 per cent. The picture of the EEC becoming more liberal in market access terms while the UK became less so after entry is also apparently evident in the fall in the share of the UK market held by non-Commonwealth developing countries – from 20.2 per cent to 13.5 per cent.

Every schoolboy knows that statistics can 'lie'. And this is true of trade statistics, probably more so than of any other form of economic data. The data in Tables 9.1 and 9.2 are as reported by OECD importing countries and as converted by the OECD into current US dollars. The difficulties include the technical problem of country name and grouping changes and secrecy;[5] the quality problems arising out of

TABLE 9.2   *EEC impor*

Imports to (1)	From total world (2)	From all developed countries (3)	EEC(6) (4)	EEC(9) (5)	Rump EFTA (6)	Other developed countries (7)	All developir countrie (8)
EEC(6)	88 431	66 434	42 802	47 681	5 986	14 105	18 273
EEC(9)	116 063	84 782	48 781	56 564	9 270	21 503	25 376
UK	21 678	13 257	4 264	5 698	2 148	6 593	6 460
Denmark	4 385	3 739	1 457	2 068	1 081	608	477
Eire	1 569	1 352	259	1 117	55	197	166
							Percentag
EEC(6)	99.2	75.1	48.4	53.9	6.8	16.0	20.
EEC(9)	98.3	73.0	42.0	48.7	8.0	18.5	21.
UK	94.1	61.2	19.7	26.3	9.9	30.4	29.
Denmark	96.8	82.3	33.2	47.2	24.7	13.9	10.
Eire	98.8	86.2	16.5	71.2	3.5	12.6	10.

NOTES
Column 6:   N.B. in 1970 Iceland had only just joined. Figures are included here but would not yet
            be affected by membership.
All columns as for 1980 *except:*

smuggling and incorrect source classification; and industrial action and incompetence in statistical offices. In addition, there are the problems of economic interpretation. The data reflect the impact of all the many and various influences on the prices and quantities of trade flows, and not just changes in trade policy. There are further problems associated with reducing the national currency data (itself the result of conversion from accounting data in trading currencies) into a common numeraire – the current US dollar.

The most dramatic factor influencing trade flows between the EEC (6) and (9) and developing countries over the period 1970 to 1980 was the increased price of oil. The influence of this single factor was greater than the influence of all the trade policy changes by the members of the EEC (9). Tables 9.3 and 9.4 show EEC imports in current US dollars from the same source groupings as Tables 9.1 and 9.2 except that all oil-exporting countries in the Third World have been removed from the data. All importing groups (except Denmark on its own) now show falls in shares from all developing countries as a single group: from 13.4 per cent to 12.7 per cent for EEC (6), from 14.7 per cent to 12.4 per cent for EEC (9), from 22.6 per cent to 12.5 per cent for the UK and from 7.1 per cent to 4.7 per cent for Eire. And, again, except for

70 ($ million)

ACP (9)	Yaoundé (10)	Other ACP (11)	Common-wealth developing countries (ACP) (12)	Asian Common-wealth countries (13)	Hong Kong (14)	Other developing countries (15)	COMECON centrally planned (16)
363	1 863	381	1 119	649	275	13 986	3 049
606	1 950	421	2 236	1 297	601	18 872	3 921
173	76	37	1 059	612	300	4 375	681
48	8	2	37	19	22	388	158
23	2	0	20	18	3	122	32

ares

3.8	2.1	0.4	1.3	0.7	0.3	15.8	3.4
4.0	1.7	0.4	1.9	1.1	0.5	16.3	3.4
5.4	0.4	0.2	4.9	2.8	1.4	20.2	3.1
1.1	0.2	0	0.8	0.4	0.5	8.8	3.6
1.5	0.1	0	1.3	1.1	0.2	7.8	2.0

Column 12: No figures for Seychelles, Dominica, St Lucia, Grenada, PNG, Solomon Is., Fiji, Tonga.
Column 11: No figures for Cape Verde Is., Sao Tome Principe, Comore Is. and Western Samoa.

SOURCE   As Table 9.1.

TABLE 9.3   *EEC imports 1980 (other than petr*

Imports to (1)	From total world (2)	From all developed countries (3)	EEC(6) (4)	EEC(9) (5)	Rump EFTA (6)	Other developed countries (7)	deve cou
EEC(6)	484 818	396 087	233 031	277 474	41 474	79 859	61
EEC(9)	623 364	502 156	281 353	340 411	55 568	109 020	77
UK	109 277	80 337	39 194	45 717	9 817	24 901	13
Denmark	18 652	15 830	6 971	9 327	3 913	2 611	1
Eire	10 618	9 920	2 157	7 893	364	1 649	
							Perc
EEC(6)	99.2	81.7	48.1	57.2	8.6	16.5	
EEC(9)	97.1	80.5	45.1	54.6	8.9	17.5	
UK	88.0	73.5	35.9	41.8	9.0	22.8	
Denmark	97.3	84.9	37.3	50.0	21.0	14.0	
Eire	99.5	93.4	20.3	74.3	3.4	15.5	

NOTES
Oil exporters are excluded from totals altogether. These are:
Yaoundé: Gabon
Commonwealth: Trinidad and Tobago, Nigeria.

TABLE 9.4   *EEC imports, 1970 (oth*

Imports to (1)	From total world (2)	From all developed countries (3)	EEC(6) (4)	EEC(9) (5)	Rump EFTA (6)	Other developed countries (7)	deve cou
EEC(6)	80 981	66 434	42 802	47 681	5 986	14 105	10
EEC(9)	106 333	84 782	48 781	56 564	9 270	21 503	15
UK	19 674	13 257	4 264	5 698	2 148	6 593	4
Denmark	4 167	3 739	1 457	2 068	1 081	608	
Eire	1 511	1 352	259	1 117	55	197	
							Perc
EEC(6)	99.0	82.0	52.9	58.9	7.4	17.4	
EEC(9)	98.1	79.7	45.9	53.2	8.7	20.2	
UK	93.5	67.4	21.7	29.0	10.9	33.5	
Denmark	99.7	89.7	35.0	49.6	25.9	14.6	
Eire	98.7	89.5	17.1	73.9	3.6	13.0	

NOTES
Column 15: No figures are given for Qatar.

m developing countries) ($ million)

	Yaoundé (10)	Other ACP (11)	Commonwealth developing countries (ACP) (12)	Asian Commonwealth countries (13)	Hong Kong (14)	Other developing countries (15)	COMECON centrally planned (16)
	6 453	1 356	3 027	5 618	2 986	42 007	23 215
	6 817	1 473	5 126	7 714	4 862	51 122	26 326
	278	98	1 981	1 824	1 739	7 766	2 133
	55	19	34	186	97	1 088	832
	30	0	84	86	40	262	147
.2	1.3	0.3	0.6	1.2	0.6	8.7	4.8
.2	1.1	0.2	0.8	1.2	0.8	8.2	4.2
.2	0.3	0.1	1.8	1.7	1.6	7.1	2.0
.6	0.3	0.1	0.2	1.0	0.5	5.8	4.5
.1	0.3	0	0.8	0.8	0.4	2.5	1.4

Other DVG: Saudi Arabia, Iran, Kuwait, Iraq, Venezuela, Libya, United Arab Emirates, Indonesia, Mexico, Algeria, Qatar, Oman, Angola.

SOURCE   As Table 9.1.

m oil from developing countries) ($ million)

	Yaoundé (10)	Other ACP (11)	Commonwealth developing countries (ACP) (12)	Asian Commonwealth countries (13)	Hong Kong (14)	Other developing countries (15)	COMECON centrally planned (16)
	1 749	381	610	649	275	7 159	3 049
	1 832	421	1 353	1 297	601	10 143	3 921
	73	37	716	612	300	2 717	681
	7	2	10	19	22	197	158
	2	0	15	18	3	69	32
.4	2.2	0.5	0.8	0.8	0.3	8.8	3.8
.4	1.7	0.4	1.3	1.2	0.6	9.5	3.7
.2	0.4	0.2	3.6	3.1	1.5	13.8	3.5
.5	0.2	0	0.2	0.5	0.5	4.7	3.8
.2	0.1	0	1.0	1.2	0.2	4.6	2.1

SOURCE   As Table 9.1.

Denmark, and for Eire's imports from the Yaoundé group, import shares of all ACP country groupings in the EEC (6) fell from 0.8 per cent to 0.6 per cent while the Asian Commonwealth countries' share rose from 0.8 per cent to 1.2 per cent and Hong Kong's share increased from 0.3 per cent to 0.6 per cent. All developing country groupings saw their share of the UK market fall over the period as the share of EEC (6) in that market rose from 21.7 per cent to 35.9 per cent.

It can be seen that after allowance is made for the oil price increase the earlier conclusions are mostly reversed and the EEC (6) and the UK both apparently became less liberal in terms of market access, as did Eire overall, while Denmark alone became more liberal. However the data do not show what would have happened to trade flows in the absence of the various changes in trade policy. Although Tables 9.3 and 9.4 show most major Third World to EEC trade flows falling relatively, they also show that all such flows increased in absolute terms as measured in current US dollars. The absolute increases in current dollar and percentage terms are given in Table 9.5. And now signs of moves to liberality in trade policy by the EEC (6) appear again as their imports from all developing countries rose faster (468 per cent) over the period than did trade among themselves (444 per cent), although diversion towards imports from the new members is reflected in the higher figures of 481 per cent for imports from EEC (9) and of 593 per cent from the rump of EFTA. The aggregate developing country figures hide the fact that at 295 per cent the slowest growing

TABLE 9.5   *Growth of imports by source, 1970–*

Imports to (1)	From total world (2)	From all developed countries (3)	EEC(6) (4)	EEC(9) (5)	Rump EFTA (6)	Other developed countries (7)	All developing countri (8)
EEC(6)	403 837	329 653	190 229	229 793	35 488	65 754	50 624
	498%	496%	444%	481%	593%	466%	468
EEC(9)	517 031	417 374	232 572	283 847	46 298	87 517	61 468
	486%	492%	477%	502%	499%	407%	393
UK	89 603	67 080	34 930	40 019	7 669	18 308	9 230
	455%	506%	819%	702%	357%	278%	207
Denmark	14 485	12 091	5 514	7 259	2 832	2 003	1 220
	348%	323%	378%	351%	262%	329%	471
Eire	9 107	8 568	1 898	6 776	309	1 452	394
	603%	634%	733%	607%	562%	737%	365

SOURCE   Prepared by Nancy Wall from Tables 9.2 and 9.4.

flow for the EEC (6) from developing countries is that from the supposedly most preferred group: the ACP. The UK again has a slower overall growth of imports from the total developing country group (207 per cent) and from the ACP (185 per cent) although the increase in its imports from Yaoundé ACP countries was greater at 281 per cent than the increase in its imports from Commonwealth ACP States (177 per cent) and Asian Commonwealth countries (198 per cent). This shift in the UK balance from Commonwealth to Yaoundé is the reverse of that by the EEC (6), where the 269 per cent increase in imports from the Yaoundé groups is more than matched by the increased flows from the Commonwealth ACP (396 per cent), the Asian Commonwealth (766 per cent) and Hong Kong (986 per cent).

If, then, we assess the effects of changes in trade policy in terms of relative rates of growth of non-oil imports, the EEC (6) appears to have become more liberal in access to imports from developing countries as a whole. However, its old Yaoundé associates have lost out as a result of this. The reverse is true of the UK where, when measured in these growth terms, joining the EEC appears to have made it less liberal towards the Third World in general and particularly so in the case of Commonwealth countries.

The difficulty of assessing whether or not the data indicate liberality in trade policy is compounded when an attempt is made to take account of the various price changes embodied in the data. The data used above are current monetary values data, as converted into a

:luding petroleum oil from developing countries)

CP 9)	Yaoundé (10)	Other ACP (11)	Common-wealth developing countries (ACP) (12)	Asian Common-wealth countries (13)	Hong Kong (14)	Other developing countries (15)	COMECON centrally planned (16)
6	4 704	975	2 417	4 969	2 711	34 848	20 166
5%	269%	256%	396%	766%	986%	487%	661%
1	4 985	1 052	3 773	6 417	4 261	40 979	22 405
2%	272%	250%	279%	495%	709%	404%	571%
0	205	61	1 265	1 212	1 439	5 049	1 452
5%	281%	165%	177%	198%	480%	186%	213%
8	48	17	24	167	75	891	674
0%	686%	850%	240%	879%	341%	452%	427%
6	28	0	69	68	37	193	115
3%	1 400%	0%	460%	377%	1 233%	280%	359%

common currency using a set of exchange rates. To interpret the data correctly in terms of liberality requires a knowledge of changes in the real flows of goods and services, i.e. net of the effects of inflation and exchange rate changes. To uncover these real flows in monetary data is difficult: it requires correction for price changes and exchange rate changes. Leaving aside the difficulties of correcting for exchange rate changes, the basic problem of correcting for price changes is that owing to very limited availability of data on price changes for individual trade flows, the level of aggregation at which the correction can be made is necessarily high. The choice of price deflators involves judgement on the selection of price series, on the weight of each of those series in the aggregate index, and on how many different commodity bundles and sets of weights to use when making intercountry comparisons. However, whatever deflators are used, except in the unlikely case that all prices are changing at the same rate, comparisons in 'real' data will be different from those made in 'nominal' data – sometimes markedly so. For example, all the above analysis was heavily affected by the rapid growth in trade in manufactures among the EEC (9).

Over the period 1970–80, trade among the nine increased by 501 per cent while imports of the nine from all non-oil-exporting developing countries increased by 564 per cent. The UN Yearbook of International Trade Statistics (1979 edition) shows that the unit value[6] of trade among developed market economies grew by about 235 per cent while the comparative increase in the unit values of their imports from the Third World was 381 per cent. Adjusted in this way for price effects, the comparison of real flows changes so that tests of hypotheses may reach different conclusions. In the rates of growth analysis above, for example, rates of growth of trade among the EEC states would be increased relative to the rates of growth of their imports from the Third World. Consequently comparison of real trade flows would suggest that the EEC has become less liberal than the current value data suggested. Thus the UN quantity index shows developed market economies, trade among themselves increasing by 152 per cent while their imports from the Third World grew by 139 per cent.

The process of correcting for price changes, however, uncovers two other problems associated with this type of evaluation exercise: the so-called terms of trade problem, and the aggregation problem. The terms of trade problem involves the need for a separate deflating exercise in order to arrive at a sense of the 'value' to a country of any given change in its real exports. Ignoring complications involving capital flows and servicing, a country exports in order to raise foreign exchange to finance its imports. So the relevant deflation exercise converts the actual monetary value of its exports by the price changes of its imports, giving in this way an indication of the 'purchasing power' of its export receipts. EEC (9) imports from developing countries have been growing more slowly, in quantity terms, than the growth in intra-EEC trade. Nevertheless, correction for the terms of trade effect would indicate that the value of those increased imports from the Third World is increased in terms of their purchasing power over EEC exports.

The aggregation problem refers to the fact that any analysis carried out in terms of heterogeneous groups such as the EEC (9), 'the Third World', 'ACP states', Commonwealth developing countries, hides the existence of the varying experiences of different countries within those groups. The difficulties associated with using an increased trade flow as an indication of a liberalisation of trade policy can easily be envisaged, in view of the complications already outlined. For example while the aggregate data for 1970–80 of Tables 9.1–9.4 show an overall increase in UK imports from the ACP states, her imports, in current value terms, from Mauritania, the Gambia and Zambia actually fell over that period. Similarly the unit value changes in individual country trade flows vary widely; using the UN 1975 based data for 1978 (the latest available) the range was from 203 per cent for Sri Lanka to 93 per cent for Jordan. Disaggregated data show clearly the influence on trade flows of other factors, independent of changes in trade policy: for example, the figure just quoted for Sri Lanka for 1978 was almost double its value in 1977– 109 per cent. Year-to-year variations are also affected by supply-side conditions such as the weather, strikes, the formation of monopolies (e.g. OPEC), and natural disasters, revolutions and demand-side conditions such as boycotts and abrupt fashion changes. Longer-run trends are also affected by factors other than trade policy. Changes in technology, movements of international capital, technical assistance (private and official), the growth of synthetics, intergenerational changes in taste and variations in the levels of economic activity are particularly important. The use of aggregate data tends to obscure the intercountry differential effects of these factors; for example, the data on the unit value index for developing country exports to developed market economies include trade in petroleum products for which the unit value increased by 699 per cent while the unit value of the food category rose by 269 per cent, raw materials other than fuel by 243 per cent and chemicals, machinery and all other manufactures by only 222 per cent. In other words, the single most important factor in the explanation of the increase in the overall index was a non-trade policy factor which affected only a small minority of Third World countries: the formation of OPEC.

Given the most sophisticated techniques of modern econometrics – a subject still in its infancy – we still cannot identify and isolate all the various factors affecting trade flows, and so cannot allocate a quantitative significance to changes in trade policy. In addition, as we have seen, the underlying data have defects which can affect the impression a series gives. Even with an unambiguous criterion stated in unambiguous quantitative terms, the form and structure of the data chosen for a 'test' can be 'corrected' and/or varied to give different – often conflicting – impressions. The problem is compounded when the criterion is conceptually ambiguous and has no definitive quantitative form so that, for example, a given change in a trade flow can be legitimately described as reflecting both a liberal and an illiberal change in trade policy. In other words, the size and quality of the pudding vary according to the viewpoint of the eater. We are back at the starting-point of this chapter.

CONCLUSIONS

The introduction to this chapter suggested that sufficient time has now passed since the UK joined the EEC to justify raising questions as to its influence on EEC policy. This chapter has been addressed to the question of whether Britain had a liberalising influence on the EEC's trade policy towards the Third World. It has been argued that although the question may be put, it is impossible to give an unambiguous answer. The lack of consensus over the objectives for trade policy towards Third World countries means that there is no single, simple criterion for measuring its liberality. Even if an arbitrary criterion is accepted, the problems of identifying the potential affects of trade policy changes against a multipolicy background, and of associating any given changes with any single participant in negotiations, are mostly overwhelming. The argument that actual effects of trade policy changes should be visible in changed trade flows was also examined. The difficulties associated with using trade data for such purposes were briefly outlined and the conclusion drawn that the data do not unambiguously support either position.

In situations like this economists working in the normative, prescriptive branches of their subject tend to recall with envy the yardstick fixed in Trafalgar Square and the weights and measures inspectorate.

The fact that so many of the discussions of the political economy of the real world involve such nebulous concepts as 'liberal' explains why economists can be so frequently split in their views as to the appropriateness of any given policy change. This is why at the time of the negotiations over British entry to the EEC roughly half of the economists in British universities thought that membership would be in Britain's long-run economic interests, while half did not. And although 364 academic economists signed a letter condemning the present Conservative government's economic policies, an even larger number did not.

Evaluation in such situations necessarily involves a large element of judgement. In the present author's view, British entry had a once-for-all impact on EEC trade policy towards the Third World which did in theory increase potential access to EEC (9) markets. Since entry, however, the British position has been increasingly illiberal in this sense compared to its fellow members, although it has been liberal *vis-à-vis* domestic interest group pressures and a population increasingly disillusioned with Third World governments and their representatives. To a large extent the overt liberal changes in trade policy have been outweighed by domestic economic policies which have increasingly determined the nature and quantity of trade flows. The only two apparently effective trade policy developments – the GATT-negotiated tariff reductions and the UNCTAD-sponsored GSP – would have occurred whether or not Britain had joined the EEC. The danger is that the increasingly ambitious interpretation of the 'liberality' of trade policies, pressed by the governments and representatives of some Third World countries, their supporters in the professional development lobbies in developed countries, and some international agencies, generates sterile conflicts. These divert attention away from more important issues. The quantity and quality of real resources flowing to the Third World countries, and improving the efficiency with which those resources are used to establish credible programmes for ameliorating the condition of the poor, are the fundamentally important issues. It is against this background that the concept of 'liberality' in economic relations between rich and poor countries should be seen.

ACKNOWLEDGEMENTS

Nancy Wall assisted in the preparation of the chapter. Comments on an earlier draft by Patrick Low are gratefully acknowledged.

NOTES AND REFERENCES

1. The removal of the tariff reduces the costs of production to the user of the raw materials in the importing country, and improves his competitive position *vis-à-vis* foreign suppliers.
2. The other six were already covered.
3. This applied to most products, but not to 'crisis' industries such as footwear and steel.
4. A full discussion, with examples, of how domestic UK policies have restricted UK imports can be found in *Public Assistance to Industries*, ed. W. M. Corden and G. Fels (London: Macmillan, 1976).
5. A substantial – possibly 10 per cent – share of UK imports in 1980 was classified as secret and not classified by source. This could have a marked effect on the figures for shares.
6. Unit value data incorporate both composition and price changes. No data on unit value changes for the country groupings covered in this chapter exist; the UN groupings are the closest proxy.

11 Political Institutions of the European Community: Functions and Future

JOHN PINDER

The functions of the European Community's political institutions are mainly economic, so their study must cross the frontiers of two disciplines: economics and political science. The student who is bold enough to do this risks annoying the specialists in both, by being insufficiently expert in either. But he also has the chance to identify significant elements that are less salient to those whose focus is in the heartland of one or the other discipline. In the given case such elements may be the policy instruments which are supposed to transmit the outcomes of the political process that interests political scientists into effects on the economy that are the major concern of economists.

Among the multitude of subjects that have been discussed in its institutions, the EC may be said to have had an historic impact on the economy with respect to three: the establishment of the common market, the Common Agricultural Policy and the Common Commercial (or external trade) Policy. To implement each of these policies the Community was given adequate common instruments. Where it has tried to execute policies through the several instruments of the member states, it has effected little, if any, change from the *status quo ante*; and where the common instruments have been inadequate, there have been correspondingly minor results. Thus, if there is a major function to be performed in common, the Community needs a major common instrument to perform it.

Whether radical change from the *status quo* is desirable or not is a question we will leave until later. But the founders of the Community certainly wanted radical change, much more radical than they in fact achieved. Robert Schuman, then French Foreign Minister, in announcing his plan to establish the European Coal and Steel Community (ECSC), said on 9 May 1950 that 'this proposal will build the first concrete foundation of a European federation which is indispensable to the preservation of peace'.[1] This aim explains the disparity between the scope of the Community's institutions, which look as if they are intended to be the basis for a system of parliamentary democracy, and the functions that the Community can effectively perform, which were then confined only to management of the coal and steel sectors of the economies of the six original member states. Jean Monnet, the first President of the High Authority of the ECSC, in his inaugural speech, stressed this federal character of 'the first European Community which merges a part of the national sovereignties and submits them to the common interest', showing that the High Authority, Assembly and Court were all independent of the member states, that the executive obtained its financial resources 'not by contributions from States, but from levies imposed directly on production' and that it was 'responsible, not to the States, but to a European Assembly'.[2]

This view of the Community institutions made sense only if the functions were to be extended far beyond policy for coal and steel. The attempt to do this through a European Defence Community, with the common instrument of a European Army and the institutions of a European Political Community, failed when the French National Assembly voted it down in 1954, although the treaty had been ratified by the five other member states of the ECSC. But the European Economic Community (EEC) and the European Atomic Energy Community (Euratom), established in 1958, extended the scope of the Community (EC) to a wide range of economic policies, and gave it a decisive role in policies relating to the internal market, agriculture and external trade. At the same time, however, the balance of power among the Community institutions was shifted, decisively in the event, away from the Parliament (as the Assembly came to be known) and the Commission (which the executives of the EEC and Euratom and, later, of the ECSC were called) and towards the intergovernmental Council of Ministers. The treaties gave the Commissions of the EEC and Euratom less scope for independent initiative than the High Authority of the ECSC; and, after a few years in which the Commission of the EEC nevertheless looked as if it might impel the Community towards federation as the founders had hoped, de Gaulle forced a showdown to clip the wings of the Commission and confine the Parliament to a peripheral role. The result was the 'Luxemburg compromise' of 1965, in which the French government made clear, and the other member governments accepted, that it would not be coerced by a majority vote in the Community institutions in any matter that it regarded as a vital national interest.

The EEC treaty had provided that, as the EEC passed through the three stages of its 'transitional period' of 12–15 years, the Council of Ministers would proceed from decision-taking by unanimous agreement to voting by qualified majority on a growing number of matters;[3] and it had been envisaged that the power of the Commission, with its right to put the policy proposals to the Council, would correspondingly grow. In fact the Council of Ministers, fortified by de Gaulle's *dé marche* and by the continued resurgence of the continental nation-states, increasingly imposed their will on the Commission instead. The role of the Parliament remained, as de Gaulle intended, peripheral; and the Economic and Social Committee, which could in a federal system complement the Parliament by articulating the views of the economic and social interests, became little more than a fifth wheel.

Although the federal elements in the institutions were thus much weaker than the founders had intended, the Community managed to perform the three functions for which it had been given major common instruments, as well as to facilitate a great deal of useful cooperation in other fields. The functions have often been performed slowly or weakly, as we shall see; but it cannot be said that the Community has failed to deliver a common market (even if many distortions and imperfections remain), a Common Agricultural Policy and a Common Commercial Policy. What the institutions have not been able to do is to secure major new policy instruments for the Community or major reforms of the existing policies: the Community has shown the capacity to continue its policies with the instruments it was given at the start, but not to initiate new or reformed policies that could approach these early ones in importance. The Community has been living on the capital with which its founders endowed it. The consequences of this will be considered as we examine the performance of the EC's institutions and instruments in the main fields of Community activity.

A COMMON MARKET SECURED BY COMMUNITY LAW

The founder governments of the EEC agreed that 'a merger of the separate markets is an absolute necessity' in order to achieve 'a powerful unit of production ... continuous expansion, increased stability, an accelerated raising of living standards, and the development of harmonious relations among the participating States'.[4] The function of the common market was to provide a large single market to accommodate the member countries' industrial development. How much of the tremendous subsequent growth of production was due to the common market is a matter of debate among economists. But it can hardly be denied that the removal of so many barriers and distortions from trade among the member states had major consequences for industry and trade; and these great changes were brought about by the instrument of common Community law.

For the removal of tariffs and quotas from trade among the member states, this law was embodied in detail in the original treaties. Where enforcement has been required, the agents have been the Commission in its role of 'watchdog of the treaties' and the Community's Court of Justice as the ultimate judicial authority. Since the Community does not dispose of its own police, armed forces, prisons or other means of physical coercion, it has to rely on the coercive powers of the member states to enforce the law on their citizens and other legal persons; and where, as in the case of tariffs and quotas, the perpetrators of any illegal acts are the states themselves, the states must be relied upon to comply voluntarily. So far they have usually done so, and the historic liberalisation of internal trade has been secured with little intervention by the Community institutions, save the Commission and sometimes the Court.

Tariffs and quotas are far from being the only distortions of economic transactions that cross frontiers, however. Markets for agricultural products and transport services are regulated; economic activity is subject to national laws relating to tax, competition, standards and many other matters; there are barriers to the movement across frontiers of services, capital and economic agents. The treaties provided for the removal of distortions in all these fields. But the changes in regulations were too complex to be defined in detail in the treaties, which could do no more than lay down a framework of principles and procedures to enable the Community institutions to make the necessary laws. Beyond the removal of tariffs and quotas, therefore, the creation of a common market depended on the Community's law-making capacity, which centred on the relationship between the Commission and the Council of Ministers.

The compromise which the founders of the Community devised between federal intentions and the fact of the nation-state was to give the Commission the initiative in proposing legislation and the Council the power to enact the proposals or reject them. Some very important laws were enacted in this way in the early years of the EEC, including the completion of the common external tariff, the structure of the Common Agricultural Policy and the basis of the competition policy. This inspired some political scientists to regard the Commission – Council relationship, which was for a time called the 'Community method', as an epoch-making innovation in international relations.[5] But even in those early, euphoric years, the decisions on agricultural and competition policy were forced through only thanks to a circumstance that gave the governments wanting those policies a special bargaining strength. The move at the end of 1961 from the first to the second stage of the transition period required the unanimous agreement of the member governments. All wanted the move to take place, but the French only on condition that agricultural decisions were taken; and the Germans insisted on the competition policy.[6] After these major decisions, the pace slowed, as de Gaulle curbed the Commission's initiative, the early euphoria evaporated and the practice of unanimous voting became entrenched. Thus agreement on a common form of value-added tax took some fifteen years to reach after being first mooted by the Commission.[7] While many other decisions on the removal of distortions did not take so long, the case of the form of VAT is far from unique, and there is now little talk of arriving at a common VAT rate as the Commission originally proposed. Nor is there much talk of the 'Community method'. The relationship between Commission and Council does not ensure a speedy taking of decisions, whenever these decisions would impinge on some interest in a member state, as the removal of non-tariff distortions is increasingly seen to do.

It might be expected that, where the hurdle of agreement in the Council no longer has to be negotiated, the Commission could ensure that Community law is executed without impediment. Thus once the Council had issued the regulations to give practical effect to the principles of competition policy enunciated in Articles 85 and 86 of the EEC treaty, the Commission was 'able to build up a policy incrementally and independently without continuous reference to the Council of Ministers and without the need to fight to achieve a consensus amongst the member states'.[8] But this anti-cartel policy was not politically controversial in the member countries. The Commission's power with respect to state aids (or industrial subsidies), on the other hand, affects the highly political issue of industrial policy. According to Article 93 of the EEC treaty, only a unanimous vote in the Council can reverse a decision by the Commission as to whether such a subsidy is to be allowed. In theory, this 'reverse veto' puts the Commission in a most powerful position. In practice, the Commission dare not override the wishes of the member governments in such sensitive issues of industrial policy, which can spell the life or death of an industry or a community and the rise or fall of a government. The members of the Commission are appointed by the governments 'acting in common agreement' (Article 158), that is, by a unanimous vote; and although they are enjoined to 'perform their duties in the general interest of the Community acting with complete independence' (Article 157), their need to secure unanimous agreement to almost any major new initiative tends to define for them the 'general interest of the Community' as a policy to which all the member governments could agree. The Commission has in fact, therefore, relied heavily on the Council to determine the application of the articles on state aids, thus putting the responsibility for the main decisions of Community industrial policy back in the hands of the member governments.

Is there any reason to worry about this? The reduction of obstacles to a single market, or negative integration as it has been called,[9] has after all been in general a great success. While many non-tariff barriers remain to hinder industrial progress, there are also arguments against further negative integration, at least as far as the weaker economies are concerned. But a return to disintegration would hold serious dangers. The advance of technology implies greater specialisation and costlier research, development and investment, and hence a need for a larger market. At the same time it tends to imply more regulations and industrial policies, which will disintegrate the market if there is no countervailing pressure. The drift of the laws embodied in the EEC treaty and in the ensuing regulations has been to forbid such national regulations and policies, which up to a point is no doubt salutary. But beyond that point lies the suppression of industrial policies that can reasonably be held to be desirable, and of a kind which all the member governments pursue. If disintegration is to be resisted, the alternative to such a destructive *laisser faire* is, therefore, agreement on a coordinated or common industrial policy; and this is probably necessary in the long run, if the economies of member countries are to have scope for advanced technological development.

This brings us to the field of 'positive integration',[10] that is, of policy integration with aims beyond that of creating a perfectly undistorted industrial common market. The aims of positive integration with which the Community has been concerned are of three main types: management of the Community economy to achieve its stability and development; redistribution of benefits of integration among member countries; and the securing of external interests, which may imply a redistribution of power or wealth between the Community and outside countries. These aims are usually secured by instruments other than the law: by taxes, subsidies, licences and other controls, or public enterprises. Of course such instruments are established and the scope of their use is defined by legal acts. But because the circumstances of their use cannot be precisely foreseen, much must be left to executive discretion; and this again brings the Community away from enforcement of the law and towards the conduct of politics, as we shall see from three examples of the Community's principal fields of activity.

PROMOTION OF EXTERNAL INTERESTS: THE COMMON EXTERNAL TARIFF

The rationale for the common external tariff with which the EEC treaty replaced the tariffs of member countries was that 'a simple free trade area would encounter almost insuperable practical difficulties'[11] in the form of diversion of imports through the member countries with lower tariffs. As the European Free Trade Area and the EEC's special arrangement for free entry of imports from Eastern into Western Germany were to show, these difficulties can be overcome. A more important reason for insistence on a common commercial policy, whose principal instrument was to be the common tariff, was probably the feeling that 'it was important . . . to act externally as a single unit' and to have a 'bargaining weapon with third countries for a general lowering of tariffs'.[12] This has, in the event, been the principal outcome. Before the establishment of the EEC with its common tariff, the United States stood alone as a trading superpower, with no equivalent negotiating partner. The EEC with its tariff immediately became such a partner, leading to the Kennedy Round of GATT negotiations in which the US proposed that tariffs be cut by half and as a result of which cuts of about one-third by the US, the EC and other GATT members were in fact accomplished. The tariff was also the main instrument that enabled the Community to form its special relationship with over 60 African, Caribbean and Pacific countries under the Lomé Convention, although the preferential tariff favours for these countries were supplemented by other instruments including the European Development Fund, which provides Community development aid in parallel with the aid programmes of the member countries. The common tariff was also the basis for a significant act of Community policy towards the developing countries as a whole, when it was the first of their major trading partners to establish, in 1971, a generalised scheme of preferences.

Thus the Community not only became, with the common tariff, a trading superpower, but its institutions, that is, the combination of Commission and Council, also showed the capacity to negotiate with this instrument effectively and constructively. The difference between the strength they showed in this field and their weaknesses in many fields of internal EC policy may be due to the pressure to reach agreement in order to avoid a failure of the member countries' foreign policies. Thus Jean Rey, the Commissioner responsible for the Kennedy Round, was able to conclude the negotiations by exceeding the brief that the Council of Ministers had given him and securing their subsequent approval;[13] and a group of Commission officials who were promoting the generalised scheme of preferences gave the question 'so much publicity that the Community, after going beyond a certain point, was in no position to turn back without losing considerable face in the eyes of the developing countries and the rest of the world'.[14] During the years of prosperity, there was moreover less opposition from threatened interests to set against these considerations of foreign policy and a generally liberal trading stance. The slowness in agreeing upon the Community's original policy towards the Multifibre Arrangement in the mid-1970s, however, and the increasingly protectionist constraint on the renewal of the agreements made under it, demonstrated the difficulties caused by the recession that followed 1974. Trade policy has become harder to make and more apt to be aligned on the lowest common denominator of the most protectionist member government; and with the growing importance of industrial policy, both as an alternative means of protection and as a way to promote the adjustments that make more liberal trading possible, the Community's capacity for effective negotiation will be weakened unless more industrial policy instruments are transferred to it from the member states.

The intention to 'act externally as a single unit' was not confined to the field of trade. It was part of a more general desire to redress the balance of power which had, by 1945, swung so far against Western Europe. Following the shocks of the Berlin crisis and the Korean War, the six member governments of the ECSC agreed in May 1952 on a treaty to establish a European Defence Community, whose common European army would offer a better defence against Soviet expansionism and, eventually, less dependence on the United States. Political opposition to the treaty, on grounds of national sovereignty and of policy towards German rearmament, grew in France, however, until August 1954 when it was rejected by the National Assembly. Since then there has been no attempt to endow a European defence organisation with military instruments. But there have been moves towards cooperation among the Community governments in matters of foreign policy and defence. The first proposal for a system of intergovernmental cooperation that would include foreign policy and security was mooted by the French government in the early 1960s, under the name of the Fouchet Plan, but was rejected by France's partners in the wake of de Gaulle's veto in January 1963 of further negotiations for British accession to the Community.

After de Gaulle fell from power, the question was taken up again at the Community summit conference in the Hague in December 1969, and less than a year later the foreign ministers had their first meeting to discuss matters of foreign policy under the new system of 'political cooperation', which included a Political Committee of senior officials from the member governments' foreign ministries. Security was excluded from the terms of reference; with economics being the province of the Community, which was at first kept rigidly separate from these 'political' proceedings on French doctrinal grounds, the 'political cooperation' disposed of no common instruments; and the achievements of this activity have been useful but modest. The member governments acted jointly to get human rights on the agenda at the Helsinki conference, with significant results in East–West relations; they have often voted as a group in the United Nations; and a closer mutual understanding has probably brought their positions closer together on various more urgent issues. The title 'Political Cooperation: Procedure as a Substitute for Policy',[15] which referred to the original decision to set up the system, would not be quite a fair summary of its subsequent achievements. But there is something in it. Officials from the foreign ministries tend to speak highly of the procedure. But there may be a professional bias in favour of useful activities that do not raise any of the risks of radical change.

Intergovernmental committees without common instruments are also attractive to practical politicians who want to achieve *something* and have to secure the agreement of all the member governments in order to do so. Hence the recent Colombo/Genscher proposal for 'European Union' which would extend this form of cooperation from foreign policy to include external security, internal security, culture and law.[16] In comparison with the Community's inability to discuss

security hitherto, this can be seen as an important development –
important enough to raise objections from some member governments
that feel it goes too far in various directions. Viewed in relation to
Western Europe's security predicament, however, with a relentless
expansion of Soviet military power and a restive United States, what
Colombo and Genscher have proposed is a very small step indeed. But
there are grounds to believe that, as far as defence is concerned, it is
necessarily small. Integration of defence forces into a common instrument of security policy may well follow a deep and long experience of
economic integration; but even in classic federations, such as Switzerland and the United States, far-reaching military integration came a
long time after the federal institutions had exercised substantial
economic powers.[17]

REDISTRIBUTION: THE COMMON AGRICULTURAL POLICY

When the EEC was established, the French felt industrially weak. In
order to make sure they did not lose from a Community in which the
Germans could expect to make large industrial gains, therefore, the
French, who were strong in agriculture, insisted that their farmers
should have open access to an agricultural common market. The case is
of interest, not just because it resulted in one of the Community's most
important policies, but also because it shows how a redistributive
policy may be needed in order to secure agreement to a major initiative
of integration such as an industrial common market; and it also shows
how the continued legitimacy of the Community institutions may be
affected by such redistributive policies.

Whereas laws against trade barriers were the main instrument to
establish an industrial common market, instruments of market organisation were required for agriculture. Each member country entered
the Community with a market organisation, and none would have been
willing to expose its farmers to a completely free market. The form of
common organisation that was agreed had as its main instruments
support prices, funds to buy and store farm produce if prices fell below
them, levies to prevent imports from undermining the price levels, and
subsidies to facilitate exports at lower world market prices. Given the
number of principal products and the complexity of their markets,
securing agreement on the structure of the Common Agricultural
Policy was an enormous task, comparable, a representative of the

German government said at the time, to negotiating 'a new Treaty of Rome'.[18] Yet it was accomplished, because without it France would not have agreed to the establishment of the EEC or, as we have seen, to its passage at the end of 1961 from the first to the second stage. The institutions have, moreover, managed to maintain the policy since. The Commission and Council have arrived each year at a set of prices and the Commission has executed the policy effectively. The intensely interested and often angry farmers, with their powerful lobbies and their electoral clout, have provided enough pressure to ensure that the Council took the decisions; and for this purpose the Council has comprised only the ministers of agriculture, without the ministers of finance, so that there has at certain crucial moments been insufficient restraint to taking the easy way out, by fixing prices higher than economic logic or financial prudence would suggest.

The Common Agricultural Policy fulfilled the function of helping to secure and maintain French loyalty to the Community; and it allowed the farming workforce to decline by half, from seventeen million in 1960 to eight million in 1980, without the brutality with which it was reduced in nineteenth-century Britain. But after two decades in which this transformation has taken place and France has become industrially strong, the redistributive function of the policy has become perverse, both socially and nationally. Socially, the greatest gainers are now a class of rich farmers; nationally, with the exception of the Irish Republic, they are rich countries: Denmark, the Netherlands, France. Italy has never been greatly helped by the CAP. Since the focus was on France, the more 'northern' products have gained the most; and since Italy was less necessary to the Community, the instruments that were established by the EEC treaty to redistribute in favour of Italy – the Investment Bank and the Social Fund – have never had a comparable importance. Awareness grew that the redistribution had become hard to justify and the cost should be cut; and the Germans, who had paid the budgetary price as the greatest industrial gainer with the strongest economy, began to call for change. But it was the end of the transitional financial arrangements for the first five years of British membership that raised the distributional issue in an acute form.

Unless special arrangements are made, a net payment of the order of £1 billion a year now has to be made from the British economy to the Community budget, because of the relatively low receipts by British farmers and the relatively large payments of duties and levies by British importers; and in addition British consumers pay high prices for most of the food they buy from the other Community countries. This was foreseen when Britain joined the Community and the amount was fairly accurately forecast, if allowance is made for inflation. In order to secure their gains from the agricultural policy, the French exacted the 'financial regulation', which guaranteed the Community its own financial resources of import duties and levies and up to 1 per cent of added value in the member countries, as a price for accepting British entry. The British, for their part, secured acceptance in principle on the establishment of a regional fund from which they expected to derive considerable benefit; and Mr Heath took part in the Paris summit meeting in 1972, when the heads of Community governments planned a wide range of developments in Community policy, from which Britain could hope to gain. The British aim was, then, to secure a reduction in the proportion of the Community budget spent on agriculture from its high level of between two-thirds and three-quarters, and thus by the 1980s to erode the financial disadvantage; and the government also expected that membership would ensure industrial prosperity.

In the event, the French were right to put their faith in the power of a common Community instrument, in the form of the EC's own tax resources; and the British were wrong to hope that the Community institutions would produce major new policies with the common instruments to make them effective, or major reforms of existing policies relating to agriculture or the budget. A regional fund was established, but much smaller than had been hoped and on no scale to compensate for the agricultural and budgetary deficit. Progress with most of the other policies discussed in 1972 has been disappointingly slow. While agricultural prices have been squeezed in real terms over a number of years in which increases were less than the rate of general inflation, the majority of member countries, led by France and Germany, showed themselves unwilling to allow the farm price level to be used as a lever for serious reform, when they forced a majority vote over Britain at the 1982 agricultural price review. It is hard not to conclude that the Community institutions, as at present constituted, can maintain existing policies in their present form and satisfy the existing vested interests, but have much less capacity to start major new policies or reform the old ones to take account of new circumstances and interests.

Temporary arrangements have been made to compensate Britain in part for its budgetary loss. But their negotiation has taken up much time in the European Council, which was established in 1975 to put the Community summit meetings on a regular basis and thus enable the heads of governments to consult each other and plan ahead.[19] This has diverted the Council from more constructive discussions; and there is a serious danger that the repercussions of failure to agree could lead to disruption of the work of the Community institutions and, in certain circumstances, British departure from the Community. The issue of redistribution has come full circle and it is once again urgent that a solution be found.

A lasting solution is not likely to be based on the assumption that distributive justice is a problem that arises only in the British case. The difficulty has arisen now because of a similar assumption that was earlier applied to France. If a special deal for Britain were to lead to two decades of stability, as did the agricultural deal for France, that would doubtless be permanent enough. But similar issues have already been raised by Greece and will certainly result from accession by Portugal and Spain. Such problems cannot be resolved within a Community whose major policies are confined to an industrial common market, a Common Agricultural Policy and a Common Commercial Policy. Permanent mechanisms to compensate for member countries' budgetary deficits have been proposed, although the governments of countries that gain from the present budget show scant sign of agreeing to them.[20] But even if they did, the problem would remain of ensuring the acceptability and legitimacy of a Community in member countries which feel, for a time at least, that they lose from integration in other ways. The weaker economies in particular are likely to feel this in a period of prolonged recession.

There are, in principle, two ways to resolve this. One is to allow member countries to opt out of some aspects of integration until they are confident that they will gain from them. This has in practice been the relationship chosen by Britain and Greece with the exchange rate mechanism of the European Monetary System. But if the habit were to grow of opting out of policies already accepted, such as the industrial common market, there would be a grave risk of economic disintegration, a recrudescence of autarky, and a permanent damper on technological progress in Western Europe. This danger leads us to the second way of resolving the distributive problem, through a wider range of Community policies and instruments, that can help the weaker countries to build on their strengths and reduce their weaknesses.

The MacDougall Report on the role of public finance in European integration[21] considered this possibility. The committee of experts chaired by Sir Donald MacDougall concluded that equilibrium could be maintained among the different countries and regions of the Community through a budget equivalent to $2-2\frac{1}{2}$ per cent of Community GDP, spent on cyclical, structural, employment and regional policies. The problem of divergence has if anything got worse since MacDougall reported in 1977, which might point towards his suggestion that, as integration proceeded, expenditure could rise to 5–7 per cent of GDP; meanwhile, however, attitudes towards public expenditure have become more restrictive.[22] But despite this dilemma, MacDougall's approach may be the only one that can combine the technological and industrial benefits of integration with the social and political cohesion that are needed to support it. The question of distribution leads us, therefore, directly to that of the management of the Community economy.

MACROECONOMIC MANAGEMENT AND COMMON MONETARY INSTRUMENTS

It was, ironically, the classical liberals, although they were such convinced internationalists, who provided the idea that a single market did not require a common economic management. Although the principle of *laisser faire* lent a certain logic to their position, for if there is no official intervention in the economy there is no need for a government to undertake it, they were castigated for this by the greatest of modern economic liberals;[23] and if there is economic policy other than *laisser faire*, the tension between national policies will rise as market integration proceeds. One country's policies will distort the market in ways that annoy another country, or will affect its economic stability or development. Coordination of national economic policies is difficult and may be found inadequate, so that the case for a common economic policy to cover the whole market becomes increasingly strong. It is not surprising that there have been successive moves to enhance the Community's role in the making of economic policy.

The EEC treaty provided that the member states should treat their policies relating to 'economic trends' and to exchange rates as 'a matter of common interest' (Articles 103, 107). But in contradistinction to its provision for the common market, Common Commercial Policy and Common Agricultural Policy, the treaty did not envisage the creation of any Community instruments to embody that common interest. Thus any agreements arising from the cooperation have to be implemented by the instruments of member states. In the search for unanimity, agreements tend to be weak. But when they come to be implemented, cooperation is liable to become weaker still. For economic policy cannot be precisely stipulated in advance; any agreement has to be interpreted in the light of changing conditions. Since the instruments are located in the member states' political and economic systems, the interpretation will be influenced by national political, economic and social pressures. National positions that diverged at the start, even if the differences were bridged by a form of words, are likely to diverge increasingly if they are subject to divergent pressures. Small wonder that the Marjolin Group, established to consider proposals for economic and monetary union, found that 'the coordination of national policies is a pious wish which is hardly ever achieved in practice'.[24] There is a useful exchange of information and views, but little approach towards common economic management.

The first major attempt to establish a system of common economic management was initiated by the Hague summit in 1969 and articulated in the Werner Report on economic and monetary union.[25] The Werner Report proposed the eventual locking of parities and abolition of controls on movements of money among the member countries, which is the equivalent of replacing the member states' currencies by a common Community currency. Since such a central instrument of economic management was to be transferred to the Community, the report logically stressed the indispensability of 'a centre of decision for economic policy'; but at the same time it allowed that the 'role of the Community budget as an economic instrument [would] be insufficient', so that the 'centre of decision must be in a position to influence the national budgets especially as regards the level and direction of the balances and the methods for financing the deficits or utilising the surpluses'.[26]

It may be doubted, for the reasons just given, whether Community control of member states' budgets would be practicable. It was difficult for Mr Heseltine to control the local authorities' spending even in such a centralised polity as the UK. But no such doubts were put to the test, because the negotiations to establish the system broke on the issue of the centre of decision. The Germans, who expected to be called upon to finance other countries' deficits, insisted on a strong Community control of monetary policy; the French, still insistent after de Gaulle on national sovereignty, held that decision by intergovernmental or inter-central bank agreements would be enough. The episode illustrates the danger of separating consideration of functions from that of institutions. The Werner Committee recognised the need for a 'centre of decision' but apparently not its political significance. There was no intellectual preparation for what would have amounted to a giant leap to federation. It is not surprising that the member governments failed to agree to leap.

Instead, a small step was taken to cooperate on exchange rates, known at the time as the 'snake in the tunnel'. Even this almost foundered in the economic turbulence of the early 1970s, when Britain left it in 1972 and France in 1974. But the idea of monetary union was revived in 1977 by Roy Jenkins, then President of the Commission.[27] This time both France and Germany set much store by the more powerful mechanism for exchange rate cooperation that was established as the centrepiece of the new European Monetary System (EMS) in 1979; and all the member states have continued to participate in the mechanism save Britain and Greece, neither of which has joined it. Beyond the exchange rate mechanism, the member governments agreed to establish, after a transitional period, a European Monetary Fund, to which the member states would transfer one-fifth of their gold and dollar reserves, and at the same time to use the European Currency Unit (ECU) as both a reserve and an instrument for settlement.

The European Monetary Fund (EMF) has not yet been established. But it represents an idea that could enable the Community's institutions to expand their role in economic management without the great leap to a quite centralised federation that the Werner Committee envisaged but the member governments refused to make. This is the idea of a Community monetary instrument that does not replace the member states' instruments, but is used in parallel alongside them.[28] Thus the EMF could implement a Community policy towards the dollar or the yen, and could influence the currencies of member states, without depriving them of their right to use their own reserves. If the member states' reserves were used for the same purposes as the Community's, the result would be very powerful; and they would be more likely to coalesce around a Community policy that disposed of its own instrument for action. But their monetary sovereignty would not be abandoned. There has already been some development of the idea of parallel financial instruments, with the Ortoli bonds (officially called the Financial Instrument), the denomination of some loans in European units, and the operations of the European Investment Bank. The establishment of the EMF could be a very significant further step.

MICROECONOMIC MANAGEMENT AND THE COMMUNITY BUDGET

Whether we considered the common market, the Community's external economic policy or the distributive problem, the conclusion was that many of the opportunities for further integration are blocked unless the Community can strengthen its structural and industrial policies, for which a principal instrument would be the Community budget. In order to provide the Community with a tool of economic management that corresponds to the present stage of the market integration, moreover, the MacDougall Report recommended the development of a much more substantial Community budget, from the present size of less than 1 per cent of GDP to a level of $2-2\frac{1}{2}$ per cent, which would still leave it as a parallel instrument much smaller than the budgets of the major member states. Such a budget could have a macroeconomic function to supplement that of any parallel monetary instruments; MacDougall envisaged that it would contribute to cyclical policy. But at such a modest size its contribution to short-term equilibrium would necessarily be small. Its major functions would be to promote structural adjustments that would strengthen the weaker parts as well as the Community economy as a whole.

Any substantial expansion of the budget would require a decision in the Council to increase the Community's tax resources, whether by raising the contribution from value-added tax above the present limit of 1 per cent of added value or by new Community taxes. While some official attitudes are opposed to this at present, this is, on the British side at least, partly a tactic to force reform of the agricultural policy by keeping a ceiling on expenditure. Several member governments favour breaking the 1 per cent limit and the objections of the others do not seem deep-rooted. More profound is the problem that a substantially larger budget would pose for the Community institutions.

Although the European Parliament already has a role of co-decision with the Council of Ministers in approving the Community budget, this does not extend to the expenditure on the Common Agricultural Policy, so the sums that the Parliament can influence are quite small. A large expansion of spending on other policies would change this situation radically and give the Parliament a much more important role. At the same time, the Council's already severe difficulties in making effective decisions would be sharply aggravated by the growth in its workload, as should not indeed be surprising if the Community broadens its focus from three major specific fields of policy to that of a more general economic management.

The issue that the Community's functions raise for the future of its institutions may be put quite simply. If a larger role for the Community in economic management is not adopted, the existing institutions can manage well enough, though improvements are doubtless possible along the present, predominantly intergovernmental lines, and something must be done about the distributive problem as it affects Britain and, probably, the prospective Iberian members. But more radical reform of the institutions would hardly be justified for that particular purpose alone. If, on the other hand, the Community does come to play its own part in economic management alongside that of the member governments, this implies at least a much more substantial Community budget and probably parallel monetary instruments as well; and if the Community disposes of these instruments, a more radical review of its institutions will be required. If the member states then find they wish to proceed from parallel monetary instruments to an exclusive common currency that in effect replaces the separate currencies of the member states, there can be no burking the need for federal institutions to manage the Community economy.

INSTITUTIONAL CHOICES: WHO IS TO MANAGE THE EUROPEAN ECONOMY?

Hardly anybody admits to being satisfied with the Community institutions, and there have been numerous proposals for improving them without presupposing any decisive change in the Community's functions such as could follow from the transfer to it of an important policy instrument. The European Council of heads of Community governments and the system of European 'political', or foreign policy, cooperation are examples that have been adopted. The Commission asked Mr Spierenburg to report on its own functioning, and he made a variety of proposals, such as a strengthening of the role of the Commission's President and a reduction in the number of Commissioners.[29] The European Council asked a Committee of Three (Berend Bisheuvel, Edmund Dell and Robert Marjolin) to report on the European institutions as a whole.[30] They supported much of what Spierenburg recommended for the Commission and concentrated their attention on the Council of Ministers; their recommendations included the restoration of a strong coordinating role to the Council of Foreign Ministers, which had been undermined by the newer European Council, and, again, a strengthening of the role of the (rotating) President among the foreign ministers. Then there are the Colombo/Genscher proposals, already mentioned, which recommend intergovernmental cooperation on external and internal security, culture and law, as well as on foreign policy, together with a more formal relationship between the European Council and the Community institutions.

The main trend of contemporary political science, in so far as it pays attention to the Community, supports the rather conservative character of these changes, actual or proposed. Interdependence and trans-nationalism are the labels which categorise much of the present thinking, and they imply a fairly stable system of international relationships.[31] There is a tendency in the US to play down any distinction between interdependence within the EC and in the wider international system.[32] This may be a reaction against the error of the earlier, neo-functionalist school, who supposed that integrating one sector of the economy would 'inevitably lead to the integration of other economic and political activities',[33] a process which they called automatic spillover. De Gaulle and the member states proved them wrong, and the Community's institutions and instruments have been fairly static for the past two decades. There is a temptation, evidently, to replace the idea of automatic spillover by that of automatic *immobilisme*. It might be more realistic to conclude that extrapolation of current trends projects the least likely of futures, given the flux and turbulence of contemporary economic and political conditions.

Economic bad times and strategic uncertainties provide an unstable background for the Community. Technological and industrial advance continue to press steadily against the centrifugal tendencies of international politics. More likely than *immobilisme*, in these circumstances, would seem to be either a disintegration of the Community, whether gradual or sudden, or a renewal of policy, and hence of political, integration. It is interesting to speculate which is the more probable, even if it may be feared that 'pessimism of the intellect' will prevail. But it may be as useful, and more congenial, to exercise some 'optimism of the will' and consider what institutional reforms might be required, if the member countries do summon up the courage to introduce the common instruments and policies that would enable them to perform the function of a common economic management.

It has been suggested that the pace of decision-taking that has characterised much of the Community's business would not serve for the purposes of managing the economy, and that the institutions with their present procedures, and the Council of Ministers in particular, might be unable to deal effectively with the additional work. Proposals for a 'two-speed Europe',[34] in which a core of the stronger members would press ahead with further policy integration, as eight of the member countries have done in the EMS, would do little to alleviate this problem. It has also been noted that an expansion of the Community budget would at the same time expand the role of the Parliament. A number of proposals have been made for strengthening the capacity of

the institutions by enhancing the Parliament's role. A working group
chaired by Professor Georges Vedel[35] proposed in 1972 the principle
of co-decision by Parliament and Council. Instead of just being
consulted before the Council decides, the Parliament's approval of
Community laws and policies would equally be required. In 1975, an
Amending Treaty, building on an earlier Amending Treaty of 1970,
gave the Parliament powers of co-decision with the Council on that
part of the Community budget defined as 'non-compulsory' expenditure, the 'compulsory' expenditure being that arising from commitments in the EC treaties, and in particular from the Common Agricultural Policy.[36] In June 1979, the Members of the European Parliament
were for the first time directly elected to it by the voters of the member
states.[37] In July 1982, the Parliament passed, by a large majority, a
resolution on the 'achievement of European Union', which proposed
that the Council and Parliament should 'jointly exercise legislative
power ... jointly ratify treaties ... together constitute the Union's
budgetary authority' and that Parliament should 'exercise political
control over the Executive and ... participate, in appropriate ways, in
its constitution'. Thus the Parliament is proposing that co-decision
with the Council, instead of being confined to a part of the budget,
should become the general rule. At the same time, in order to avoid the
Council's sometimes interminable delays, the Parliament proposed
that 'the Council must be enabled, by means of appropriate procedures, to take promptly decisions which lie within its powers'.[38]

Unfortunately political scientists, with their sights kept low since the
failure of the neo-functionalists' ambitious predictions, have done
little to help us judge whether the institutions as they stand now could
cope with the quantity and quality of business involved in an expansion
of the Community's function of economic management, or whether a
reform on the lines proposed by the Parliament would serve the
purpose of strengthening the institutions if that is necessary. A model
of clear analysis of such a problem is to be found in a body of literature
produced between 1939 and 1941 by a group of distinguished British
scholars, including Beveridge, Jennings, Robbins, Wheare and
Wootton,[39] in which they identified the reasons for the failure of the
League of Nations in its lack of institutions and powers independent of
the national governments, and proposed a federal system for post-war
Europe, around a core comprising Britain, France and a Germany
restored to democracy. Although this literature is hardly remembered
in Britain, it had a considerable influence on post-war developments
on the continent.[40] Circumstances are different now and, if a federalist

analysis were to be relevant again, it would have to take the form of a neo-federalism, showing what minimum of instruments may be required for the management of a Community economy at the present stage of market integration, what minimum of changes in the Community institutions may be necessary to ensure those instruments' effective use, and what conditions might enable the instruments to be transferred to the Community and the institutional reforms to be accomplished. One such condition is clear thinking on the subject. It is to be hoped that British scholars may find it possible to emulate their predecessors of four decades ago in this respect.

NOTES AND REFERENCES

1. Statement made on 9 May 1950, reproduced in Roy Pryce, *The Political Future of the European Community* (London: Marshbank and the Federal Trust, 1962) pp. 97–8.
2. Speech to the Inaugural Session of the High Authority of the ECSC, 10 August 1952, cited in Jean Monnet, *Les Etats-Unis d'Europe ont commencé* (Paris: Robert Laffont, 1965) pp. 56–7 (my translation).
3. Some 46 matters were listed as requiring unanimity in the first stage, 34 in the second stage and only 27 in the third and final stages. See Roy Pryce, *The Politics of the European Community* (London: Butterworth, 1973) p. 61.
4. *Rapport des Chefs de Délégation aux Ministres des Affaires Etrangères* (Spaak Report), Comité Intergouvernemental Créé par la Conférence de Messine (Brussels: 21 April 1956) p. 13 (my translation).
5. This line of thinking derived from the neo-functionalist school, whose most representative works were Ernst B. Haas, *The Unity of Europe* (London: Stevens and Sons, 1958); Leon N. Lindberg, *The Political Dynamics of European Economic Integration* (Stanford University Press, 1963); and Leon N. Lindberg and Stuart A. Scheingold, *Europe's Would-Be Polity: Patterns of Change in the European Community* (New Jersey: Prentice-Hall, 1970).
6. See Miriam Camps, *Britain and the European Community 1955–1963* (London: Oxford University Press, 1964) pp. 390–1.
7. See Donald J. Puchala, 'Worm Cans and Worth Taxes: Fiscal Harmonization and the European Policy Process', in Helen Wallace, William Wallace and Carole Webb (eds), *Policy-making in the European Communities* (London: John Wiley & Sons, 1977).
8. David Allen, 'Policing or Policy-making? Competition Policy in the European Communities', in Wallace, Wallace and Webb (eds), ibid., p. 93.
9. See John Pinder, 'Positive Integration and Negative Integration: Some Problems of Economic Union in the EEC', *The World Today*, vol. 24 (March 1968) pp. 88–110.

10. Ibid.
11. Spaak Report, p. 21.
12. Camps, *Britain and the European Community*, pp. 38, 39.
13. See David Coombes, *Politics and Bureaucracy in the European Community* (London: George Allen & Unwin, 1970) p. 195.
14. Glenda Goldstone Rosenthal, *The Men Behind the Decisions: Cases in European Policy-making* (Lexington, Massachusetts: D. C. Heath, 1975) p. 47.
15. By William Wallace and David Allen, in Wallace, Wallace and Webb (eds), *Policy-making in the European Communities*.
16. See European Parliament, proceedings of the sitting of 19 November 1981.
17. See K. C. Wheare, *Federal Government*, 2nd edn (London: Oxford University Press, 1951) pp. 200–1.
18. Herr Lahr, Under-Secretary of State in the German Ministry of Foreign Affairs, cited in Camps, *Britain and the European Community*, p. 391.
19. See Annette Morgan, *From Summit to Council: Evolution in the EEC*, European Series 27 (London: Chatham House and PEP, 1976).
20. Problems relating to such mechanisms are discussed in Geoffrey Denton, *The British Problem and the Future of the EEC Budget* (London: Federal Trust, 1982).
21. *Report of the Study Group on the Role of Public Finance in European Integration*, 2 vols (Brussels: Commission of the EC, April 1977).
22. See also Helen Wallace, *Budgetary Politics: The Finances of the European Community* (London: George Allen & Unwin, 1980) pp. 107–8.
23. In F. A. von Hayek, 'Economic Conditions of Inter-State Federation', *New Commonwealth Quarterly*, vol. v, no. 2 (London: September 1939) pp. 131–49.
24. *Report of the Study Group 'Economic and Monetary Union 1980'*, EMU–63, II/675/3/74 (Brussels: Commission of the EC, 8 March 1975) p. 1, cited in Wallace, Wallace and Webb (eds), *Policy-making in the European Communities*, p. 83.
25. *Report to the Council and the Commission on the Realisation by Stages of Economic and Monetary Union in the Community* (Werner Report), Supplement to Bulletin 11–1970 of the European Communities (Luxemburg: Council–Commission, 8 October 1970).
26. Ibid., pp. 12, 13.
27. First Jean Monnet Lecture, *Europe's Present Challenge and Future Opportunity* (Florence: European University Institute, 27 October 1977).
28. This idea was developed in *European Monetary Integration*, report of a Federal Trust working group (Giovanni Magnifico and John Williamson rapporteurs), (London: Federal Trust, 1972); and in Giovanni Magnifico, *European Monetary Unification* (London: Macmillan, 1973).
29. *Proposals for Reform of the Commission of the European Communities and its Services* (Spierenburg Report) (Brussels: Commission of the EC, 24 September 1979). This and other reports mentioned here are summarised in Stanley Henig, *Power and Decision in Europe: The Political Institutions of the European Community* (London: Europotentials Press, 1980).
30. *Report on European Institutions* (Brussels: Council of the EC, 1979).

Political Institutions of the EC

31. The current schools of thought are analysed in Carole Webb, 'Introduction: Variations on a Theoretical Theme', in Wallace, Wallace and Webb (eds), *Policy-making in the European Communities*.
32. See for example Gordon Douglass (ed.), *The New Interdependence: The European Community and the United States* (Lexington, Massachusetts: D. C. Heath, 1979), cited in Roy Pryce, *New Research on European Integration*, paper for the XIIth World Congress of the International Political Science Association, August 1982, p. 27. See also Roy Pryce, ibid., p. 22.
33. Lindberg, *Political Dynamics of European Economic Integration*, p. 10.
34. A two-speed Europe was first proposed in *European Union: Report to the European Council* (Tindemans Report), (Brussels: Council of the EC, 1975). With the problems raised by Greece and the prospect of accession by Portugal and Spain, the idea has recently been revived; see for example *Financial Times*, 29 July 1982.
35. *Report of the Working Party Examining the Problem of the Enlargement of the European Parliament* (Vedel Report), (Brussels: Commission of the EC, March 1972).
36. See Wallace, *Budgetary Politics*, pp. 67, 76–8.
37. On some of the implications of this, see David Coombes, *The Future of the European Parliament*, Studies in European Politics 1 (London: PSI/European Centre for Political Studies, 1979) and David Marquand, *Parliament for Europe* (London: Jonathan Cape, 1979).
38. European Parliament, proceedings of the sitting of 6 July 1982.
39. This literature included Sir William Beveridge, *Peace by Federation*? (London: Federal Union, 1940); W. Ivor Jennings, *A Federation for Western Europe* (Cambridge University Press, 1940); Lionel Robbins, *The Economic Causes of War* (London: Jonathan Cape, 1939), and 'Economic Aspects of Federation', in M. Chaning-Pearce (ed.), *Federal Union* (London: Jonathan Cape, 1940); K. C. Wheare, *What Federal Government Is* (London: Macmillan, 1941); Barbara Wootton, *Socialism and Federation* (London: Macmillan, 1941).
40. See for example Walter Lipgens, *A History of European Integration 1945–1947* (Oxford: Clarendon Press, 1982). See also Jean Monnet's speech at the Inaugural Session of the High Authority of the ECSC, op. cit.

12 Political Cooperation in Europe

ROGER MORGAN

INTRODUCTION

A chapter with this title might be expected to deal with any one of a number of different subjects: the theme could be defined, for instance, to designate the system of loose intergovernmental consultation and cooperation which most of the governments of Western Europe have pursued since 1949 through the Council of Europe; or alternatively the various forms of cooperation in which the states of both Eastern and Western Europe have worked together, whether on the relatively limited basis (statistical fact-gathering and practical cooperation on transport) represented by the United Nations Economic Commission for Europe based in Geneva, or on the much more ambitious basis represented by the 1975 Helsinki Final Act of the 35-nation Conference on Security and Cooperation in Europe. Although these broader dimensions of cooperation between the states of Europe must not be neglected, this chapter will deal with European Political Cooperation (EPC) in the more limited sense of the system of cooperation, essentially on diplomatic issues, which has developed in the last decade among the member states of the Community.

HISTORY AND STRUCTURE OF EPC

The systematic attempt at the coordination of the foreign policies of the member states of the European Community, known in general as European Political Cooperation (and to the British Foreign and Commonwealth Office as PoCo), was adopted in principle by the six member states of the then European Community at the Hague summit conference of December 1969, on the same occasion as their final decision to move towards accepting Britain as a member. The broad procedures were laid down at a conference in Luxemburg in October 1970 (based on a report by the then Permanent Secretary of the Belgian Foreign Office, Viscount Etienne Davignon), and further elaborated by a decision taken in Copenhagen in July 1973, after Britain had become a member. Unlike the activities of the member states which are governed by the Treaty of Rome, and which take effect in Community policies in the strict sense, EPC is a loose and informal system of intergovernmental consultation and coordination, with no binding effects upon the policies of the member states. Participants in the process, and outside observers of it, have seen in this flexible structure a source both of strengths and of weaknesses in EPC.[1]

The formal 'summit' of the EPC procedure is represented by the meetings of the foreign ministers of the Ten, which take place four times a year, twice in every six-monthly presidential term. Although the chairmanship is in the hands of the state holding the presidency of the Community, these meetings are not held in Brussels, but in the capital of the presidency. This underlines the fact that they are not meetings of the Council of the EC, and that Community business is not discussed or transacted at them. The Commission is represented at these meetings, but is not a formal participant: EPC is essentially an intergovernmental affair, which is legally distinct from the procedures of the Community. Here again is a source of potential strength but also of serious weakness.

In addition to these four formal meetings each year, at which the foreign ministers are accompanied by the officials of their respective foreign ministries responsible for political cooperation, the ministers also meet twice each year (i.e. one in each presidency), in informal surroundings, without the presence of officials. As these meetings are informal, they may range over the entire field of European Community *and* political cooperation problems, or they may be focused on some specific problem or problems of general importance to the Community.

After a period in which the distinction between European Community business and the discussions on political cooperation was most rigorously maintained, especially on French insistence (a period which was symbolised by the ludicrous episode in 1973, when the foreign ministers of the Nine flew from Copenhagan to Brussels to hold two distinct categories of meetings on the same day), agreement has been

reached – particularly since the first British presidency of the first half
of 1977 – that brief sessions on political cooperation might be held by
ministers in the course of meetings of the EC Council in Brussels or
Luxemburg. The relationship between Community business and EPC
thus became more natural, even though it should be underlined that
the officials who support their ministers at EC Council meetings are
not the ones responsible for the conduct of EPC business. This makes it
difficult for ministers to switch at will from Community business to
EPC affairs and back again.

Although, as stated above, the quarterly meetings of foreign ministers represent officially the 'summit' level of discussion in EPC, these
meetings are in fact 'outclassed' by the thrice-yearly meetings of the
European Council of the heads of government of the Community's
member states. In the European Council, more explicitly and more
systematically than in meetings at the foreign minister level, the heads
of government look at world affairs both from the Community and
political cooperation angles, and it is expected of them that they make
the necessary links between the two (usually on the basis of last-minute
preliminary meetings by their foreign ministers).

At the level *below* the regular meetings at foreign minister level is
the Political Committee of EPC, which consists of the 'Political
Directors' of the ten foreign ministries. The designation of the 'Political Directors' from the various foreign ministries has posed some
problems for those ministries – e.g. the British Foreign and Commonwealth Office – which have not traditionally been organised on the
basis of a rigid separation between 'political' and 'economic' responsibilities, but these difficulties have in practice been overcome. The
Political Committee meets every month in the capital of the presidency
state, and it also meets once a year in New York in September, at the
opening of the UN General Assembly. (The particular purpose of this
New York meeting is to enable the senior officials to put finishing
touches to the part of the speech by the foreign minister holding the
presidency which is made not in his national capacity but as the
spokesman of the Ten.)

At their monthly meetings, which usually last two days, the Political
Directors are accompanied by the 'European Correspondents'
(medium-rank officials responsible for the day-to-day communications with other member states – see below), and also by one or two
other officials. In order to maintain the link between political cooperation and Community affairs, the UK delegation sometimes includes a
member of the staff of the UK Permanent Representation (UKREP)

at the seat of the Community in Brussels, though this is difficult if the Political Committee meets, as it often does, on the same day as the Committee of Permanent Representatives (COREPER) in Brussels. At meetings of the Political Committee, as of ministers, the EC Commission is represented, though the Commission has no standing as a member of the system.

The role of the European Correspondents within each foreign ministry is to provide continuity between the meetings of the Political Committee, to supervise the flow of direct telegraphic communication between foreign ministries in the so-called 'Coreu' (an arrangement by which several hundred telegrams every month pass between the foreign ministries of the Ten, on a variety of EPC issues), to maintain close contact with one another by telephone, and to ensure that their respective foreign ministries contribute as required to the labours of the working groups of EPC, sometimes known as 'expert' groups.

These working groups, which represent quantitatively the largest part of EPC activity, have no fixed status or procedure. They consist of experts from each of the foreign ministries who work on particular topics designated as important by the Political Committee, to which the working groups report. In the course of the 1970s, regular working groups were established to deal with the following issues:

- East – West relations
- the Conference on Security and Cooperation in Europe
- the Eastern Mediterranean
- the Middle East
- Africa
- UN affairs

These groups have met fairly regularly and frequently, as often as once or even twice a month if their work demands it. The EPC system has also led to the creation of groups dealing with Asia, Latin America and disarmament, but these have met less frequently than the others: this is also the case with a working group on protocol questions and another on communications, established chiefly to control the development of the Coreu system.

As well as these standing groups of officials from ministries of foreign affairs, it is most important to note the existence of a group of senior officials from ministries of the interior and ministries of justice, who have been considering problems of judicial cooperation among the Ten, including the particular problem of concerted action against international terrorism. This incorporation in the EPC process – essentially one limited to the diplomatic milieu – of representatives of national ministries essentially concerned with internal affairs represents a most significant reminder of the context of high enthusiasm for the European ideal in which EPC was launched in the early 1970s – a theme to which this chapter will return.

The working groups provide a forum for an increasingly intensive pooling of information and opinion between the Ten member states of the European Community in matters of foreign policy. The fact that the foreign ministry officials concerned, say, with African questions, are constantly in touch with their opposite numbers in the other foreign ministries of the Ten provides the basis for common assessments of international problems, and does much to justify the assertion made by the proponents of the EPC system that it precludes 'surprises' between the member states, resulting from the actions of any one of them. Even though – as will be seen – the activities of politicians occasionally produce such surprises, it is in the working groups of EPC that the foundations of an eventual common foreign policy for the European Community – if there is ever going to be one – are being laid.

A corollary of the intensive cooperation between foreign ministries with the EPC system– from ministerial level down to that of specialist working groups – is that the diplomatic representatives of the Ten in other parts of the world work together in an increasingly intimate manner. All over the world the embassies of the country holding the presidency arrange meetings of the ambassadors of the Ten as often as seems desirable and convenient, usually at least once a month. Occasionally the Political Committee calls for a joint report from the ambassadors of the Ten in a particular country, but such reports are said to have been disappointing through their lack of vigour, and to pose the problem of disagreement between those in favour of the report and those against it at the level of the Political Committee. The most important examples of cooperation between the Ten in overseas locations are probably the consultations which take place between the missions of the Ten at the United Nations in New York (which occur more or less daily), and between the embassies of the Ten in Washington.

In sum, the structure of EPC provides an increasingly full exchange of information and assessments between the foreign ministries of the European Community's member states, and potentially for a common foreign policy on the part of Western Europe towards the outside world. This question of what is 'potentially' in EPC leads to a contrast of the somewhat prosiac reality with the ambitious claims made for EPC in the political context of its birth and development.

AMBITIONS, ASPIRATIONS AND CLAIMS

As noted above, the EPC system was conceived and developed during the years of relative euphoria, the late 1960s and early 1970s, when the decision was finally taken to enlarge the membership of the European Community from six to nine by the incorporation of Britain, Ireland and Denmark (to be followed a few years later by Greece, though not by Norway as intended in the 1960s). Re-reading the communiqué issued at the end of the summit conference of the Community's member states in Paris in October 1972, the reader of ten years later is struck by the highly ambitious programme set out: political cooperation between the member states of the Community was only one thread in an elaborate tapestry which promised that by the end of the 1980s the member states of the Community would 'transform the entire complex of our relations into a European Union'. Much play was made with the idea – both at the 1972 summit conference and in public statements by European political leaders at the time – that the Community of nine or ten countries, endowed with an economic potential comparable with that of the United States, would emerge as a sort of economic superpower on the world scene.

Similar rhetoric from outside the West European area enhanced this notion of Europe as a power in the world system: for instance, when President Nixon and his adviser Henry Kissinger launched the 'Year of Europe' in 1973, they did so partly with the justification that Western Europe was now emerging as a centre of power in a 'pentapolar' world system, a power to be measured alongside the United States and the Soviet Union, and in some ways at a higher level than the other two power centres, Japan and China.

After the oil shock of 1973, which suggested that the real emerging power in the international system might be the Arab oil-producing states rather than the still disunited and energy-dependent member states of the European Community, the political atmosphere surrounding the development of EPC became less assertive and more defensive. How could the West Europeans defend their interests, it was argued – whether against the OPEC countries, or against a more expansionist Soviet Union, or against US administrations which pursued policies contrary to Europe's interest in one way or another – if not through the systematic attempt to develop a common West European foreign policy?

This question, in numerous variations, has underlain all the attempts made since 1973 – in British terms, from Heath and Home to Carrington and Pym – to create the preconditions for 'a European voice' to have its say in world affairs, and for European actions to carry some weight. How far have the achievements of EPC in fact measured up to the ambitious claims which Europe's political leaders have voiced on its behalf?

ACHIEVEMENTS OF EPC

When one recalls that the instruments through which the Ten can actually operate in political cooperation are very limited, the achievements of the system are by no means negligible. Building on the creation of a consensus through the procedures described above, the Ten can often speak with one voice through the mouth of their president, either in *ad hoc* situations or in such international fora as the United Nations. They can agree a common line on which the nine governments will base public statements by their respective ministers, and they can follow an agreed line in press briefing, either severally or through the presidency alone or through the presidency with the support of some or all of the other partners. Such methods of diplomatic action may be less effective, because they are concerned essentially with the definition and expression of broad policy lines, than the more subtle and pervasive methods of daily diplomatic contact pursued by 'normal' national embassies and foreign ministries, but these methods have succeeded in establishing a 'band' within which all member states can act in harmony and without excessively constraining the national freedom of action enjoyed by each of them.

Among the undoubted 'success stories' of EPC, the most often cited is the cooperation of the Ten (for most of the time the Nine) in the proceedings of the Conference on Security and Cooperation in Europe in Helsinki and Geneva, leading to the signing of the Helsinki Final Act in 1975, and in the subsequent review conferences in Belgrade and Madrid. Among other points in this highly complex multilateral negotiation the EC member states succeeded in establishing a common line on economic cooperation (the so-called 'Basket Two' of the Final Act) and on the extremely sensitive question of human rights (Basket Three) on which West European approaches differed considerably from that of the United States.

Another example of fairly successful cooperation is to be found in the application of EPC in the United Nations in New York. Here, however, the record of voting shows something falling very far short of unanimity between the member states of the Community.

Other examples could be added to the record of relatively successful outcomes of the EPC process, including most recently the way in which most of the EC allies of the United Kingdom supported the British position in the Falklands dispute, and carried this support to the lengths of imposing economic sanctions on Argentina.

Perhaps the achievements of EPC are best summarised by saying that, even though the member states of the European Community are far from having agreed that they should pursue a common foreign policy, they very often act – thanks to their increasingly intimate consultation through the EPC process – *as if* such a commitment existed. Supporters of the 'European ideal' who are not convinced of the virtues of the institutional approach might argue that this evidence of *de facto* consensus suggests that a non-institutional approach is the best route towards a true European union. It might be argued that, just as the multiple constraints of interdependence in the international system as a whole compel states to behave much of the time *as if* they were subject to a binding rule of international law (even though it is well known that *de jure* they are not), so the habit of cooperation and the growing realisation of interdependence within the Community will induce the member states of the Community to behave *as if* they were component parts of a European federation, even though this is legally and institutionally not the case.

There is something in this argument, but it needs to be set in perspective by recalling that EPC as it is now conducted is essentially an affair of the foreign ministries of the EC member states, and it is fair to argue that, in a world where these foreign ministries are made aware of their relative impotence both by the rise of the non-European superpowers and by the claims and demands of other centres of power within their respective national systems, it is only natural for them to enter into a system of collusion in order to pursue together a role to which none of them can aspire individually.

STRENGTHS AND WEAKNESSES OF EPC

The main strength of the EPC system is suggested by the point referred to above, namely that it is a flexible instrument which provides for the maximum degree of political consultation between the states concerned – maximum, that is, in terms of the degree of confidence and consensus prevailing between their respective political leaderships – while at the same time being without any ultimate binding effect in terms of action. This very flexibility – the fact that states can in the last resort refuse to accept a common line of action as a result of EPC discussions, or that even a successfully-accomplished joint action does not provide any binding precedent for the future – may well explain why a group of states with such differing interests (despite all their common ones) have been willing to go as far as they have. The strong points of the EPC system should not, however, blind us to its very considerable weaknesses. Six of these may be singled out.

First, the fact that the EPC system precludes any binding commitment to action imposes a serious limitation on it, judged by the standards of what a common European Foreign policy would need. The member states of the EC may, as argued above, be willing to go along with a system of foreign policy cooperation only on the under-standards of what a common European foreign policy would need. of such a system have been made glaringly apparent by some of the failures of the Ten to achieve a common front: by, for example, the refusal of the British Parliament to impose economic sanctions *retrospectively* on Iran after the seizure of the American diplomatic hostages, although the foreign ministries of the member states had agreed that this should be done; or, again, by the way in which Ireland and to some extent Italy defected from the common front of EC sanctions against Argentina in the Falklands affair.

Second – and this weakness is directly linked with the economic issues raised by the question of sanctions – the EPC system is still not linked closely enough with the economic and commercial activities of the Community on the world scene. Even though the grosser absurdities of the early 1970s are now things of the past (e.g. the insistence of France that EPC should be discussed in Copenhagen and European Community affairs in Brussels on the same day); and even though the diplomatic resources of EPC are often used to good effect in explaining to the Community's external partners the implications of EC policies in such delicate areas as agriculture, trade or the protection of Europe's steel industry; still the fact remains that the 'political' and 'economic' dimensions of Europe's foreign relations are still too much conducted in separate compartments. The 'economic giant' which the Community represents on the world scene is still in many ways a 'political dwarf'.

Third, the EPC system is still very far from having entered effectively into the vital area of foreign policy represented by military defence and security affairs. Even though the EPC discussions on the CSCE agenda touched on certain areas of security (for instance, the military 'confidence-building measures' agreed in Basket One of the Final Act) and the Ten have finally agreed – in the so-called 'London Paper' of October 1981 – that EPC should henceforth be allowed to discuss 'certain important foreign policy questions bearing on the political aspects of security', still the fact remains that the central issues of military defence and disarmament, war and peace, are regarded as lying within the purview of NATO rather than of the European grouping which meets in EPC. There are many reasons for this state of affairs, including the historical legacy of the premature attempt at European defence integration in the European Defence Community of the 1950s, and also the fear of many European members of NATO that too much European discussion of these matters would alienate the United States and divide the Alliance – not to mention the reluctance of some EC member states (Ireland and Greece in particular, for different reasons) to become involved in discussions on the military defence of the West. It is however, striking – and an obvious weakness in the EPC system – that even the sort of European *consultations* on military security which might be held if the defence ministers of the Ten met on the same basis as the foreign ministers (as was proposed by the British Conservative Party in the European Parliament election campaign of 1979), are inhibited for whatever reason. A system of European Political Cooperation which – as well as having only a tenuous grip on the *economic* instruments of foreign policy – is totally unable to command any of the *military* instruments, is very far indeed from living up to its original claim to provide the basis for a European foreign policy.

Fourth, it must be doubted whether the existing system of EPC is effective in conducting a dialogue between 'Europe' and some of Europe's most powerful interlocutors in the outside world. In relation to the United States, for instance – to mention the most important outside partner with which 'Europe' has to deal – the EPC system, while it provides for an effective link between EPC discussions and the officials in charge of the Bureau of European Affairs in the Department of State, disposes of no direct channel to the much more powerful hierarchies of the National Security Council, the Bureau of International Security Affairs in the Department of Defense, the Office of the President's Special Trade Representative or the Departments of Commerce or Agriculture. It is true that the European Community has other means of communicating with some of these power centres – and also with the legislative branch of the US government – but this multiplicity of channels represents a further weakening of the effectiveness of EPC.

Fifth, the EPC system, despite recent improvements, is still not good at inducing a quick and effective response on the part of Western Europe to pressures and problems arising outside. Even though the working groups of officials from the foreign ministries concerned may have successfully laid the groundwork for a collective decision by collecting and collating the necessary information and assessments, the act of taking a decision is often much too long delayed. After the Soviet invasion of Afghanistan in December 1979, for instance, there was no meeting of European foreign ministers for a period of three weeks, and the response of European governments to more recent developments in Poland has been only slightly more speedy. The EPC system could be said to be mainly one designed to allow the European governments to make a collective *response* to outside pressures, rather than to undertake significant European *initiatives* (the attempts to lay down a collective policy towards the Middle East, culminating in the Venice Declaration of June 1980, have remained essentially declaratory): but there must be considerable scepticism as to the degree to which even a reactive joint European posture can be established.

Sixth, and last, there is the important point that 'Political Cooperation', despite its ambitious title, remains essentially a system of *diplomatic* coordination between Western Europe's ministries of foreign affairs. The 'aberrant' case of cooperation between officials from ministries of justice or ministries of the interior, cited above, goes only a very short way towards the ambitious objective of creating a 'European Union' which the governments of the Community set themselves in 1972. EPC could more accurately be described as 'European *diplomatic* cooperation', at least until Europe's governments succeed in establishing a much more intensive network of communication between other parts of their respective political and administrative systems, in addition to the purely foreign policy establishments.[2]

THE FUTURE OF EPC

Many of the weaknesses listed above have of course been the subject of concern on the part of the ministers and officials responsible for running the present system. By endorsing the suggestions of the 'London Paper' of October 1981, already cited, the foreign ministers did in fact commit themselves to considerable improvements in the administrative functioning of EPC: for instance, they agreed to strengthen the administrative staff at the disposal of the presidency of the system, and to facilitate the spreading of the workload on the foreign minister of each presidency by allowing him to associate either his predecessor or his successor with some parts of his work.

More ambitious developments, such as the incorporation of the military security dimension in EPC discussions, were endorsed only in the extremely cautious way indicated by the quotation given above.[3]

The Ten are still very far from being ready to endorse the much closer connection between foreign policy and defence policy envisaged, for instance, in the Genscher/Colombo proposals, or even the more modest suggestions for facilitating emergency meetings of foreign ministers, put forward by Lord Carrington in a speech in Hamburg in November 1980. If the Ten are to fulfil their potential as an actor on the world scene by going beyond these first stages of cooperation towards a true foreign policy for Europe, a new act of political will is necessary.

NOTES AND REFERENCES

1. This study draws extensively on a privately-circulated paper on EPC by Sir Reginald Hibbert, Director of the Ditchley Foundation and formerly HM Ambassador in Paris: the help given by his paper is gratefully acknowledged.
2. See further Philippe de Schoutheete, *La Cooperation Politique Europeénne* (Paris: Fernaud Nathen, 1978), and D. Allen, R. Rummel and W. Wessels (eds), *European Political Cooperation* (London: Butterworth, 1982).
3. See Christopher Hill, 'Changing Gear in Political Cooperation', in *Political Quarterly* (Jan–March 1982).

Index